MONTH-BY-MONTH GARDENING

DEEP SOUTH

First Published in 2019 Cool Springs Press, an imprint of The Quarto Group, 100 Cummings Center, Suite 265-D, Beverly, MA 01915, USA.
T (978) 282-9590 F (978) 283-2742 QuartoKnows.com

Cool Springs Press titles are also available at discount for retail, wholesale, promotional, and bulk purchase. For details, contact the Special Sales Manager by email at specialsales@quarto.com or by mail at The Quarto Group, Attn: Special Sales Manager, 100 Cummings Center, Suite 265-D, Beverly, MA 01915, USA.

EAN: 978-1-59186-585-8

Library of Congress Cataloging-in-Publication Data

Neal, Nellie.
  Deep South month-by-month gardening : what to do each month to have a beautiful garden all year : Alabama, Louisiana, Mississippi / Nellie Neal.
     p. cm.
  Includes bibliographical references and index.
  ISBN 978-1-59186-585-8 (softcover)
  1. Gardening--Alabama. 2. Gardening--Louisiana. 3. Gardening--Mississippi. I. Title. II. Title: a Deep South month by month gardening.

  SB453.2.A2N43 2014
  635.09761--dc23

                    2013039029

Acquisitions Editor: Billie Brownell
Design Manager: Brad Springer
Layout: Kim Winscher

MONTH-BY-MONTH GARDENING

DEEP SOUTH

**What to Do Each Month to Have
a Beautiful Garden All Year**

NELLIE NEAL

COOL
SPRINGS
PRESS

Dedication

To Pamala, who lives with a writer and loves me anyway. As always, to Dave.

Acknowledgment

I owe a great debt of gratitude for this book to my family and the Deep South states that tell our story. My family had the foresight to migrate here from Wales via Scotland and Ireland and to stop when they reached the only part of this country as green as they had known. Thankfully, Alabama, Louisiana, and Mississippi became their garden, and mine.

It's impossible to learn much about gardening without taking advantage of other gardeners' open gates and willingness to talk plants "'til the cows come home." Pete Maucelli of Greenville, Mississippi, makes me proud to be a plant nerd.

My colleagues in horticulture and media know that I live at their crossroads, a tenuous intersection at times. The professionals in both disciplines are generous with their wisdom and opinions, yet treat me with respect when we disagree. My thanks go to Billie Brownell, acquisitions editor at Cool Springs Press, to Tracy Stanley at Cool Springs Press, and to the horticulture editor, Troy Marden, for making this book possible.

Book authors cannot exist without people who buy books, and I am humbled every time you do. Especially in the Deep South, we prize the written word like we do our beloved blues, jazz, and heritage music—daily.

Contents

How we Garden

We take gardening very personally in the Deep South. We celebrate the first tomato of the year and the greenest lawn in the neighborhood right along with our favorite sports teams. Sometimes it's a family tradition and you do what Daddy did. Times change but you respect those lessons so much you may not tell him when you decide to grow a different azalea or tomato variety. If your family didn't mow or grow at all, gardening becomes a healthy way to express generational differences. The first time you pick an armload of your own zinnias can be a rite of passage to self-identification and adulthood. And if it makes Mama flinch a bit to see your hands get dirty, so much the better.

Deep South gardens can be huge, tiny, fancy, Spartan, serious, whimsical, or somewhere in between. They range from a few pots on the deck in summer to manicured landscapes, from elegant courtyards to wild, wooded glades. We grow all sorts of plants in containers everywhere—fancy ceramics flank the front door, cuttings root in a row on the kitchen window, and big black plastic pots hold pepper plants out back. Our delicious sense of humor can often be found in the everyday objects we turn into containers, too, especially when the project involves repurposing. A broken child's wagon, an old washtub, or even a watering can that leaks quickly becomes the centerpiece of a clever garden scene. You might plant an old mailbox or sink, or sometimes even a toilet or tire. Or a wicker chair with a broken seat gets fitted for its own pot with a sign bemoaning the expense of recaning. These projects and so many more get done in our states because our kind of gardening appeals to your heart, head, and stomach, and not necessarily in that order.

Some plants, ornaments, and architecture just seem to belong in our gardens, and we feel the sense of place they bring to it as much as we see it. That feeling is expressed when you choose tall shutters or a wrought iron fence, opt for a brick barbecue pit and tables under high pine shade, or buy a house for its hipped roof and wraparound porch. Equally potent mood enhancers might be palm trees, azaleas and gardenias, crepe myrtle trees, and the fragrant rose you remember from childhood. More than anywhere else, here we bring ourselves into the garden and try every day to live the concept of indoor-outdoor harmony.

There is strength in the great diversity of our gardens because it means no matter what direction you take, there are good examples to lead the way. Some swear by row and furrow planting when there's space but readily shift to raised bed and container gardens to make room for swing sets or to downsize for retirement. If you are devoted to 360 degree views of garden beds and the neighbor builds a fence, you put that backdrop to good use and plant a border. We get our backs up a bit when anyone tells us we can't grow a particular plant, can't be organic gardeners, can't possibly grow heirloom vegetables, or anything else because of where we live. Once you start, you won't be surprised to find gardeners already busy at it right here in our states without fanfare or benefit of a support group.

When you settle in the Deep South, the potential for twelve-month gardening looms large and sometimes you wonder when to rest. January's out—there are fruit trees to prune—but so is July if you're putting in flowers and vegetables for fall. The key to twenty-first-century gardening here is flexibility. We hedge our bets against challenges— from harsh weather to difficult soils and beyond. In some places, you garden outdoors almost all year and drag a few pots indoors or protect them on the screen porch behind a plastic drape when needed. Those who experience more of the four seasons might go for a sunroom or greenhouse but still need shade on the structure during the summer months. All of us improve our odds with smart plant choices, temporary covers, and true season extenders like hoop gardens and high tunnel gardens to shield plants from the extremes. We plant old favorites, the latest releases, and sometimes what happens to be available with surprisingly good results. The transitions between seasons can be blurry as when autumn cools steadily until it's late December without a true killing frost. Or things can change overnight as they often do in late winter and early spring. It seems like you light the fireplace one night and turn on the air conditioner the next. And sometimes we *do*.

Deep South gardening is a vibrant gumbo of home horticulture where your age and station in life matter less than pure desire and a willingness to break a sweat. You might be out on your own for the first time or surprised to find yourself back at home with new responsibilities. First time homeowners, folks with families to feed, new retirees ready for a new hobby—if you want green, gorgeous, and delicious, gardening's your game.

You might decide to turn backyard space into profit, like the teenager at the farmers market who grows hanging baskets on the back porch for his college fund. It all comes down to you, the joy you feel in the accomplishment, the comfort you find in doing what so many have done before, and the legacy in sharing what you know.

Spoken or not, there are prejudices against gardening in our world. Friends visit in August, swoon when they get off the plane, and refuse to go anywhere without air conditioning. They complain of hurricanes and hail storms, tornadoes and drought—and those are folks that live here but don't garden. Be kind to them, and hope that one day they'll come around to the good exercise, serious stress relief, and sheer joy found in our pursuits.

CLIMATE

There are three USDA Hardiness Zones included in this book—7, 8, and 9—and their boundaries continue to change as the climate warms. Conditions may not be exactly the same within zones on a given day, but their lowest temperatures fell within the same averages across thirty years. While each zone has plants specific to it, many are found throughout our states. Those bloom first in 9b, the zone at the very southern tip of Louisiana where average annual low temperatures just brush freezing. In most years, the flowers of these common plants bloom seven to ten days later as you go north through each subzone. Thus, about a week later, the same plants bloom in 9a where the average annual extreme minimum temperature (AAEMT) range is 20 to 25 degrees Fahrenheit. This zone now includes Lake Charles and Houma but also Opelousas and Slidell, Louisiana, and Biloxi, Mississippi. Several miles north of Interstate 10 in Hancock and Harrison (Mississippi) counties are in 9a, as well as the southern tips of Mobile and Baldwin counties in Alabama.

Zone 8 has pushed north. Zone 8b (15 to 20 degrees Fahrenheit) extends into Beauregard parish and goes over to Alexandria, Louisiana, but also runs up the Red River to Shreveport where it dips down to include Winn parish on its way to Monroe and Bastrop. In Louisiana, 8a (AAEMT 10 to 15 degrees Fahrenheit) is now restricted to northwest and north central parishes and the cities of Minden and Ruston.

Zone 8b hugs the Mississippi River counties from Issaquena county south through Vicksburg and into Claiborne county, Mississippi. From there it spreads east, extending to Hattiesburg where it follows the Leaf River south to the Pascagoula and on to Mobile, Atmore, and Dothan, Alabama, plus parts of Monroe, Conecuh, Coffee, Dale, and Henry counties.

Zone 8a takes in more of Mississippi and Alabama than on previous maps. The zone now runs from Clarksdale in the north to spread south to Jackson and Meridian and then north to Starkville and on to Alabama. It continues there through Pickens county to Tuscaloosa then east to the Coosa River and includes Elmore county, and the cities of Montgomery and Auburn.

Zone 7b (AAEMT 5 to10 degrees Fahrenheit) is limited to a wedge of Mississippi from Southaven to Winona and back north to Tupelo. It continues in a wide swath across Alabama to Birmingham and Talladega, and then dips into Coosa, Tallapoosa, and Chambers counties. Only a small part of Limestone county, Alabama, and sections of Jackson and DeKalb counties are in Zone 7a (AAEMT 0 to 5 degrees Fahrenheit).

You will use this book to follow the rhythm of your own garden through the year as you plan for its care. Exactly when you can do a particular task will depend on your zone and the month's weather. For example, from south to north, we prune azaleas after their first big bloom of the year, whenever that happens. Knowing that, you wouldn't be surprised to see an azalea pruned in March following its bloom time in New Orleans, Louisiana, and the very same variety just opening its flowers a month or more later in Corinth, Mississippi.

SUN AND SHADE

People say the sun in the South feels different from other places. Sometimes, you even know it's there on cloudy summer days because your skin prickles with its power. But when that bold sun bursts through the clouds in December, its warming power is truly appreciated. Yes, it feels warmer here at the same temperature than in the Midwest, in

Evergreen azaleas deliver a bright pink message amid the spring greens of new leaves and lawn grass.

Unconventional color choices can bring out the best contrast in sweet pink geraniums and a terra cotta wall.

it to wilt daily in the summer. Recovery usually occurs overnight, but it's not a sweet sight to come home to after a day at the office.

The difference between sun and light is important to note. Many plants labeled for sunny sites outdoors actually grow better when there is abundant light but little or no direct sun. This is especially true of non-native plants that have not been grown here for many years. Where they are from and/or where they have been tested may not have our conditions.

The idea of locally proven plants rings especially true here and is a good reason to stay in touch with and/or visit trial gardens in your state. Their research and awards programs provide excellent track records for a variety of plants, especially new releases you will see at the garden center soon. Each is open to the public several days each year.

- LSU Ag Center Hammond Research Station, Hammond, Louisiana

- MSU Truck Crops Experiment Station, Crystal Springs and Poplarville, Mississippi

- AL Agriculture Experiment Station, Auburn University, Auburn, Alabama

part because of the sun's angle and path, but also the combination of its heat with humidity.

In plant parlance, full sun means six to eight hours of direct sunlight, part sun plants need less. There is also a very real difference between the effect of morning sun and afternoon sun. The earlier hours are more humid on average, but heat builds through the day to create mid-to-late afternoon's blistering sun. The same number of hours at different ends of the day can have very different effects on plant materials. Perhaps the most obvious example of this reaction happens with hydrangea (*H. macrophylla*). No matter how many or how few hours the shrub gets from dawn until about 3:00 p.m., the hours after that can cause

Shade falls into three categories: dense, dappled, and high. Dense shade never sees direct sunlight, and plants that grow there depend primarily on reflected light for photosynthesis. This deepest shade falls directly under mature trees with low canopies, between homes in zero lot line properties, and similar environs. Dappled shade occurs where beams of sunlight reach the ground, but for less than half the daylight hours. As a corollary, areas where sunlight finds the soil for more time each day may be designated partly sunny or sunny, depending on the sun's duration there. High shade casts its shadow all day long and may or may not have as much accumulated light as dappled shade. Tall trees create high shade, a lower light zone that lasts throughout the day. Of course, most properties of any size may have more than one kind of shade, and understanding their relative light qualities helps when choosing plants and locating hardscape.

SOIL

Dirt is dirt, but soil is an ecosystem that also includes roots and the underground atmosphere. The three act together to power plant growth when they get along; when plants decline or fail to grow, the reasons can often be traced to soil issues. Soil has organic matter, rock, water, nutrient minerals, and microorganisms, but it also has roots that use the oxygen in its atmosphere and give off carbon dioxide to it. When you water deeply so water percolates through soil (or potting mix), you enable healthy exchange of these and other gases in the soil atmosphere.

Each component of soil plays its role in nurturing your plants, but the reality is that our soils are often heavy and usually waterlogged at some time of the year. To understand why our garden beds are at least slightly elevated above ground level and sometimes truly raised, understand what happens in soil.

Leaves use photosynthesis to make sugar, which then moves to roots and other plant parts as energy sources. Roots bring the sugar energy to the soil party, allowing them to take up water and nutrients that, in turn, return to the leaves. Soil critters like earthworms act in harmony with busy roots as microorganisms feed on root secretions and, in turn, become food for the roots when they die. The oxygen to carbon dioxide ratio in the soil atmosphere determines how well the system works. They fill the spaces between soil particles and around roots, and water management controls them. Because our native soils are poorly drained except those that shed water like a sieve, gardeners amend them to improve conditions for roots, and thus our plants.

The old, humid soils in our states represent a range of geologic types from highly fertile to truly poor, and they all grow something or can be easily coaxed to. Their structure consists of sand, silt, and clay in varying amounts that you can feel when you wet a bit and rub it between your fingers. Sand feels gritty, silt is slick, and clay is sticky. Sand is the biggest soil particle, each about the same size in one place. It drains water rapidly and has large air pockets but little nutrition. Silt is an assortment of smaller particles with qualities in between sand and clay. Clay has even smaller particles, the fewest air pockets, and more minerals. Almost every soil in our region benefits from the addition of organic matter to soils used for gardening. They are made of mostly small particles that attract water and drain it poorly because they are humid in nature. Amending soils with the larger particles of compost and other organic materials gives the sand, silt, and clay something to hold onto. Garden beds made with amended soils will drain well and be slightly higher than ground level. Well-managed sandy soils hold water in root zones long enough and clay opens larger pockets so that water can drain soon enough to grow plants.

You will find more information about improving and keeping your soil healthy throughout this book, but bear this in mind. When botanist H. J. Dittmer got done measuring in 1937, he had a winter ryegrass plant grown in 1.9 cubic feet of soil with 380 miles of roots. After all the calculations were made in this famous study, he proved that when you measure surface area, you find that less than half of any plant is aboveground. No wonder good soil is such a big deal to gardeners!

MULCHES AND COMPOST

Probably the first people who mulched were Adam and Eve. You just can't see them blowing and bagging all the leaves in the Garden of Eden. Those leaves were left to cover the ground where they decomposed over time and delivered nutritious organic matter to the soil. Voila—the first and simplest mulch was born. That same natural mulching process continues every day in the woods of our states, and if you're smart, mulch and compost are integral parts of your garden, too.

Whether you use pine straw, shredded hardwood, ground pine bark, or other organic mulches, there are many reasons to mulch:

- Suppress weeds by depriving them of sunlight.

- Give a neat and finished look to plantings.

- Add texture and color to the landscape.

- Prevent erosion on sloped beds, around exposed roots, and under trees.

■ *Bark mulches can be confusing but each size and type has appropriate garden uses. All except nuggets (2"+ solid wood chips) will decompose in 12-18 months in the Deep South. Plan to work the organic matter into the soil after it begins to decompose; it'll help preserve good drainage and prevent crusting. Shredded bark is lightweight but washes away easily on slopes. Ground bark averages 1" pieces and works well in beds and containers. Hardwood barks are used in vegetable plantings because they have a higher pH than pine barks, which are used almost everywhere else. As a rule of thumb, limit mulch depth to 1-2 inches.*

■ *Gravel mulches are underused in the Deep South but deserve attention for their good looks and ability to moderate soil temperatures and control weeds.*

■ *Pine straw is abundant and inexpensive each fall, and makes a beautiful mulch around shrubs and trees. Remove and replace it when its color darkens.*

- Create a barrier between soilborne diseases and vulnerable green stems.

- Be a ready source of organic matter to work into the soil when it decomposes.

- Moderate water in two ways: mulch holds water in the soil and also helps to shed excess amounts.

Mulch goes along with our need for slightly elevated beds because of so much rain. When a ton of rain falls at once, plenty gets through the mulch and into the soil, but the mulch helps direct rain away from the plants if there's even a couple of inches elevation.

Not all mulches are organic materials that decompose in our lifetime. Black plastic sheet mulch laid over vegetable garden rows in very early spring traps heat to warm soils to make earlier planting possible. Watch for signs of excess heat under this mulch: plants may dry out more rapidly than expected or the plastic may feel soft and very hot to the touch as summer heats up. Remove it if necessary. Clear plastic sheeting is not used for this purpose but is used to control weeds in a process called "solarization." It's a summer project detailed in July's Problem-Solve section. Gravel and stone mulches are as beautiful as they are functional for weed and water control and soil warming.

When you pile up leaves instead of bagging them as trash or set up a more formal compost system, natural rot produces the compost spectrum in these stages:

1. Each leaf is recognizable by tree species in a pile of freshly raked autumn leaves. Despite rumors to the contrary, a light layer of fallen leaves left in garden beds is not dangerous and will usually rot by spring. However, several inches left on the lawn all winter creates too much shade and moisture below.

2. Leaves and other organic materials begin to turn dark, but you can still recognize whole leaves, and not all materials are the same color or texture. You know the process has begun to heat up, to literally gather steam sometimes visible on cold days.

3. Next comes leaf mold, when components are darker and less recognizable. It is valuable for layers in no-till beds, building soil for raised beds, mulching beds of asparagus, and similar situations that call for a larger particle organic matter.

4. Finally, compost happens. The material is rich and crumbly to your hand, and you cannot distinguish leaves anymore. At this stage you can use the compost to build beds and nourish soils, or screen it to produce a finer-size product for potting mixes or seed starting.

The rate at which this all happens depends on what else you add to the compost. For faster rot, use 2 parts brown leaves to 1 part green matter by adding lawn clippings and kitchen trimmings. Add a cup of fertilizer to a new, 3-cubic-foot pile to kick it off and turn the pile weekly to add air and further increase the speed of decomposition.

WATER AND HUMIDITY

NOAA records of average annual precipitation in the United States (1971–2000) rank us the second, third, and fourth rainiest states. Only Hawaii outdoes us with 63.7 inches, and we follow close behind:

Louisiana	60.1 inches
Mississippi	59.0 inches
Alabama	58.3 inches

Like most averages, these numbers can be deceptive. If it just rained the same amount each month, we'd be set and, like much of Hawaii, we would need little supplemental irrigation. But reality harkens to the Three Bears: too wet, too dry, and occasionally just right. Your job is to manage rainfall, irrigate as needed, and moderate conditions in the garden so the extremes have less effect on your plants. Information about projects for water collection and storage, irrigation methods and systems, and soil preparation for good drainage is included elsewhere in this book.

Let's bust these popular myths about watering plants:

- *If you don't water native plants, they will adapt to wet and dry conditions.* Not true for bog plants. True for others if they survive the transplant to your garden and, in the case of shrubs and trees, the first two years of life in the garden. Water natives as you would any new plant and taper off as they mature.

- *Lawns can stand drought or flood by going dormant and come back to life.* Not only is this not true, it is ugly to watch. A better strategy is great drainage under the lawn and enough water in dry times to keep it alive.

- *If water drains out the bottom of the pot, you haven't overwatered.* The thinking is backwards here because soggy soil happens when you water too often or let water sit in the saucer below the pot so that it stays wet constantly.

- *Watering late in the day contributes to leaf diseases.* If this were strictly true, there would be outbreaks after every nighttime rain storm. Water in the morning if you can but do not stress yourself or the plants if your schedule means late day irrigation. Automated systems and manual timers make it easy.

- *Good plants don't need extra water.* The implication here is that you are either growing the wrong plants or doing something essentially wrong as you garden. Neither is true, although well-adapted, healthy plants are better prepared to face extreme water conditions.

Among the advantages of an inground irrigation system is that you control both the spray pattern and frequency of watering.

Humidity is the measure of water vapor in the air, and our vocabulary for its worst effects include words like *sticky, cloying,* and *downright stifling.* The average annual humidities measured at 6:00 a.m. local time in our states range from 84 to 91 percent, and daily averages sit in the 70 percentiles. We relish the days of low humidity and tolerate the rest, mindful that fast, lush plant growth and soft skin are among its benefits. Not every plant can stand up to the combination of humidity and heat in our states, even though it is hardy in our zones. Plants with marginal tolerance are the jewels of northern Mississippi and Alabama, like some daphnes (*Daphne odora*) and *Forsythia.*

FERTILIZER

Fertilizer is nothing more—or less—than plant nutrients. You make sure that the plant gets what it needs and reap the rewards of beauty and sustenance. When you consider how many kinds there are plus the ways and times you are told to fertilize, it's remarkable that anyone ever gets it right. The information can be confusing on its face when words like *specialty* take on horticultural definitions. Add more designations—slow-release, acid-producing, organic, and conventional—and it's no wonder some people vow to garden using only compost or nothing at all. When you look at the subject from the plant's point of view, however, fertilizer is easy to understand and provide. Then you can select a few kinds to use and set up a schedule that suits your garden and your schedule.

Plants use lots more of three particular elements than any others: nitrogen, phosphorus, and potassium, designated N, P, and K. While all act in concert, each has a primary role: nitrogen for leafy growth, phosphorus for flowers, and potassium for cell wall strength in roots and stems. The numbers 10-10-10 on a fertilizer bag indicate a balanced formula, or one that has all three of the major elements in equal amounts. There are effective minor elements, also called trace elements because only a little is needed, that are essential to plant growth. Seven are added to NPK to create complete fertilizers and are mixed together as a specialty fertilizer: sulfur, boron, magnesium, manganese, zinc, iron, and copper. Complete fertilizers have both major and minor elements in

Bricks laid end to end make a sharp, colorful edge that is easily maintained – sweep or hose it off after you work in the bed. A 1 inch layer of composted manure in spring adds important organic matter and nutrients to Deep South soils.

them; specialty fertilizers may have one or more elements in them and are designed for specific plants or issues.

Fertilizers may act so quickly that leaves get greener in just days, such as those made to be mixed in water or fast actors like ammonium sulfate. Or they may be released slowly over a period of time as they degrade naturally, when water reaches them, or soil temperatures rise to activate their ingredients. Some have both modes of action. Individual elements like aluminum in fertilizer accomplish specific goals like changing the color of hydrangea flowers.

Conventional fertilizers are those produced in chemical plants from laboratory formulas; they may be liquid or granular. They are consistent in content and easy to use by hand or in spreaders.

Labels are very specific as to formula, appropriate plants, amounts and intervals for use. Some product lines are made for particular regions while others are not.

Organic fertilizers are those produced from natural sources in a plant, at a farm, or in your compost pile. They supply nutrients and have a positive effect on the life of your soil but work more slowly than conventional fertilizers. Sources vary widely as do production methods. If you compost, you know the materials and process you use determine its nutrient outcome and the quality of the finished fertilizer. The same factors are at work in commercial composts and organic fertilizers. Animal litters and manures, fishes, oils, and plant extracts are among the ingredients on organic labels and the best will include details of contents, process, and nutrients.

Note: Lime is not a fertilizer or a soil conditioner. Its use is detailed in October.

PESTS AND IPM

The major pests of our gardens can be grouped into categories by how they feed. Piercing and sucking insect and mite pests have beaks that enable them to feed on your plants. They damage by dehydrating and discoloring plant parts. Common pests of this kind include spider mites, scales, whiteflies, beetles, and aphids. Chewing pests are cutworms, caterpillar larvae, web builders, and the non-insects snails and slugs. Their damage is often painfully visible as they can strip leaves, chew into stems, and even digest entire plants in a short time. Mammals sometimes eat but more often disrupt the garden in search of food. For example, voles do eat plant roots as they burrow under mulch, but moles tunnel to root out white grubs living under your lawn. Armadillos poke around looking for grubs and other insects while squirrels dig up bulbs and pinch tomatoes, and possums and raccoons forage in the compost. Their paw prints can help identify the intruders and direct your actions to remove food sources or repel the critters.

■ *When you limit the use of pesticides in the garden, you also encourage beneficial insect populations like these ladybugs busy lunching on aphids.*

The professional concept of Integrated Pest Management (IPM) readily translates into home gardening with a method and a mindset for effective pest control. Here's how it works:

- **Monitor.** Make a daily garden walk your priority. Smell the roses but look for insects and watch what they are doing. Check out leaves to notice blemishes, color change, or spots that might indicate a pathogen is present in them.

- **Identify.** Know your enemies and your friends—identify the insects, arachnids, reptiles, amphibians, and mammals in your yard. Fewer cause trouble than you might realize, and you want to encourage the nice guys.

- **Evaluate.** Assess the damage being done and if it is considerable, go directly to action. But one chewed leaf does not necessarily mean you are under attack. Watch for a few days to learn more about what's going on.

- **Act.** Take action if necessary and use the least toxic, least intrusive method of control first.

When you decide there is a pest to be controlled, use physical measures initially. You might pick off blighted leaves, pluck caterpillars and stomp them, blast a strong stream of water to deter aphids, or catch beetles sleeping. And you may decide to fence out larger mammals, put out repellants to run them off, or grow other plants. Oil sprays are considered physical controls because they smother insects and their eggs and should be used annually within the temperature range stated on the label.

The second tier of pest control relies on natural predators and short-lived organic products. You can purchase predators, such as ladybird beetles and aphid lions, or move them from one part of your garden to the problem area. The predatory bacillus used to control caterpillars and more general purpose sprays like insecticidal soaps are also in this category. The issue with these controls is that they act slowly and so should be used in concert with physical measures. For example, the predatory *Bacillus thuringiensis (B.t.)* will be effective if you spray right after you pluck off the first caterpillars you see. But if you wait until there

is a swarm actively feeding, the damage will be done before the *B.t.* can work.

After other measures fail or when a devastating outbreak of insects or disease threatens the life of a plant you cannot live without, use organic or conventional chemical sprays. Few of these products have targeted action and are used when flying insects are relatively still such as whiteflies at dusk or when crawling insects like aphids are present on the plant. Some insecticides act systemically; the plant is drenched with a solution of the product and drawn up through the vascular system. Systemic insecticides should be reserved for serious and ongoing insect pest problems and used with the awareness of their long-term threats to desirable pollinating insects.

Fungicides act preventively and do not cure the diseases they attack but rather slow their progress. Their prompt use can forestall further damage unless the disease shows up long after the plant is inoculated. Commonly used fungicides include:

- Biologicals introduce beneficial microbes into the soil that attack soil-borne fungi.

- Botanicals are formulated from plants with natural fungicide potential and one of these, Neem oil, also has insecticide and miticide properties.

- Mineral and metal-based fungicides may have longer active working life than the other naturals but are often more toxic to plants and users.

- Chemical formula fungicides have active ingredients produced in a laboratory and are effective when used as directed but are not organic.

Always read and follow label directions when using pesticides of any kind.

Step into gardens in the Deep South at any time of year to see plants of every description in beds and pots, from courtyards to estates. No matter what month, you can find all the colors in the crayon box and a panorama of shapes, textures, and seasonal features. The gardens we love are welcoming places, ready year-round with drama, mystery, and tasks to keep us busy. Whether you're looking for a calendar of what and when to do common garden chores or searching up strategies for greater garden success, you've come to the right place. Month by month, from lawns to treetops and everywhere in between, you'll know what to do.

HOW TO USE THIS BOOK

When you purchase any book or get one as a gift, you open it to see if it will be relevant to your life. If it is a book about gardening where you live, it had better be—or it will be relegated to a shelf in the hall. That is not the purpose of this book and it is why the concept of month by month works so well. Some gardening can go on anytime, but other important activities are time sensitive. By referring to any month, you can quickly plan for both. This is not a book about plants, garden style, or philosophy, though they play an integral part. Here you will find the what, how, and when to do a range of garden chores presented with clarity for each month of the year. This book brings together successful strategies and methods used for years in our states, with others developed in recent years as we face a changing climate. The information has been gleaned from personal experience, from professors and professionals, plus from a host of individuals and groups including master gardeners, garden club members, and plant society veterans. It is intended to be a friendly reference that you will want to keep close by your to-do list, or your honey-do list.

You can read the book cover to cover, or pick a month and start from there to maintain and improve your plants and their care. Task areas focus your attention to plan, plant, and care for the garden, as well as details about watering, fertilizing, and problem-solving during that month. Each of those areas is divided into familiar plant categories: annuals, bulbs, edibles, lawns, perennials and ornamental grasses, roses, shrubs, trees, vines and groundcovers, and water gardens. You will find simple tasks to check off your list and more complex ones that may take time but need doing that month.

In 2012, the USDA released new Plant Hardiness Zone Maps for every state and ours are included here. They are drawn to show the average low temperatures in a given place, and it's important

to know if your zone has changed but also to note statewide and regional trends. In that vein, precipitation maps and frost/freeze charts are included. The index is intended for quick reference to topics, plants, and major tasks to take you directly to that information.

Much traditional garden wisdom from other parts of the nation and world gets short shrift from anyone who has gardened even a little bit in our states. Whatever the claim, we have to see it to believe it in our own backyards because so much written about gardening in other states simply does not apply here. No information is presented here that has not passed the backyard test, right here in the Deep South. Use it with confidence and, I hope, find inspiration to keep on growing.

■ *Give yourself the gift of a place to work with your plants. A potting bench needn't be in a shed, and doesn't have to be big to keep necessities close at hand.*

USDA COLD HARDINESS ZONES FOR ALABAMA

ZONE	AVERAGE ANNUAL MINIMUM TEMPERATURE (°F)		
7a	0	to	5
7b	5	to	10
8a	10	to	15
8b	15	to	20
9a	20	to	25

■ *USDA Plant Hardiness Zone Map, 2012. Agricultural Research Service, U.S. Department of Agriculture. Accessed from http://planthardiness.ars.usda.gov*

USDA COLD HARDINESS ZONES FOR LOUISIANA

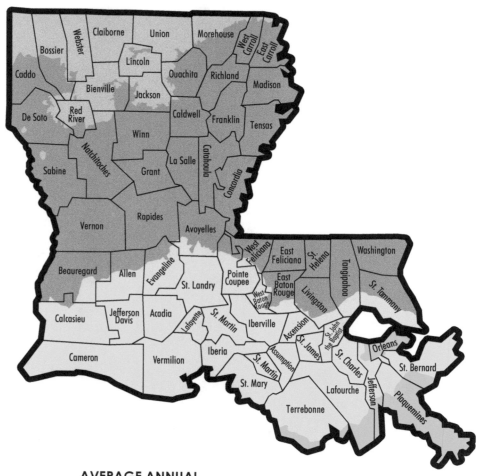

ZONE	AVERAGE ANNUAL MINIMUM TEMPERATURE (°F)		
8a	10	to	15
8b	15	to	20
9a	20	to	25
9b	25	to	30

USDA Plant Hardiness Zone Map, 2012. Agricultural Research Service, U.S. Department of Agriculture. Accessed from http://planthardiness.ars.usda.gov

USDA COLD HARDINESS ZONES FOR MISSISSIPPI

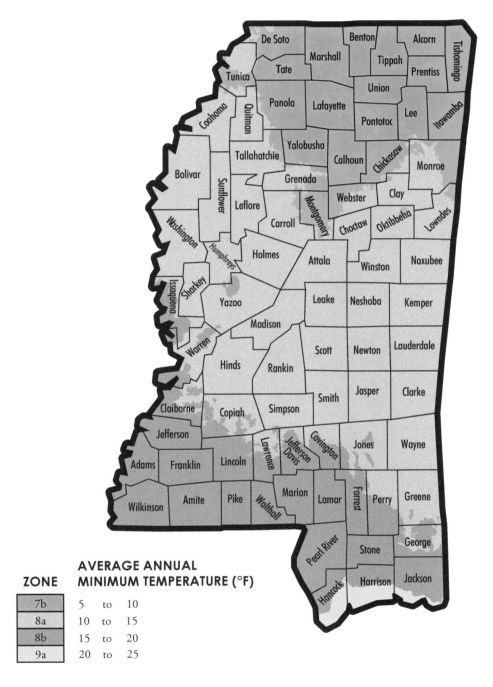

AVERAGE ANNUAL

ZONE	MINIMUM TEMPERATURE (°F)		
7b	5	to	10
8a	10	to	15
8b	15	to	20
9a	20	to	25

■ *USDA Plant Hardiness Zone Map, 2012. Agricultural Research Service, U.S. Department of Agriculture. Accessed from* http://planthardiness.ars.usda.gov

January

If you find a Deep South gardener sitting fireside perusing seed catalogs for days, then it's a very wet, very cold January. Our idea of winter sets in this month: cold weather fronts sweep from west to east while others push much warmer air up from the Gulf of Mexico. Occasionally the weather makers collide to bring frightening storms, but more often, a warm week brings rain and then colder temperatures follow. Plants that require true dormancy or chilling hours to perform may be unsuccessful in the Deep South, even if they are supposedly hardy in our zones, because conditions vary so much. We may wear flip-flops one day and heavy coats the next. Still, it's a good time to have a warm greenhouse or sunroom, especially if there's a lemon tree in bloom.

There will be some days when conditions are good for transplanting shrubs and trees to a better place in the garden, including hydrangeas that are in too much sun. This soil-to-soil transplanting is best done in cold weather to give disturbed roots plenty of time to recover before top growth begins again. Pick the right tool for these tasks—a sharp shovel is best to dig around shallow-rooted shrubs growing in flowerbeds because it digs wider and lifts more soil. Be sure to sharpen the long, narrow-bladed sharpshooter shovel to harvest young trees from the woods for the garden. Slice into the soil at an angle on each side of the trunk to form a long, triangular wedge of roots. As long as the soil does not stick to your shovel, it is a good day to dig up plants or work the soil for their new location.

You may not call it a "garden journal," but find the notes and photos you took last year of your garden and review them now. Grab a calendar and make plans for this year's gardening season. Set practical goals in broad terms—to have more zinnias this summer, to get ahead of the weeds in the backyard so the lawn can grow, or perhaps to switch to containers for this year's tomato plants. Whatever you didn't like, devise a new plan.

Indoors, it's time to start seeds for the spring garden flowers and vegetables. The selections and colors available as established plants are good at local nurseries and plant centers, but for custom color and variety choices, seeds offer more variety.

PLAN

ALL

Whether your garden was designed by experts or not, you will learn a lot about your gardening space by looking at the "big picture."

Understanding your garden site will guide you to wiser planting choices. Every space, large and small, has different microclimates that fit one of these profiles in relation to the others: sunny and wet, sunny and dry, shady and wet, shady and dry. These areas may be natural, such a steep slope in

HERE'S HOW

TO DRAW A SITE SURVEY

- Get a sheet of graph paper and fold it in quarters. Open the paper and orient it so you can mark north, south, east, and west. Understand how the sun moves across your property and what impedes it. This helps define your property's shade.

- Few spaces are truly flat and windless. Observe and note the direction of water flow in heavy rainfall as well as that of prevailing winds or breezes. Mark these observations with small arrows.

- If power lines cross your property, draw them in as dotted lines.

- Locate your home and other structures as they relate to the rest of the property. Draw their shapes and mark the sidewalk, driveway, patio, and deck with solid lines.

- Mark hardscape features with an "X" such as trellises, arbors, columns, garden walls, and seating areas that are permanent.

- Add in existing trees and garden beds. Use a dot or circle for the trees and roughly draw the shape of the beds.

- Mark irrigation zones if you have an in-ground system, or note the places in the garden that stay dry or wet on their own or with your watering methods.

- Look at the drawing with a critical eye, paying attention to the balance of elements in your garden's microclimates.

- Use the drawing as you plan additions and modifications to the garden to best choose what and where to plant.

HERE'S HOW

TO CREATE A NEW GARDEN BED

1. Use a sun-warmed garden hose to lay out your proposed garden, following the topography of the site. Most gardens look best with gentle curves rather than straight lines.

2. Remove existing vegetation, either by hand (digging) or by chemicals (a non-selective glyco-phosphate-based herbicide such as Roundup). Which way you choose depends on how much time you have and how you feel about using herbicides.

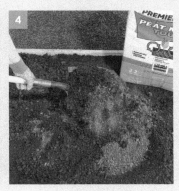

3. Turn in soil amendments to a depth of 6 to 10 inches. Once the existing vegetation is dead or removed, turn the soil by hand or with a tiller, and add soil amendments. Do not use a tiller without killing all existing vegetation first—it may look like you've created a bare planting area, but all you've done is ground the roots into smaller pieces that will sprout into more plants than you started with. Even after multiple tillings spaced weeks apart, you'll be haunted by these root pieces.

4. Install edging to keep lawn grasses from invading your garden. The best option is to install a barrier of some type. When it comes to barriers, it's worth paying more for a quality material. Metal edging buried 4 inches or more into the soil effectively keeps turf from sneaking in. If you go with black plastic edging, use contractor grade to avoid having to replace it in a few years.

5. Cover the new garden with mulch. Mulching your new garden will not only help keep the weeds from settling in, it will also help maintain soil moisture and prevent the soil from washing away until you can get the plants established. Cover the entire prepared garden bed with 2 to 3 inches of an organic mulch such as shredded bark, pine bark nuggets, cocoa bean hulls, and shredded leaves. Avoid using grass clippings; they tend to mat down and become smelly.

full sun that stays dry, or created by structures, such as the shady space between two tall houses that never quite dries out. Make an informal site survey for the specifics in your garden.

For example, you will see that some areas, such as a long fence, may be devoid of plants. You know the site is in sun and rainfall runs across it, but does not linger. It would be the ideal place to plant the roses you've always wanted.

ANNUALS

Close your eyes, or open your photo gallery to recall the colors of the annual flowers that touched you last year—your own or someone else's. Decide whether you want a deliberate mix of hues or to feature one color across the garden this year. Either choice takes planning to accomplish, so begin with a list of colors and plants. For example, you may want to paint a bed in blue and white for spring and add deep purple for summer. Consider sweet alyssum (*Lobularia maritima*) and blue pansies (*Viola* x *wittrockiana*) in spring followed by white Cape daisies (*Osteospermum*), light blue plumbago (*P. capensis*), and purple Io (*Iochroma cyanea*) for color all summer. Knowing the colors that appeal to you informs both seed starting and plant purchases.

If pansies or snapdragons didn't make it, there's a color void in pots and beds. Shop for more of these plants now to fill in the gaps and sow seeds for calendula, cornflower, and nasturtium in Zone 9 beds. Elsewhere, start them in peat pots for transplant to the garden next month. When reseeded larkspur (*Delphinium ajacis*) beds have grown into a strong stand, weed the bed and mulch around the plants for another showy display of color in the early season.

BULBS

Plan to shop locally and order gladiola bulbs (*Gladiolus*) by the dozens to plant in the cut flower garden next month, along with caladiums to start in pots soon after. If you have never grown dinner-plate-sized dahlias, plan to order their tubers soon. Few things are certain in gardening, but you get what you pay for in bulbs—always purchase premium quality, top-size bulbs, tubers, and rhizomes.

EDIBLES

Take a survey if necessary and do the math to plan edible plantings. Use graph paper or sketch out a plan to grow enough edibles for the family to eat, plus some to share. Average harvest amounts and the space needed are readily available, but plan accordingly for your family. If no one but you likes eggplant (*Solanum melongena*), two plants will be plenty. Make space for more berry bushes for growing appetites.

It may seem like a waste of space to plant at the recommended spacing, such as a minimum of 4 to 6 feet apart for blueberry plants. The suggested spacing is based on the mature size of a plant when grown in optimal conditions. Plan to use the "empty" space between new fruit plants to grow annual vegetables or flowers until the berry plants reach maturity in a couple of years.

LAWNS

For a much better summer of lawn care, take care of lawn equipment problems while time is on your side. Locate a shop or do-it-yourself guides to replace worn blades, sharpen edgers, and repair string trimmers and blowers.

PERENNIALS & ORNAMENTAL GRASSES

Find room for divisions of crowded clumps of perennials and ornamental grasses, keeping spacing and texture combinations in mind. Make notes, tag those to be dug up, and plan to amend soils several weeks ahead of planting, if needed.

ROSES

Tea roses are unparalleled in sheer beauty, but the effort comes at a price. Most tea roses lose their "oomph" after a few years and must be replaced. Put rose beds on a three- to five-year rotation plan so new ones are added as others age. Browse new releases and classic varieties this month at garden centers and in gardening catalogs so you can plant them in the garden in February.

SHRUBS

Take time to lay out new beds, note needed rejuvenations, and list potential replacements

■ Camellia *'Guilio Nuccio'*

among your shrubs. Incorporate their lasting beauty into the garden and plan to repeat some in containers to carry your theme throughout. For example, you might reinforce the impact of tall sasanquas (*Camellia sasanqua*) with dwarf varieties in pots on the patio.

TREES

It's a wise idea to take pictures of your trees each January to compare their growth and decline from year to year. You will see changes that need attention such as leafless stems, broken branches, and webs. Set goals now for new plantings and consult an arborist or tree surgeon about maintaining older trees with timely pruning.

VINES & GROUNDCOVERS

When trellises lean and pergolas slump, determine better anchor systems and reinforcements for the structures. Soft winter soils and sometimes-leafless vines ease the task when the weather cooperates.

When you are looking for a vine, consider natives like coral honeysuckle (*Lonicera sempervirens*) and Carolina jessamine (*Gelsemium sempervirens*). They are vigorous, flower in earliest spring, and imbue a strong sense of place.

Get wise and decide to stop fighting when encroaching shade overtakes lawn grass. Plan for groundcovers and mulch beds instead. Choices abound, but nothing beats low-growing perennial ferns in the shade:

- Hollyleaf fern (*Cyrtomium falcatum*) is tolerant of salt spray and is popular where mild winters are the norm. Grow in shade or part sun.

■ *Holly Fern* (Cyrtomium falcatum*) brings evergreen texture to every kind of shade – dense, dappled, and high.*

- New York fern (*Dryopteris novaboracensis*) grows well in drier soils under competitive trees like maple and oak that also provide needed shade.

- Male fern (*D. filix-mas*) and spinulose fern (*D. spinulosa*) are quite different but equally lacy. Both grown in damp, shady beds.

WATER GARDENS

Every garden benefits from a water feature, whether it is a wall fountain in the courtyard, ponds in pots, or inground with cascading waterfalls. The elements and installation will take some time, so learn more about each component.

- Rubber pond liners give control over the water garden's shape and depth, are UV and puncture resistant, as well as long lasting. The flexible material also works to line old, leaky concrete fountains, and to turn almost anything into a water garden. Investigate different brands and the underlay that goes with each one.

- Pumps are essential to water quality and to prevent mosquito breeding. Direct drive submersible pumps send water soaring but can be expensive. Magnetic drive submersibles cost less to run, last longer, and aerate well. External pumps require waterproof housing at the pond's edge but are very efficient at moving water in larger features. They are not swimming pool pumps.

- Some pond designs and some gardeners' tastes require additional filtration. Two kinds of filtration dominate the market: mechanical and biological. Mechanical filters are made of foam, fiber, or paper designed to capture particulates in the pond. Bio filters are more complicated and made for bacteria to dine on as they clean the water.

- Skimmers are handy floating baskets that remove floating materials. Ultraviolet clarifiers may be useful in full sun gardens or where other methods prove inadequate.

The biggest complaint voiced by those with water gardens is that the installation is too small. Avoid this dilemma by planning for more square feet of water in a new feature or to add on to existing gardens. Consider a waterfall, second pond, or boulders and more plants for a bigger impact and more growing space.

PLANT

ANNUALS AND EDIBLES

Seed sown indoors now for annuals and vegetables that will be ready for transplanting to the garden in six to eight weeks. Start seeding now and keep at it, sowing at intervals that will

HERE'S HOW

TO START SEEDS

- Inadequate light will produce stretched, pale green seedlings that fail to grow. Seed starting setups with lights are widely available or make your own: one cool white light bulb and one daylight fluorescent light bulb mounted in a shop light fixture deliver the full spectrum of light needed to start seeds.

- Purchase fresh seed and choose varieties not available locally. Try a bigger pepper, a new tomato, or an heirloom zinnia with green flowers.

- Start seeds in new or recycled plastic containers. To reuse pots or flats, wash them in hot, soapy water, rinse well, and dip in a bleach solution mixed with water at a ratio of 1:10 for five minutes.

- You can also start seeds in peat cups.

- Always use fresh seed starting mix in pots and peat cups to prevent damping off and other diseases. Dampen the mix before use.

- Fill each container to the top, water once, and allow the mix to settle before sowing seed.

- Peat pellets are best used for annuals that suffer most from transplant shock, such as poppies (*Papaver*) and morning glory and moonflower (*Ipomoea*).

- Do not let seedlings dry completely out! Put pots, cells, or pellets into a tray under the lights and water from the bottom most of the time. Keeping the seedlings covered will also help retain moisture in the seed-starting mix.

- Heating mats for seed starting can speed germination and growth.

- Keep seedlings 3 to 4 inches underneath the lights at all times and turn the lights on for eight to ten hours each day.

HERE'S HOW

TO POT DUTCH IRIS BULBS

- Select containers that are 4 inches deep and 8 inches wide—one pot for every dozen bulbs.

- Prepare a loose potting mix. Fill one pot 3 inches deep with the mix.

- Nestle twelve bulbs into the soil so they are close together, pointy end up, and not touching each other. Label the pot with the date of planting and the date eight weeks later.

- Add more potting mix until the tips of the iris bulbs are showing.

- Water well; add a starter solution to promote rooting such as liquid rooting hormone, compost tea, or root stimulator fertilizer.

- Take advantage of cold weather and store the pot outdoors where it will not freeze but will be exposed to cool temperatures and no sunlight.

- Check the pot weekly and water if the soil feels dry.

- In eight weeks, the sprouts should be a few inches tall and the plants can be moved into bright light and warmer temperatures. Water as needed.

- If you like, each week, start another pot of twelve Dutch iris bulbs so their bloom time will be a week later.

meet their needs for warming temperatures in the spring and summer gardens.

BULBS

This is the last opportunity to plant any tulips (*Tulipa*) you stored in the refrigerator last fall. Plant them twice as deep as they are tall for bright pops of color in beds and outdoor containers. Use a bulb planter to avoid damaging nearby roots; its handy ruler can be used to check the depth of planting.

Potted bulbs make fine gifts, but what to do with them after the flowers finish can be a dilemma. You hesitate to throw them away, and not all will become reblooming perennials in the garden. Daffodils, amaryllis, and hyacinths forced in pots are good candidates for transplanting, but tulips and paperwhite narcissus may regrow but seldom bloom again. Consider them annuals and when their flowers finish, compost the bulbs.

Plant a rotation of Dutch iris bulbs (*I. x hollandica*) for cut flowers over many weeks.

EDIBLES

Plant fruit trees of all kinds this month when conditions permit. Wet, cold soil and very windy days will compromise your success, so avoid them. Not all fruit trees are alike. Figs (*Ficus carica*) and persimmons (*Diospyros virginiana, D. kaki*), like

It's hard to imagine this small fruit tree providing your family with fruit, but with time and care, you'll reap the benefits.

blueberries (*Vaccinium*), grow everywhere and are among easiest to grow. In Zone 9, loquat (*Eriobotrya japonica*) and strawberry guava (*Psidium cattleianum*) are also low maintenance and the growing season is long enough for them to bloom and fruit. Plums (*Prunus*) and pears (*Pyrus*) take more time and attention, while apples (*Malus domestica*) and peaches (*Prunus*) will seldom fruit without a regular spray program to control predictable insects and diseases.

Choose apple varieties with disease resistance that matches your zone's conditions such as these and other local favorites:

- Zone 7—'Granny Smith', 'Grimes Golden', 'Liberty', 'Freedom'

- Zone 8—'Anna', 'Adina', 'Granny Smith', 'Grimes Golden'

- Zone 9—'Adina', 'Anna', 'Dorsett Golden', 'Ein Shemer'

LAWNS

If you're involved in new home construction and the lot barely gets cleared when it starts to rain again, take a chance and try seeding perennial ryegrass or alfalfa to hold the soil in place. They won't grow much, but provide "green manure" when it's time to plant a lawn or make beds.

PERENNIALS & ORNAMENTAL GRASSES

From huge pampas grass (*Cortaderia selloana*) to graceful maiden grass (*Miscanthus sinensis* 'Gracillimus') and its cultivar, zebragrass (*M. Sinensis* 'Zebrina') to pert dwarf zebra grass and fountain grasses (*Pennisetum*), ornamental grasses need dividing every third year. Without it, they crowd, overgrow, and stop flowering. Pot or replant

---

HERE'S HOW

TO PLANT BARE-ROOT ROSES

- Remove all wrapping and packing materials as soon as you get the plants.

- Prune an inch off of the bottom of roots and the top of stems.

- Fill a bucket with warm water and soak the bare-root rose overnight. If you want to add a root stimulater to the water, do so now.

- Prepare a planting hole in the garden or get a big black nursery can and container growing mix. Amend either soil to improve drainage and fertility as needed.

- Backfill the hole or fill the container with a raised cone of soil in the center.

- Spread the rose roots over the cone and finish filling so that the roots are entirely underground and the crown is at or just above ground level.

- Adjust as needed for position and stability.

- Water well. Use root stimulator fertilizer, compost tea, or liquid rooting hormone and mulch beds and pots to lessen transplant shock.

HERE'S HOW

TO PLANT TREES AND SHRUBS

Determine if your soil can be dug. If it is sticks to your shovel and won't shake off, wait a few days or risk damage to the soil structure and further impede drainage.

- Whenever possible, pick a day that is mild in temperature, cloudy, and windless. If the weather is very sunny, plant after midday.

- Dig a hole deeper and wider than the rootball you will plant. Amend the soil you dig out to improve drainage, if needed, by adding organic matter and/or sand.

- Prune new shrubs back by one third of their overall size and shape new trees to start them in the right direction.

- Slip the rootball out of its pot and snip or slice down the sides if the roots are crowded.

- Spread roots in the hole or loosen the rootball by rubbing its sides and bottom.

- Backfill the hole enough to place the shrub or tree at-or slightly aboveground level. Halfway through, tamp the soil down to prevent air pockets that can collapse and sink the plant.

- Water once, deeply and slowly, to soak the rootball. Use a root stimulator, compost tea, or liquid rooting hormone and mulch the new planting.

- In windy or sharply sloped areas, stake young trees for the first year to direct their growth and surround them with a loose ring of wire fencing to prevent bark damage from wildlife.

new divisions in sunny garden beds right away to prevent dehydration, which can slow their rebound.

In Zone 9, take advantage of a warm week to divide and replant the hardiest perennials like cast iron plant (*Aspidistra*), montbretia (*Crocosmia*), purple heart (*Setcreasea*), and Queen Anne's lace (*Daucus carota*).

ROSES

Bare-root rose bushes appear for sale everywhere this month and offer a wide variety of sizes, habits, and flower types at very reasonable prices. The tradeoff is the extra work you do to get them started on the right root.

SHRUBS AND TREES

Fruit trees and the banana shrubs (*Michelia figo*) you rooted last year, the magnolia (*M. grandiflora*) tree you dug up at Daddy's place, and the wealth of shrubs and woody vines for sale in garden centers can be planted now, unless the soil is very wet.

The Deep South needs more trees to replace those lost to storms, age, and pests, and to maintain our verdant green reputation. Solve this problem by growing trees for your property and to give away. The acorns and buckeyes you dropped into a drawer last November are still quite viable, so get to work.

HERE'S HOW

TO START TREES FROM SEEDS

- Mix garden soil with leaf mold or ground bark and fill a one-gallon nursery pot.

- Push each seed 2 to 3 inches into the pot and water if the mix is dry.

- Leave the pots outside and water them monthly but do not let them freeze. An unheated shed or garage works well during very cold spells.

- When new growth emerges, add a slow release fertilizer to the pot. Continue to water regularly, grow until cool weather, and transplant to the garden.

VINES & GROUNDCOVERS

Woody vines transplant like shrubs and trees, with two additions:

- Prune vines hard (cut back quite a bit) to reduce transplant shock, especially those you dug up.

- Install trellises and other supports at planting time to prevent root damage later.

In Zone 9 and parts of Zone 8, transplant groundcovers this month. Cut back trailers like Asiatic (*Trachelospermum asiaticum*) and star jasmines (*T. jasminoides*) to encourage new growth and mulch around new plants of clumping groundcovers like liriope (*L. muscari*) and bugleweed (*Ajuga reptans*) to control weeds until the plants grow together.

WATER GARDENS

Every water garden needs submerged plants that help oxygenate the water and maintain its quality. You can grow plenty for your pond by visiting an aquarium store now for hornwort (*Ceratophyllum*), *Anacharis*, and other hardy plants that live entirely underwater. Transplant small plants to pond pots with fresh water and fertilizer; grow them until you can move them into the water feature.

CARE

ALL

If you make no other New Year's resolution, plan to walk the garden daily this year. A quick turn or a leisurely stroll, depending on the weather, gives you exercise and a close-up view of exactly what's happening in the garden. You will see problems in their early stages when they can be readily addressed but also observe the critters that live there or those that help control pests. Most important, the first flower buds to open, the first seeds to sprout, and the first fireflies will be yours. Don't miss a minute!

Indoors and on the porch, potted plants will lean toward the sun, especially when winter skies are gray. Rotate each pot if you see a slight tilt so light exposure and growth stay even.

ANNUALS

Overwintering flowers like pansy and snapdragon (*Antirrhinum*) in Zone 9, along with foxglove (*Digitalis*) and Canterbury bells (*Campanula*) farther north, tolerate stormy weather with great aplomb. Groom the plants in pots and beds outdoors to remove damaged flowers and leaves, fertilize them, and freshen the mulch if it has washed away.

BULBS

Dry amaryllis (*Hippeastrum*) bulbs growing inside in pots to prepare them for rebloom. Lay pots on their side and remove leaves as they brown out. After a month or so, the bulb will sprout a green nose signaling the return of active growth. That's your cue to resume watering and fertilizing.

To prevent disease spread, check dahlias, caladiums, and other bulbs in storage and discard any that have soft spots. Dust those nearby with sulfur.

EDIBLES

Prune fruit trees to increase the amount of sunlight that reaches every branch. This improves their ability to make and sustain fruit. Begin by removing dead and diseased wood, one of any two

Prune fruit trees to open up interior areas so sunlight can reach all the branches.

branches that rub against each other, and those that crisscross the canopy.

- Fig trees should look like big round blobs but not solid ones. Select and space branches so sunlight reaches each one. Shape, but avoid excessive pruning, as figs will be late or skip a year if pruned very hard.

- Plum trees produce all along their branches if they are sturdy and sunlit. Envision an open vase shape for plum and peach trees, too, with branches beginning 2 feet above ground level. Above that, select branches that are well spaced around the main trunk and remove

the rest. Shorten each stem slightly to keep a pleasing shape.

- Let pear and apple trees develop a taller trunk before leaving side branches to mature. Both can be shaped wider at the bottom of the canopy to form a loose teardrop shape. Apple trees have right angled side shoots called "spurs" that grow along each branch. Trim these to 2 inches for better fruiting.

LAWNS

If you cannot tolerate lawn weeds, one or two clumps of clover will spur you into action. Most people can live with a few weeds, but when more than one-third of a lawn is covered in weeds, during summer, winter, or both, it is time to act. Understand that weeds thrive where turf grass does not. So act accordingly to favor lawn grass over the weeds. Dry areas, wet areas, slopes and holes, compacted soils, and very sandy soils challenge lawn grass to overcome the weeds that thrive there. Address your lawn's underlying issues now.

PERENNIALS & ORNAMENTAL GRASSES

When the fuzzy plumes of ornamental grasses have passed their peak and the blades of grass are brown, it is time to rejuvenate them for the new year. Grab the hedge shears, protect your eyes and limbs, and cut the grass down. After the initial cuts, turn the hedgers over to trim the clump neatly into shape. In the end, the clump should look like a squat mushroom even if it takes a chainsaw to get through it.

If it has grown too large for its space, dig up the entire clump with at least a shovel's depth of roots and more, if possible. Split it into sections 1 square-foot-sized or slightly smaller.

ROSES

Even the hardiest roses benefit from annual sprays of horticultural oil to smother insects and their eggs. Use a pump sprayer with an adjustable nozzle to create a spray that you can control and direct. Spray all parts of the rose bush—from its base to

Cut back ornamental grass, avoiding any new growth.

TO PRUNE CREPE MYRTLES

- Look at the knobs that have formed where the tree has been pruned in the past. There will be numerous small branches emerging from the knob.

- Choose three to five strong, well-spaced branches to become the new canopy and cut a few inches off of each one.

- Remove the rest of the branches entirely.

- Inspect the knobs occasionally and remove any additional branches that emerge.

the tip of every cane. If leaves are present, spray both upper and lower sides with a mist of oil. Always check the label of your product for the most effective, safe temperature range.

SHRUBS

Weed underneath shrubs now while the soil is soft and invaders are small. Use a gloved hand, sharp hoe, or a string trimmer as the situation demands, taking care not to dig deeply. With a little practice it is not difficult to weed around shrubs without disturbing shallow roots. If vines or trees invade a shrub, get them at ground level or slightly below for best control.

TREES

Sharpen the shears and loppers and get to work on crepe myrtles. Remove old flower heads and a few inches from each stem to encourage the natural grace of their form. If your crepes have been severely pruned annually for years, it is challenging to change that pattern but not impossible.

VINES & GROUNDCOVERS

Much of the joy of growing vines is getting them to bloom prolifically and/or make fruit and seeds without watching them grow out of sight. For example, winter pruning wisteria (*W. sinensis*) controls its vigor and flowering. Shorten the vines to fit their pergola or maintain their globe shape and to keep them out of nearby trees. Look along each vine to see a right-angled side branch (called "T" for its shape) and trim those to 3 inches long to promote flowering.

Shortening the "Ts" also works to bring flowers and fruit to that Deep South favorite, muscadine and scuppernong grapes (*Vitis rotundifolia*).

WATER GARDENS

Where water features were drained for the winter, check for leaks and gaps in liners and remove and/or repair them this month.

Replace and reposition gravel and rocks that have loosened or broken away.

Groom water plants in storage and fertilize if you are growing them in a heated greenhouse. If yours is a year-round water feature, give it a gentle cleaning—groom the plants, scoop out leaves and debris, and clean the filter.

WATER

ALL

January brings an average of 4.5 to more than 6 inches of rainfall to our states. There may be exceptions at your location, but this month usually gives irrigation systems and water bills a welcome break. In dry years, winter watering still should be done with caution to accommodate most plants' slower growth and semi-dormancy. In years of average rainfall, garden beds seldom need additional water except to ensure that new plantings stay hydrated.

For many weeks, potted plants spending the winter indoors will tolerate imperfect practices such as watering too little at random times or when the plant wilts. With just weeks to go before they return outdoors, establish a solid watering pattern.

ANNUALS AND EDIBLES

Water pots and beds of actively growing plants regularly, especially if January weather is dry or very windy.

BULBS

Water pots of tulips and Dutch iris in cold storage outdoors when the soil in their containers feels dry on top. When the sprouts are up and growing, put the pots in bright light for a few days and then in a sunny place; water completely once a week.

LAWNS

Watering the lawn now will not harm it any more than a good rain does and will help the ryegrass stay green and growing. If you plan to fertilize the perennial ryegrass overcoat this month, be certain the lawn is not dry beneath. Water the day before you fertilize, if needed.

PERENNIALS & ORNAMENTAL GRASSES

Pulling mulch up around perennial crowns to protect them from cold weather has its merits. Some insulation at ground level can be helpful, especially if the site is exposed, hilly, or subject to prevailing north winds. But too much mulch can be counterproductive—inspect those clumps monthly to be sure the soil underneath the mulch

HERE'S HOW

TO WATER OVERWINTERING INDOOR POTS

- Poke the soil, and if it is dry and hard, put the pot in a sink or tub and use a hand cultivator or a fork to loosen the surface crust.

- Water the pot thoroughly with tepid water and let it drain. Water again to fill the space between the soil and the top of the pot.

- Ideally, this leaching process happens monthly or more often if you use constant feed fertilizer programs. Leaching allows the necessary air exchange in the soil and removes salts and other contaminants that can slow growth.

- When a pot needs water in between leachings, fill its saucer with water and the soil will absorb it through the drain holes.

- More water is not better in this case. Empty saucers an hour later or use a turkey baster to extract excess water.

- Pick a pleasant day to check on pots of tropical plants in storage outdoors and water them well once this month.

is not extremely wet or dry. Pull some of the mulch away to let it dry out or water, if needed.

ROSES
Where rosebushes do not lose their leaves, watch for wilting to know if they need water.

SHRUBS
Watch for unexpected withering on tips of young shrubs, especially thin-stemmed beauties like spireas. Windy, cold weather can dry them out, so monitor the soil, and if it is dry, water well.

TREES
When you are trying to establish trees and must depend on rainfall to water them, consider using a reservoir bag. Durable and easy to use, the bags drip slowly to make sure the soil does not dry out. If rainfall is plentiful, close the drip valve on the bag until you need it again.

VINES & GROUNDCOVERS
Water only if the weather is very unseasonable and rain is less than half the usually expected amounts.

WATER GARDENS
Water features in courtyards and indoors that are not turned on all the time can allow algae to grow in them. Replace, circulate, or aerate the water regularly to keep them clean.

FERTILIZE

ALL
Like cliques of teenagers in the school cafeteria, organic and conventional products sit on separate aisles at the garden center. They may be there for the same reasons but want nothing to do with one another. Fertilizing plants has gotten contentious even though it simply involves supplying the nutrition they need to grow.

- You don't have to call yourself an organic gardener to appreciate the value of organic matter and organic fertilizers, those derived from once-living resources such as animals, fish, and plants. Most organic products depend on interaction with soil life to become active and so their results are not seen as quickly as some conventional fertilizers. Organics last longer and are much less likely to burn plants if overused or applied to dry soils. Because they contain organic matter, they benefit the soil over the long term.

- Consistent, dependable, and easy to use, conventional fertilizers enable you to readily provide specific nutrients and programs without inventing your own formulas. Their results are predictable and depend only on your ability to mix them properly and coincide their use with plant growth stages. Both liquid and granular forms are available in individual elements and endless combinations that can do more than fertilize, such as maintaining an acidic soil condition. They are widely available, affordable, and show their results sooner than organics.

After you water indoor plants, water them again with a soluble fertilizer included, if you do not have a slow-release formula pellet in the pots. Newly rooted cuttings can be fertilized with balanced soluble formulas, such as 16-16-16. Mix at half the recommended strength to maintain growth in these young plants.

ANNUALS
To enjoy traditional spring annuals in the Deep South we plant them in the fall and grow them over the winter. Depending on where you live, plants in this category include pansy, snapdragon, Canterbury bells, English daisies, calendula, most foxgloves, and some hollyhocks. Yellowed leaves on overwintering annuals remind you that pots and beds need fertilizer. When nitrogen is depleted, older leaves give theirs up to the new growth above and turn yellow in the process. Soluble formulas deliver a faster re-greening, which is particularly important in wet weather when all nutrients, but especially nitrogen, can wash out of the root zone.

BULBS
As daffodils and other spring-flowering bulbs emerge, fertilize established clumps with a granular

formula made for bulbs or a general-purpose garden fertilizer. Use your gloved finger to draw a circle 1 inch deep around each clump and sprinkle about 1 tablespoon of granular fertilizer evenly in the groove. Cover it and water if a soaking rain is not forecasted.

EDIBLES

Fertilize actively growing vegetables, except for those you will pick this month, such as Brussels sprouts and cabbage in parts of Zone 8 and Zone 9. Add 1 inch of compost/manure to beds that are resting now and turn under alfalfa or other green manure crops once the stand is 3 inches tall.

LAWNS, PERENNIALS & ORNAMENTAL GRASSES, ROSES, AND WATER GARDENS

Please do not apply fertilizers in January to these garden plants growing outdoors. It is fine to fertilize any cuttings you are rooting indoors.

SHRUBS, TREES, AND VINES & GROUNDCOVERS

If plants in these categories are newly planted, continue using the same root-stimulating formula you applied at transplant time. Plants recovering from stresses like storm damage or pest invasions can be fertilized with no-nitrogen formulas such as 0-10-10.

PROBLEM-SOLVE

ALL

Look out your windows! If there is nothing to see, no focal point to draw your eye at midwinter, it is past time to get one. A tree can be that steady focus, as can an evergreen hedge. But neither is as compelling as well placed statuary, big wooden arbors, an elaborate bird feeding station, an elegant pergola, a seating group that beckons to you, or a row of gorgeous pots atop your garden wall. Nonliving landscape elements, known as hardscape, lend continuity to the garden because they do not change with the seasons. That repetition adds a comfort level to the scene and is the reason to use one material for paths and edging rather than a diverse collection. Make a statement

with hardscape that stands out in the winter garden and enjoy the view.

Reports of fire ants in January are more common than anyone would like to believe. Treat mounds that appear this month to slow down the ants' march across your property and consider applying bait as a neighborhood project this spring.

EDIBLES

Wet soil can delay planting next month unless you take steps to solve the drainage problems now. Add a perforated pipe to raised beds, dig a ditch to drain rows, or shovel a swale between beds to get ready for potatoes, onions, and green peas. Raised beds that aren't as raised as they were may just need a solid edge to reinforce and hold their soil in place. Use landscape edging, bricks set on end, or boards nailed together to form a neat, useful edge.

LAWNS

White grubs thrive along the drier edges of your lawn, especially near sidewalks and driveways. Identify the pests and take action to control

■ *Use milky spore powder to get rid of grubs in your lawn.*

them. A combination of milky spore treatments and conventional pesticides will work sooner than milky spore alone and can begin this month in the warmer parts of Zones 8 and 9. Milky spore products contain a bacterium that is a predator of white grubs. Apply milky spore three times yearly, in January, June, and September. If you are an organic gardener, stop at this step. Otherwise spread a conventional grub control product in the spring. Both products should be applied to the lawn with a spreader for even distribution.

PERENNIALS & ORNAMENTAL GRASSES

Though you might not plant bamboo, it can invade your garden if a neighbor has the running variety. Control running bamboo as soon as it sprouts by stomping on the cone-shaped shoots when they appear. Do this everywhere the bamboo pops up and there will be less to stomp each year.

ROSES

Collections of similar-size plants are not as interesting as those with a variety of heights, colors, and flower shapes. Every rose garden needs an arbor or trellis to lift the eye as well as to support the roses. Without an element of height, the rose garden looks flat, a problem solved by installing an architectural element. With a sturdy arbor in place, plant a vigorous climbing remontant (reblooming) rose:

- 'Crepuscule': Rare apricot shades cover this noi-sette rose, a stiff climber introduced in 1904.

- 'Lamarque': This white noisette was intro-duced in 1830.

- 'Mermaid': A species rose introduced in 1918 with single white flowers and bright yellow centers.

- 'New Dawn': Subtle shades of pink color and a blowsy flower on this 1930 introduction.

- 'Old Blush': A China rose with stunning, big pink flowers.

- 'Peggy Martin': This rose found blooming after Hurricane Katrina delivers bunches of perfectly pink flowers on nearly thornless vines.

- 'Red Cascade': A miniature rose in flower size only with hundreds of deep crimson, dime-sized flowers.

- 'The Fairy Cl.': A pink polyantha with rounded leaves like the shrub variety.

SHRUBS

The dominant winter garden colors are green, gray, and brown, a palette that looks best decorated with Christmas lights. After New Year's, though, when camellias (*C. japonica*) begin to bloom, nothing equals the natural show. Evergreen, broad-leaved, and well suited for shade or dappled sun, camellia is long lived in rich, fertile, well-drained soil. Keep the shrubs mulched and water weekly in dry seasons. Choose among flower shapes—single, semidouble, or fully double—in white, red, pink, and many other hues. More than 3,000 named varieties exist; here are some to consider:

- Zone 7: 'Winter's Dream', 'April Blush', 'April Tryst'

- Zone 8: 'Purple Dawn', 'Pink Perfection', 'Betty Sheffield'

- Zone 9: 'Lady Clare', 'Professor Sargent', 'Alba Plena'

Float short-stemmed camellia flowers in a bowl and let one adorn a suit jacket for a classic look to brighten up gray days.

VINES & GROUNDCOVERS

Keep aggressive vines like wisteria from taking over at ground level by cutting sprouts off just below ground level to suppress regrowth. Cover the area with deep mulch, if possible. Alternatively, watch for resprouts in warm weather and spray or paint the new vines to control them. Use grass shears, hedge shears, or a string trimmer to cut down groundcovers that have crept out of their bed to keep the edges neat. When they resprout, dig up the new shoots and plant them back in the bed or share them.

February

This month reminds everyone that winter exists, even if only for short spells. February keeps us on guard, threatening, and sometimes delivering, frigid temperatures and endless waves of rain. Somehow the pruning and planting gets done in between. Days in the shortest month can be glorious, too—crisp air, blue skies, and flowers aplenty. On average, temperatures range from freezing or a bit below it to the mid-50s in Muscle Shoals, AL, and Clarksdale, MS. As you travel south into Zone 8, cities such as Shreveport, LA, and Meridian, MS, are warmer by 7 to 10 degrees but are still subject to freezing, ice storms, and rare snowfalls. Mobile, AL, New Orleans, LA, and the rest of Zone 9 rarely see freezing temperatures, with temperatures ranging from 40 to 65 degrees Fahrenheit. Still, there are days when wind and cloudy skies conspire to make conditions feel colder and snow sometimes makes a brief appearance.

The Deep South boasts some color all winter, but the real show starts early along our coasts, steadily spreading the signs of spring to our northern borders as the month ends. Flowering quince (*Chaenomeles*) brightens gray days. Native red maples (*Acer rubrum*) burst into bloom to fill swamps and backyards with powerful shades of crimson and maroon. By the end of the month, they are followed by the glassine flowers of native redbud (*Cercis canadensis*), a showstopper in lilac-purple shades.

Snowdrops (*Leucojum*) start the bulb parade, followed by the littlest daffodils (*Narcissus* 'Tete a Tete', for example) and then their trumpeted relatives, the roadside daffodils. These remind passersby where homes once stood, defying the odds and tempting gardeners. Among the most reliable daffodils for the Deep South are:

- Yellows: 'Carlton', 'Hawera', 'Dutch Master'
- Whites: 'Mt. Hood', 'Thalia'
- Bicolors: 'Ice Follies', 'Jack Snipe', 'Einstein'

Indoors, foliage plants are at their peak or should be, and some may be in bloom, such as orchids (*Dendrobium*), moth orchids (*Phalaenopsis*), and peace lilies (*Spathiphyllum*). If you made space in the sunroom for big pots of tropical plants such as shower orchid (*Congea*), your efforts are rewarded now with sumptuous flowers.

PLAN

ALL

Time is running out to plan new beds that will grow most plants—from roses to tomatoes and beyond. Start digging when you can, or layering for no-till beds, but plan well so you have everything you need to get the job done. Called "pre-prep," it shows you that a rich, organic, well-drained soil takes more than muscles.

ANNUALS

Flower beds can be planted with dozens of identical, long-blooming annuals for a sweeping, dramatic effect or with a diversity of plants and colors to interest the eye. But neither succeeds as a last-minute decision, either falling flat or creating visual chaos. Make basic decisions now and tuck your plan for color(s) and numbers of plants needed into your wallet. It'll be there when you need it to shop.

BULBS

Big bulbs deserve big attention when it comes to planning their space. Elephant ears (*Colocasia,* *Alocasia*) and crinum (*Crinum* hybrids) bulbs can be softball sized or have diameters to rival a football. Their clumps will soar and spread, and they deserve to be focal points, such as crinums ringing a birdbath or elephant ears used as a backdrop to the patio. Plan for the "big boys" to grow near equally strong-textured, muscular plants such as banana plants (*Musa*) and cannas (*Canna*) with red or striped leaves for contrast. Look at red Abyssinian banana (*Ensete* 'Maurelii') and cannas 'Tropicanna', and the old timer, 'Pretoria'.

If you are searching for an alternative to caladiums (or impatiens) in the shade, meet *Achimene*. Oddly, this precious plant is called Japanese pansy or orchid pansy, but it is none of those (which are in the *Viola* genus). It boasts velvety leaves and sophisticated flowers mostly in shades of pink, coral, and purple. Grow it from cone-shaped rhizomes you start this month and transplant to the shade garden in late March or April. Harvest them late in the fall for winter storage.

HERE'S HOW

TO PREP SOIL FOR PLANTING

- Do a soil test if you are having problems with plants growing or if the property is new to you, to learn the soil status and what its needs may be.

- Test drainage by digging a narrow, deep hole that resembles a posthole and fill it with water.

- Watch the time. If it does not drain away in an hour, plan to grow a bog or amend it.

- Know what you are planting to decide about soil amendments and strategies. If a very well-drained soil is needed for the plants you want to grow, plan for it.

- Plan slightly raised beds or rows for vegetables, herbs, and cut flowers wherever you live in the Deep South.

- Find the amendments you will need and how much you require of each, then plan a time to get the new bed made. Lime and fertilizer may be on your list as should organic matter, such as ground barks, composts, and manures. A mix of organic material works better than individual ones to improve water management in our soils.

TO PLAN A FLOWER BED

- Check the ultimate size of your chosen plant(s). Small annuals, such as french marigolds, need about 1 square foot each; big ones like cleomes will take up 2 feet square or more of space.

- Figure the area for planting either in one swath or as sections for different plants. Measure length times width to find the area of the entire bed or split it up and calculate its components.

- For example, a square foot along the front of a bed is adequate for narrowleaf zinnias. If the bed is 20 feet long, that means twenty zinnias. Behind them might be clumping sunflowers like 'Teddy Bear' that need slightly more space to accommodate their girth, or fifteen plants to provide 1.5 square feet each.

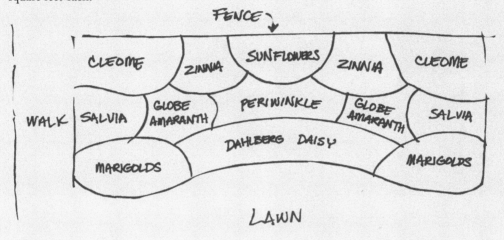

Sample Garden Plan—Annuals

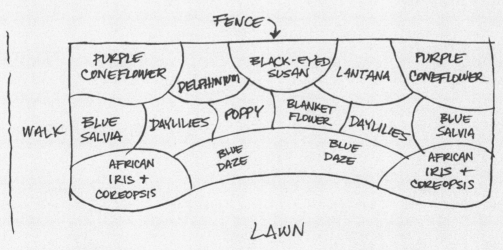

Sample Garden Plan—Perennials

■ *Community gardens can be a great idea for people with no space to raise their own edibles.*

EDIBLES

Planning for the spring and summer gardens can be daunted by lack of space or heavy shade at home. Community garden plots can be the answer and also offer the camaraderie of other gardeners. Seek out local groups now so you can get on board in time to plant the vegetables that need the most space, such as corn, melons, and pumpkins. If no such garden exists where you live, find a few folks and start one—anywhere there's empty space, sunlight, and water, there's garden potential.

LAWNS

If last year's lawn was disappointing, conduct a soil test so you can plan for a lusher, greener lawn this year. Soil test kits are available from each state's Cooperative Extension Service or can be purchased at garden centers or online. The results from the Extension or County Agent's office will be tailored by the information you provide and help you plan for liming and fertilizers, if needed.

PERENNIALS & ORNAMENTAL GRASSES

Think ahead for a succession of perennial color through the seasons. Once you see a bed of Lenten rose (*Helleborus orientalis*) in bloom for weeks during winter, you know it is a "must have" plant for shady gardens. The most reliable *Helleborus* for our zones, this perennial can be followed by Indian pink (*Spigelia marilandica*), another long-blooming shade plant. Summer brings on toad lily (*Tricyrtis formosana*) and hidden ginger (*Curcuma petiolata*), jewels of color in your shady fern grotto.

ROSES

Check the color palette in your rose collection and plan to expand it this year, reinforce your favorite shades, or change the mood entirely. In classic roses, red is for passion, white for purity, yellow for loyalty, and pink for friendship. Decide what you want to say with your roses and plan colors before you plant.

Butterfly rose (*Rosa mutabilis*) could be called "shape shifter" because it mutates through a rainbow of colors on each flower. These single flowers open yellow, turn orangey, then rose pink, and finally deep crimson red. Because they open over days and weeks, all the colors appear at once on this lovely China rose. Vigorous enough to grow as a hedge, butterfly rose easily reaches 6 feet tall in a sunny bed.

SHRUBS

If shrubs spend much of the year as solid green background plants, start thinking about variegation as a way to break up the monotony. You can't change azalea leaves but a row of shrubs in front of them, like dwarf variegated abelia, has plenty of pizzazz to keep the view interesting, even without flowers.

Foundation plantings can cause boredom, a serious problem especially when it happens on small properties. Make a strong statement at the front of the house, even if it means replacing what's there, to establish your garden style at first glance. Matching beds of boxwood (*Buxus*) or hollies add an air of formality, and while flowering shrubs like Indian hawthorn (*Raphiolepsis*) and fringe plants (*Loropetalum*) can be friendlier, they may be more casual than you intend.

TREES

Because deciduous trees are often the backbone of the winter garden, it's important to appreciate their barks—ridged, slick, notched, slippery, or peeling. Decide what's missing and where you can use more winter interest, and then plan for these in all zones:

- Crepe myrtle 'Natchez' (*Lagerstroemia*) has deep cinnamon-colored bark now and white flowers later.

- Lacebark elm (*Ulmus parvifolia*) sheds bark to show gray, green, brown, and beautiful red.

- American sycamore (*Platanus occidentalis*) bark peels back from brown for glimpses of white underbark.

■ *The butterfly rose* (Rosa mutabilis) *changes color as its petals age. They open yellow and quickly go to orange then pink and finally deep maroon; all shades can be visible at once.*

In Zone 7 and upper parts of Zone 8:

- Stewartias are tall with camellia-like flowers. (*S. pseudocamellia, S. malacodendron*) brings rich cinnamon color to both zones and Japanese stewartia peels back to show gray, red, and orange.

- Kousa dogwood (*Cornus kousa*) has patchy gray and brown bark highlighted by orange.

- Paperbark maple (*Acer griseum*) exfoliates its cinnamon bark dramatically as it ages.

Crape myrtle bark provides an interesting view in the winter garden.

During some years, saucer magnolia trees just begin to open their glorious pink and white flowers only to freeze overnight. The classic pink and white flowers of *Magnolia soulangeana* turn brown and fall off into a messy litter and hearts drop at the sight. Prevent this lamentation with named varieties, such as these that will do well in your zone:

- Zone 7: 'Verbanica' is very hardy and its purple-rose buds open to white. It blooms late and seldom, if ever, suffers freeze damage.

- Zone 8: 'Lennei' waits until relatively late to bloom in big purple globes with white interiors.

- Zone 9: 'Alexandrina' blooms with dark pinky purple outer and white inner petals. A mid-season bloom makes it less susceptible to freeze damage in this zone than the classic species.

VINES & GROUNDCOVERS

Summer shade can be hard to find in full sun gardens, so plan now to grow plenty of shade plants. Stand and face the setting sun to locate where you want a row of trellises or columns to support the vines that will offer shade later. Plan *now* for their acquisition and installation—it will be hot before you know it.

WATER GARDENS

To take a drawing or rough plan to the next step, grab spray paint first. Yes, you will make a complete plan, and then use stakes, string, and a level even before you start digging. But refine your plan by outlining the shape and size of the future water feature in spray paint to begin making it real—and to tweak its location right away, if needed.

PLANT

ANNUALS

Garden beds may be cold and wet, but potting mixes are not. For the earliest color in outdoor pots, watch garden center racks for early arrivals, such as pansy relatives Johnny jump-ups and violas, plus petunias, snapdragons, twinspur (*Diascia*), and English daisies. Every potting soil mix is different and may have some or all of the following components:

- Organic base of peat moss or forest products make up the majority of potting mixes.

- Other organic matters like humus, composts, and coir may be in the mix.

- Drainage additives including perlite, vermiculite, sand, or ground barks allow water to flow through the mix and roots to grow into it.

- Perlite is white, very porous volcanic glass that has been exploded.

- Vermiculite is tan, a little shiny, sort of spongy, and made from mica.

- Sand must be rather orange, gritty, and sharp, not the soft white type.

- Ground bark should be sized to ½-inch screen or slightly smaller for best effect.

- Water-holding crystals prevent drying out and can forgive your forgetfulness when it comes to watering.

- Fertilizer additions may be adequate for a while and delay the need to add more.

BULBS

Everybody likes cut flowers and the easiest to grow must be gladiola bulbs that you can begin planting this month.

While you're at it, diversify your iris collection:

- Bearded irises (*I. germanica*) are marked by upright center petals (standards) surrounded by arched or drooping petals (falls) with characteristic marks known as beards.

- Flag iris includes several species such as the ancient white flag (*I. albicans*), tall yellow flag (*I. pseudacorus*), and blue flag (*I. virginica*).

- Siberian iris hybrids grow and bloom well in light shade with thin grassy leaves. The flowers have tall standards and arching falls in purple, pink, white, blue, and pastel yellow.

- Louisiana irises are a group of species and hybrids that thrive at pond margins and garden beds with regular water, even occasional flooding. A wide range of colors appear on flat-faced flowers above narrow pointy leaves (*I. fulva, I. cuprea,* et al).

- Roof iris (*I. tectorum*) sprouts foot-tall fans of leaves and flowers that have falling white crests and slightly fringed blue petals in part shade and rich, damp soil.

EDIBLES

Vegetable gardeners may take January off, but much needs doing this month, whether you are growing now or later. Depending on your method, you will

HERE'S HOW

TO PLANT GLADIOLUS

- Purchase four to six dozen gladiola bulbs and store them in a paper bag indoors.

- Set aside a row or make one at the back of any sunny garden bed with enough room to plant the bulbs 4 to 6 inches apart, depending on its ultimate size.

- Beginning this month, plant a dozen gladiola bulbs weekly for six to eight weeks.

- Slip a bamboo stake next to each bulb of tall varieties when you plant to avoid root damage later. Keep plant ties nearby and use them to loosely attach gladiola stems to the stakes.

- Fertilize and water regularly, and control pests such as chewing caterpillars.

- Pick entire stems when the first flower buds show color.

In many areas of the South, potatoes can be planted now.

been exposed to the elements all winter are good candidates for the early activity, whether they have sprouted or not. And as soon as the old timey bearded iris finish their flowers, you can dig, divide, and move them as weather permits.

ROSES

Every kind of rose is available this month in hybrid teas and numerous shrub or antique types. Each rose you see can be identified as to its type, and that information should be on every label or on a sign at the nursery. However, you can look up its type once you have the name. When you know which types of antique roses originated where, you can choose wisely with your zone in mind:

- Cool climates in northern Europe, Japan, Korea, and in the mountains gave rise to hybrid rugosa, Portland, alba, damask, and moss roses.

- Warm regions in southern Europe and Asia are home to some species roses, hybrid perpetual, noisette, tea, China, and Bourbon roses.

SHRUBS

Big, thick-walled pots make perfect homes for shrubs like dwarf barberry, gardenia, and sasanqua. On a winter day, the sight of them outside the window or by the front door is sure to brighten your mood. Add tulip and hyacinth bulbs to the pots each fall for early spring color, fill in with petunias, million bells (*Calibrachoa* hybrids), and lotus vine, also called "parrot's beak" (*Lotus maculatus*), to trail from them all summer.

TREES

Continue planting—and transplanting—trees along with woody vines, shrubs, and perennials plants. To hold plants harvested from the wild, mix their native soil with your own leaf mold and pot them. Or build a big pile of compost and leaf mold to keep them hydrated until you can plant them, called "heeling in." Slide the newly dug plant into the pile and put mix around it for about a month of safe storage. Do not tamp down the soil nor let the plants wilt. Replant soon, before new roots make the task difficult.

want to add new layers of newspaper and compost to no-till beds, dig in fertilizer to existing plots, till up new ones, or mix up container-growing soils.

Plant this month:

- Zone 7: At mid-month, head and leaf lettuce from seed or plants, onion sets or plants, Irish potatoes, spinach, rutabaga, and kohlrabi seeds

- Zone 8: Beets, carrots, collards, Swiss chard, mustard, and radishes from seed, plants for broccoli, cauliflower, and Brussels sprouts, and Irish potatoes

- Zone 9: First half of month, turnips, radishes, mustard, Swiss chard, kale, collards, plants for broccoli, cabbage, and cauliflower

LAWNS

Sod trucks begin rolling on the coasts with good conditions to plant dormant sod and to patch bare areas. Get new turf in place as soon as it is practical for best root development and growth at green up.

PERENNIALS & ORNAMENTAL GRASSES

By mid- to late February, most gardeners have itchy planting fingers. Perennials in pots that have

VINES & GROUNDCOVERS

Not every vine deserves or can fill a columnar space like coral honeysuckle (*Lonicera sempervirens*), which blooms off and on year-round with tubular red flowers on a mostly evergreen vine and draws hummingbirds like a magnet. In sun or part shade, surround a light pole or a similar column with a circle of 4x4 mesh galvanized wire. Cut the wire almost as tall as the support and long enough to place it 1 foot away from the pole, surrounding it. Plant three or four vines around the outside of the wire, depending on their size, and train them onto the wire.

WATER GARDENS

Expand plantings around water features with the marginal plants that can grow at the water's edge to help stabilize it—both physically and visually. Use a combination of edging plants and those that move the eye upward, like low growing solid or striped sweet flag (*Acorus gramineus*) and canna lilies in solid green or red or wild stripes. Plant a canna combination and let a few striped cannas call out a full row of variegated sweet flag in the same colors. With a pleasing combination of leaf patterns, canna flowers will be icing on the cake.

■ *Coral honeysuckle (*Lonicera sempervirens)

CARE

ALL

More than any other month, February means pruning for good plant health. Whether you are pruning young trees, evergreen shrubs, roses, or woody perennials, sharpen your saws and get busy.

ANNUALS

Seeds sown indoors last month for summer annuals should demonstrate steady, stocky growth with two sets of true leaves. If you want multi-stemmed plants of coleus, angelonia, and impatiens, pinch the tip of seedlings at this point.

BULBS

The crocus and hyacinth bulbs you planted last fall may be short lived or small flowered in a mild winter even if you chilled them. Pull the mulch away from them when you see sprouts. This will keep the ground cool and perhaps prolong the blooms.

EDIBLES

Cut down browned asparagus ferns and fertilize the beds this month to stimulate new growth. Let female, berried asparagus ferns mature only if you want their seedlings. They will reseed in or out of the bed if you let them.

Leaf lettuce may need protection at times this month, but most days it's perfect for picking at least a few leaves. Cold weather makes them spicier than usual, but they keep on growing.

LAWNS

Mow perennial ryegrass this month and catch or rake the trimmings this time to add green matter to the compost pile as you turn it.

PERENNIALS & ORNAMENTAL GRASSES

Trim damaged leaves off of clumping groundcovers, such as liriope, and shape them before new leaves shoot up from their middles. Late in the month, cut

TO PRUNE IN GENERAL

- Sharpen your tools to make clean cuts and avoid broken tools and personal injury.

- Choose the right tool for the job. Hand pruners are not meant for tree limbs, and loppers and saws have their limits. Each is rated, so use them appropriately.

- Look at the plant and see its future—a nice shape made of strong, well-spaced branches that allow sunlight and rainfall to reach all its parts.

- If needed, shorten the height of the plant and its spread.

- Remove dead branches or sections entirely. Test by cutting into a branch or scratching back some bark. If it is green, it is alive.

- If large areas are dead, remove some other areas to balance their loss.

- Clip out dead twigs and thin out remaining branches if needed to open up the canopy or to produce thicker flowering stems in roses and woody perennials, such as butterfly bush.

- Step back and adjust what you have done to match your vision.

TO ROOT ROSES

- Use canes of thinner caliper than a pencil and take them from the tip or top third of the cane.

- Trim to 4 to 6 inches with a slant cut at the bottom end to maximize the area where roots can emerge.

- Roll the slant end in a rooting hormone, or willow water if you are a traditionalist.

- Stick into a small container of loose mix and water well.

- Put the pots in a cool, brightly lit place, add a plastic cloche if the air is very dry, and keep their soil evenly moist.

- Tug gently after one month. If the stem resists, it is rooting and will be ready to move up in another month.

back butterfly bushes that bloom on new wood (*Buddleia davidii*) to remove and reduce non-blooming branches. If this woody perennial has frozen to the ground, cut away the mess and watch for new shoots soon. Reminder: if any browned perennials remain, cut them down entirely.

ROSES

Prune roses—hybrid teas; shrub, landscape varieties; and aggressive, reblooming climbers—to stimulate new canes and new flowers. Do not prune climbers that bloom only once such as 'Lady Banks', 'Silver Moon', and 'Fortuniana'.

- Hybrid tea roses: Remove all but three or five widely spaced canes and all side growth along them. Shorten each cane to 18 to 24 inches tall depending on vigor.

- Shrub, antique, and old roses: Cut back by one-third overall and remove at least some of the twiggy growth in the interior of the rose.

- Landscape roses such as Knockout, Carpet, and Drift: Prune less severely to shape and stimulate new growth only.

- Aggressive, remontant climbing roses: Thin canes as needed and prune lengths to maintain the vines on their supports.

The many ways to root roses can fill a chapter, but one school of thought is to make cuttings when you prune this month.

Few roses leap onto their supports, and it can really be a challenge to keep them up. Use jute to loosely tie the canes to arbors and trellises rather than wrapping them around the structure. This way simplifies maintenance and shows off the flowers to the best advantage.

SHRUBS

Evergreen shrubs grow leggy and thin without annual pruning and can become twiggy skeletons with leaves only at their tips.

TREES

More trees are damaged by people operating lawn mowers and string trimmers than any other cause. Scrape grass and weeds away in a wide circle around the trunk and cover it with mulch to keep the tools at a safe distance.

HERE'S HOW

TO PRUNE SHRUBS

- Prune established evergreen shrubs lightly to neaten their shapes and stimulate new growth.

- Take off up to one-third of an evergreen's overall size right before new growth starts to thicken it.

- Plan to prune lightly again in summer to continue thickening new growth.

- When shearing a short hedge, remember to slope it slightly wider at the bottom to help sunlight reach lower branches.

Mulching around a tree not only helps keep it from drying out, it also protects it from lawn mowers.

VINES & GROUNDCOVERS

The best vines, like Carolina jessamine, bloom even more when you maintain their growth with routine care very soon after flowering. Trim off old flowers and the tips of each vine; remove old canes entirely if they did not bloom. Use the same strategy later in the year for early clematis, trumpet vines, and passion flowers.

Not all vines grow upward, and aggressive ones like Asiatic jasmine are often sheared to maintain their edges. Unfortunately, the result can be woody twigs with leaves only on top and no healthy new growth to continue the stand. Solve this problem by shearing the new growth as you would a shrub to thicken it lower on the stem. Start by going around the bed as usual and then take a few inches off the top. Fertilize the bed after pruning.

WATER GARDENS

Concrete fish ponds can be fascinating but need complete cleaning annually. If you are able to overwinter your fish in the pond, move them to a holding tank and drain the pond. Arm yourself

■ *Rainwater collected in a rain barrel is perfect for plants and lawns.*

with nylon bristle brushes, a scoop, and a garden hose with a pressure nozzle. Clean all the surfaces thoroughly but gently and remove any broken concrete. Refill the pond and treat the water as usual for the fish and let it regain a safe temperature before you return the fish.

Pots of unusual, desirable water garden plants can show up at garden shows and retailers before it is wise to put them into the pond. Because they may be hard to find later and are often crowded into small containers, move them up to larger pond pots. Keep the new collection outdoors in a protected site, such as a shed or enclosed garage.

WATER

ALL

Water, its lack or overabundance, can make the difference in garden success or failure. Evaluate how water drains around plantings of perennials, roses, and woody plants and take steps to correct any problems.

ANNUALS

Keep pots and beds watered if they need it. You can rely on the index-finger soil-moisture test—except for cacti, bog pots, and plants resting without water for the winter, such as potted amaryllis that just bloomed. Irrigate when the top inch of soil feels dry to the first knuckle of your index finger.

BULBS

Take garden bed bulbs off your list of plants to worry about watering this month. Tucked safely in the ground, they'll be fine with any level of rainfall.

EDIBLES

If you must open a ditch to drain puddles out of a bed, do so, but leave the soil you remove piled nearby so you can dam the flow when needed in dry weather.

LAWNS

Grass that stays too wet never quite stops being squishy to walk on and soon loses its vigor. Sometimes you can dig a ditch or enlarge a swale, but French drains work well. They are major projects but worth it for big drainage problems and

TO EVALUATE WATER SYSTEMS

- Test in-ground irrigation systems for output and efficiency; be sure rain sensors and other energy conservation measures are working.

- If you did not store soaker hoses, inspect them for gaps and holes; repair or replace them before they will be needed.

- Watch where rainfall travels across the entire property, including unguttered roofs, to know where you must divert it.

- Locate places that can take the overflow and channel the water in that direction.

- Consider adding a cistern or rain barrel to capture rainfall and store the overflow from gutters for later use.

- Deal with drainage issues, but take a moderate approach. Some areas may need all available water at the height of summer. Do a drainage test to determine how well your soil drains.

- Dry sites can be as troublesome as wet ones if they deprive young plants of what they need to get established and grow. Build a low-profile dam of soil and leaves around newly installed plants, especially if you are not able to monitor their water.

because grass grows on top of them, the drainage is almost invisible.

PERENNIALS & ORNAMENTAL GRASSES

In wet weather, watch for mulch washing away in the perennial bed. If the crowns of the plants are buried under wet mulch, new growth can be delayed. Use a leaf rake to sweep the mulch back into place.

ROSES

Leaf diseases, especially blackspot, are ugly. Even if they do not damage the rose in the long run, ruined leaves mean fewer and smaller flowers. Use soaker hoses, lowered spray nozzles, or better timing, but keep rose leaves as dry as possible when watering.

SHRUBS, TREES, AND VINES & GROUNDCOVERS

Water these plant categories sparingly if at all this month except to promote rooting in young plants.

WATER GARDENS

Test water-quality levels in fish ponds after heavy rains, especially in urban gardens.

ANNUALS

Feed a balanced, complete formula such as 20-20-20 to promote growth in all parts of the plant. Mix soluble formulas with water to maintain steady growth. Fertilizer labels are wordy, but there are important terms on every one. Complete fertilizers are those that have the "Big Three" elements—nitrogen, phosphorus, and potassium—needed in large amounts. The good fertilizers also have the minor or trace elements that are necessary for plant growth but in relatively minute quantities. A balanced fertilizer is one that has equal parts of the "Big Three," such as 20-20-20. When those numbers are not equal, the fertilizer is known as a specialty formula because it is made for a particular purpose or plant groups.

When your pansies don't look as good as the neighbor's, it is a problem. Check the plants to see if the crown is growing at ground level. If it is not, use a wide-bladed trowel to lift each one out of the bed or pot. Add a cup or so of soil mix to the hole and replant. Water in, dress with mulch again, and fertilize with a flower formula. Flower formula fertilizers provide higher relative amounts of phosphorus (P) and potassium (K) than nitrogen (N) to stimulate bud production. It takes the leafy growth favored by nitrogen fertilizers to produce enough energy for plants to bloom. At that point, if there is not enough P and K or too much N, the plants can't flower. Product labels list NPK amounts in that order such as 10-30-20, indicating it is 10 parts nitrogen, 30 parts potassium, and 20 parts phosphorus. It will boost blooms on healthy annuals.

BULBS

Fertilize bulbs growing in pots indoors such as freesia and amaryllis with a flowering formula mixed in water. Use a general-purpose granular formula such as 10-10-10 to encourage established stands of bulbs as their leaves appear.

EDIBLES

Fertilize greens with a balanced, soluble formula each time you pick to keep new leaves coming on lettuces, kale, and chard. Or work in an organic fertilizer made for vegetable gardens after each picking.

Citrus trees are best nourished with specialty formula fertilizers made for them because they benefit from a particular balance of major and minor nutrients. Feed citrus trees growing in pots and protect them from the weather. Wait until closer to spring to fertilize citrus trees growing outdoors.

LAWNS

Spread lawn fertilizer to nourish ryegrass stands now. It is too early to affect the bermudagrass and right on time to feed the rye for the rest of its season. All other lawns benefit from ½ inch of composted manure spread over them this month. Spread it and then use a stiff tine rake to send it into the thatch. It takes time for the organic matter to work its way into the soil, and it will have no effect on fertility now.

PERENNIALS & ORNAMENTAL GRASSES

Repeat root-stimulator formula fertilizers for ornamental grass clumps and groundcovers you divided last month.

Other actively growing perennials and ornamental grasses can be fertilized with some granular fertilizer this month.

VINES & GROUNDCOVERS

Mature groundcovers use fertilizer to keep new growth healthy and maintain the stand. Use a complete-formula flower garden fertilizer for established beds of coralberry (*Ardisia crenata*) and big blue periwinkle (*Vinca major*) every other year.

ROSES

Spread a 1-inch deep layer of composted manure under roses after you prune them. Follow two to three weeks later with a complete, balanced granular fertilizer or one made for roses. If you use a specialty formula and find that rose leaves are smaller or the bush is not growing well, switch to a balanced garden fertilizer such as 10-10-10 or use an organic fertilizer to gain added nitrogen.

Rose fertilizers often have insecticides incorporated into them that can be effective against serious, predictable pests. They may be less toxic to use than weekly sprays for hybrid tea growers who face an onslaught of insects and diseases. But few other roses require this level of intervention, and its use can limit the populations of useful pollinating insects as well as the pests.

SHRUBS

Use fertilizer formulas made for acid-loving plants like azaleas and hollies if your soil tends to be alkaline, a measurement you will learn in a soil test or from seasoned gardeners nearby. Incorporate organic mulch as it rots, and put on early season composted manure blankets to help maintain properly acidic conditions for this group. Apply ½ to 1 inch of organic mulch this month so it will be actively working in the root zone when new growth starts.

TREES

Fertilizing young trees insures that adequate and appropriate nutrition is available to their roots, trunk girth, and lush leaf canopy. Trees planted last spring or fall can be fertilized this month, preferably with formulas made for trees. Do not overfeed trees—use the recommended amount to promote steady, healthy development.

WATER GARDENS

Monitor lilies and other water plants in storage and remove rotten leaves so they do not foul the water.

A little organic matter is good, but in this case too much is a problem. If you have to add or change the water, add a half-strength amount of your aquatic fertilizer.

PROBLEM-SOLVE

EDIBLES

All citrus trees can grow in pots with varying amounts of winter protection throughout our states. A few can grow in the ground outdoors year-round in the warmest microclimates of Zones 8b and 9. Most citrus trees that could be hardy are lost to cold damage in the first two seasons. Protect yours with an insulated blanket (like you would take camping) or a thermal blanket from the linen closet topped with a layer of thick (6 mil), clear plastic. Remove each day to prevent overheating. Do not fertilize citrus trees outdoors between August and late February or March. From hardiest to most tender, our favorite citrus include:

- Kumquat: 'Meiw' (sweet), 'Nagami' (tart)

- Satsuma: 'Owari', 'Armstrong', 'Brown Select'

- Calmondin

- Sweet Orange: 'Hamlin' aka 'Louisiana', 'Moro' blood orange

- Navel Orange: 'Washington Navel', 'Red Navel'

- Mandarin: 'Cuties', 'Ponkan'

- Grapefruit: 'Ruby Red'

- Lemon: 'Improved Meyer', 'Ponderosa'

- Lime: 'Persian', 'Key' (bartenders' lime)

LAWNS

Different weeds seem to sprout every month, and many seek to suppress them with pre-emergent herbicides, but when to treat the lawn can be a challenge. If different weeds sprout in your lawn in spring and summer, no matter when you pre-emerge, try this: split the herbicide amount into two applications, half now and half in May.

PERENNIALS & ORNAMENTAL GRASSES

Bearded iris leaves make a strong statement in shady beds without ever flowering, but when there are no blooms and sunny iris beds decline, something is wrong. Often the problem is that the iris crowns have sunk below ground level over time, but there may be another reason. Brush away leaves or mulch to expose the iris clumps and inspect the rhizomes for holes that indicate borers have invaded. Use sulfur dust to deter them, but if the damage is severe, you will need to replace the rhizomes with healthy ones to regain good health and flowers.

■ *Long-term, trees must adapt to local conditions but temporary covers can be helpful for marginal choices like citrus and oleander in northern zones. Like tree stakes, they should be limited to a couple of seasons.*

March

*March cracks the egg on spring in the Deep South. Garden borders, roadsides, and woods take on familiar lighter shades as new leaves emerge in concert with exotic purple wisteria (*W. sinensis*), deciduous native azaleas (*Rhododendron canescens, R. *hybrids), and red buckeye (*Aesculus parvia*). Star magnolia (*M. stellata*) and dogwood (*Cornus florida*) bloom bright white along with bearded iris and baby's breath, and then bridal wreath spireas (*S. thunbergii, S. vanhouttei*). You can pick a bouquet in almost any backyard and use lush, deep green viburnum leaves (*V. davidii, V. tinus *in Zone 9) as filler, and you can plant to your heart's content in containers and garden beds.*

Dreaded pollen comes along with the flowers, and tissue sales are as strong now as in the fall, not to mention remedies found in and out of the doctor's office. Your bane may be junipers, cypress, and the more obviously flowering ornamental pear trees. Or it might be henbit, wild onions, clover, or any of the other "lawn weeds" in bloom now. You may consider growing plants that do not produce pollen, and that might help, but the woods and roadsides would probably get you anyway. If you think you are suffering alone, watch local television meteorologists mispronounce that week's pollen-rich plant names. Those who suffer most wear paper masks when gardening and then strip and shower when the day's chores are done. When you go to bed with lingering pollen, you're likely to wake up with sneezes and worse.

Traditional wisdom says that March "comes in like a lion and goes out like a lamb," and that can be true. Sometimes, though, the month seems to steadily progress toward weather warm enough to plant tomatoes, only to dash our hopes. Late March and early April can have surprising cold spells that make you grab a coat even if it doesn't match the Easter dress. We live and garden with caution this month, knowing the Easter freeze might await, and perhaps oddly, that edgy tension can be joyful. Gardening, after all, is a gamble, and most roll the dice, expecting the best the month can offer. The desire to grow, mow, and fertilize leads to tension between what is and what the gardener wants. It can lead to sheer foolishness like planting okra in cold soil, or to the wisdom of patience and plant covers.

PLAN

ANNUALS

Pansies are at their peak now, and in most places, you can expect strong flowering for a month or more. As the season heats up, all the overwintering annuals go to seed. You can tell the end is near when pansy flowers decrease in diameter weekly and the stems begin to stretch. Now is the time to plan for summer annuals, beginning with a style decision. The same bed or container can be a unifying element or it can sing a different tune altogether.

If you love the round shape of pansy plants amid a mix of flower colors and faces, consider moss roses (*Portulaca*) for the summer. The plants are interesting on their own and very different, yet similar enough in size and shape to offer continuity across the seasons. But you may want to go big for summer and use that bed by the patio to create a cottage garden scene with cosmos, cleome, celosia, and sunflowers.

Plan seed and plant purchases now while there's time to do both and plan to keep bags of ground bark and composted manure handy for use when the time comes.

■ *Enjoy pansies before the heat sets in.*

BULBS

Tulips will bloom and die back this month. Plan to compost the bulbs when they finish because most are unlikely to naturalize. As a frustrating statement of how wrong our summer conditions are for tulips to multiply, they may send up leaves for a couple of years but never bloom.

If there is room anywhere, plan a trip to the garden center to add more gladiolas for cut flowers. When you plant, remember to add a stake that can support the glad's height and keep its flowers off the ground.

EDIBLES

Vegetable gardeners always want the first tomato or hot pepper on the block, but those who risk early planting must plant smart and be prepared to protect plants on cold nights and ventilate on warm days. Plan ahead to have covers that work for you:

- Classic cloches are big glass bell jars, the original solar heaters for plants. Invented as clay covers to protect plants in ancient gardens, bell jars evolved into glass cases for individual tender plants.

■ Tulipa *'Lady Jane'* is a good choice for those who wish to grow tulips in the south.

Any sort of plastic bottle will work to make a cloche.

A vertical mower (also called a power rake) makes quick work of the rigorous job of dethatching your lawn.

- A recycled plastic version of a bell jar uses a gallon milk jug. Slice off the bottom, slip it over the plant, and remove the cap to ventilate daily.

- PVC pipe and fittings fashioned into dome shapes trap heat with tight plastic covers over individual plants or small groups of plants.

- Set up tomato cages over vulnerable plants and wrap them in plastic covering. Secure with plastic clips to make ventilation easy.

- Commercially available, pleated tents made to be filled with water offer good protection.

- Groups of plants and small beds can be protected by low-profile plastic pop-up greenhouses, without other utilities.

LAWNS

Spongy or compacted, problems with lawns won't go away on their own. Plan now to tackle big issues this spring and provide plenty of time for the lawn to recover well this season. Two strategies to consider:

- Dethatching slices through built-up thatch and removes it to reduce useless buildup that holds water and nutrients above the lawn. When thatch grows to several inches deep and the lawn always feels spongy to walk on, plan to dethatch.

- Lawn aeration is done to reduce compacted soils by punching holes in and filling them with sand to improve water percolation. When the lawn just won't grow and feels hard under your feet, think about aeration.

PERENNIALS & ORNAMENTAL GRASSES

Some beloved perennial plants, what some call the "oddballs," require planning to acquire for several reasons. They are not widely popular in this century so few are grown for the trade, such as Indian shot canna (*C. indica*). The South American native became naturalized long ago in the Southeast but isn't as showy as modern hybrids, so it is overlooked. Other beauties are harder to root or take longer to grow or are considered common, such as the poorly named false aster (*Boltonia asteroides*). Some are an acquired taste, or smell, such as heady tuberose (*Polianthes tuberosa*).

Attend local plant sales and swaps this spring to see what's available, and talk to other fans of unusual perennials.

Just as a sequined cocktail dress looks out of place at church, some perennials need the right place to be appreciated. Because you don't recognize them or their potential uses, they get dubbed "weeds" and suffer the consequences. When you find a plant that grows without much maintenance, has qualities you like, and isn't much of a bully, incorporate it into your plan. And don't be intimidated by convention—if wild strawberry, woods sorrel, lyreleaf sage, or dichondra suit your purposes, plan to grow them.

Sometimes plants that look great together make good companions in beds and pots, and sometimes they don't. When you face such a mismatch, investigate the different needs and address them. For example, the daisy shapes of black-eyed Susan (*Rudbeckia*) and purple coneflower (*Echinacea*) contrast well with each other in flower color. Popular varieties have essentially the same size and shape clumps, the plants bloom at the same time, and they are both native perennials. All these similarities do not make for good bedmates, however, because the black-eyed Susan has better drought tolerance and greater need for direct sun than purple coneflower. Without regular water and some shelter from blistering sun, coneflowers languish. But if you have a long bed that starts in shade and ends in sun, the solution is as near as your shovel.

ROSES

Plan ahead for excellent air circulation around each rose bush to make it harder for diseases to take hold and spread. Find out the mature size of the roses when you choose them and adjust planting plans to allow space between them: 1 foot around each hybrid tea rose when in full leaf, 6 to 8 inches of open space all around for all others. For example, small shrub roses such as 'The Fairy' will grow to be about 3 feet x 3 feet, so they should be

■ *Bugleweed is a good choice for shady areas.*

spaced 1½ feet of leaves plus 6 inches air or a minimum of 2 feet apart on their centers.

SHRUBS

Families of related shrubs work to unify designs and bring a familiar comfort when used in different parts of the garden. For example, hollies (*Ilex* spp.) and heavenly bamboos (*Nandina* spp.) can be tall or short, solid green or colorful, berried, or not. Allow space for several members of one shrub family to gain harmony with their similarities and show off their individual features.

TREES

If crepe myrtle trees have sprouted a profusion of small stems from their base in past years, plan for their control in these steps:

- Switch to a lower-nitrogen fertilizer, found in most flowering tree and shrub formulas. Look for a lower first number on the label such as 5-20-10.

- Keep a watchful eye on the trees, and as soon as the sprouts appear, rub them off with your thumb if possible.

- Know that the larger the sprouts, also called whips, the more damage you will do to the trunk when you cut them off. But cut them off anyway and be more diligent.

- If the tree is growing in the lawn, clear a 3-foot circle of grass underneath it and avoid accidentally spreading lawn fertilizer around the crepe myrtle.

VINES & GROUNDCOVERS

Dry shade comes gradually as trees grow, or quickly when your neighbor builds an addition that blocks your sun. Plan to feature a secret garden or green oasis where low-growing groundcovers are a carpet under hardscape. Consider bugleweed (*Ajuga reptans*) for compact clusters and sweet flowers in a variety of leaf colors, like 'Burgundy Glow' for purple, pink, and red shades, and 'Bronze Beauty' with green and purple variegation.

WATER GARDENS

Plan to start or expand your collection of water lilies this year to add drama night and day. They are freshwater plants in the *Nymphaeaceae* family with more than seventy species worldwide that live in soil underwater. Their leaves are circular or notched pads that float on top with a rainbow of flower colors. Hardy water lilies bloom in the daytime and can be easier to maintain in our states, but for flowers both night and day, plan for tropicals.

PLANT

ALL

Those small but tempting boxed trees, vines, roses, and shrubs are entirely viable if planted very soon—they are bare root or nearly so and more easily shocked than potted specimens. Soak as usual and prune a little more before planting, particularly if the plants have sprouted.

"Right plant, right place" is a mantra for gardeners, and you are wise to remember its importance. Just as vital is the care—especially the water—that you give the plant in its first weeks or months of life. Annual flowers and vegetables that wilt soon after transplant are in jeopardy and may show ill effects almost immediately. Perennials give you signs of drought stress, too, by failing to grow or bloom. Unwatered, new lawns cannot root and will slowly die. Shrubs and trees may show fewer signs of stress, but even native and tolerant specimens will not grow well

without regular irrigation in dry times for the first year or two of their life in the garden.

To reuse and repurpose potting mixes, remember this important exception: soil that has grown tomatoes or potatoes should *not* be used for those vegetables again. Otherwise, dump the soils into a wheelbarrow, remove any roots, and mix well. Some will no doubt be heavier or wetter with peat moss or humus, others may be gritty or full of perlite. Mixing the used soils together lets their good qualities shine. Add organic matter if needed to overcome saturated soils and those that are very lightweight.

ANNUALS

Not all annuals are created equal. Your success with garden plantings and containers of annuals can depend on understanding some of their differences. The need for good drainage is almost universal, and most annuals dry out only slightly between irrigations. Richly organic, fertile soil sounds ideal, but those who thrive in drier conditions may suffer there. The first group includes angelonia (*A. angustifolia*), impatiens (*I. walleriana*), hybrid petunias, coleus, and many more. Add compost/manure and a complete-formula granular fertilizer to their beds and pots. Zinnias you grow from seed (*Zinnia elegans*) and narrowleaf types (*Z. angustifolia*), sunflowers (*Helianthus annuus*), cosmos (*C. bipinnatus*), and marigolds (*Tagetes*) can put on too many leaves and fewer flowers in such rich soil. They are good to grow in beds and potting mix you have used before or neglected to fertilize.

BULBS

Red spider lilies (hurricane lilies), golden spiders, and hurricane lilies (naked ladies) (*Lycoris radiata, L. aurea, L. squamigera*) are fall flower favorites. The bulbs send up bare stems crowned with spectacular flowers followed by neat leaf clumps that go dormant in spring to prepare for rebloom. Now is the time to dig up, separate crowded clumps, and relocate *Lycoris* clumps, before their foliage dies down for the year. Dig deep and wide to avoid cutting into the bulbs.

If you will not be able to replant the clumps right away, mark their space but do not dig them up. Wait until the leaves die down, then harvest the bulbs. Lift the entire clump, cut off the leaves, and let them dry until you can pull them apart easily. Store in a paper bag in a cool, dark place until you can plant, or up to one month.

EDIBLES

There's plenty to plant in the vegetable garden this month, but don't get ahead of yourself and the season. Cole crops, delicious roots, lettuce, and other greens go in early in March, soon followed by beans and early corn. Soil temperatures below 50 degrees Fahrenheit are too cold for summer vegetables like squash, tomatoes, peppers, and melons.

Wait until after the date of the last average frost in your area to put in warm-season favorites or be prepared to protect them well.

Whether you purchase or grow seedlings, put the pots or flats outdoors for a few days before

■ Cole crops need 12 to 18 inches of space between each plant.

transplanting. This hardening-off process helps the young plants acclimate to temperature, sunlight, and windy conditions before being uprooted and can lessen transplant shock.

Keep up with what and when to plant with publications from your state's Cooperative Extension Service. They publish planting guides in print and online. Get yours and make a planting calendar that feeds your family. Look up your county agent in the local telephone book or consult these websites:

- Alabama—www.aces.edu

- Louisiana—www.lsuagcenter.com

- Mississippi—www.msucares.com

LAWNS

Before you plant a lawn, be sure the site is well prepped to grow grass and has the proper slope so water doesn't drain back toward your house. The accepted rule for lawn slope is that the grass should gently drop 2 to 3 inches for every 10 feet of space. That means if the lawn area is 50 feet from the house to the sidewalk, it should drop about 10 inches in that space to end evenly with the sidewalk or driveway.

PERENNIALS & ORNAMENTAL GRASSES

Dig, divide, and replant early-blooming perennials as they finish blooming so new roots can get growing before hot weather sets in. The phlox family is vigorous, blooms early, and can usually be propagated by division every other year.

- Blue phlox (*P. divaricata*) spreads under-ground to form dense clumps in light shade with sweetly fragrant flower clusters. 'Louisiana Purple' has the most vibrant blue-purple flower color.

- Creeping phlox (*P. stolonifera*) does as its name suggests but with little stealth. The perfect plant for sharing, its lavender-pinkish flowers are stunning and abundant. 'Bruce's White' lights up the shade at dusk.

- Moss pink (*P. subulata*) may not bloom as early, but its needle-like leaves quickly form huge clumps that can be divided almost anytime. The old-timey loud pink flowers have competition from close relatives like the rebloomer, 'Candy Stripe'.

ROSES

Container-grown roses need a good start to bloom their best. Time spent now will pay off later with long-lived bushes that reward your efforts.

HERE'S HOW

TO PLANT CONTAINER-GROWN ROSES

- Dig a hole in the richly organic, well-drained soil you prepared that will be a bit larger than the pot it is growing in now.
- Press on the sides of the plastic pot to loosen the soil and roots and slip the rose out of its pot.
- If the soil in the pot falls away from the roots, don't worry about it. Mix what falls out in with the soil you dug and use it. You will need to build a mound in the hole as described for bare-root roses.
- Rough up the edges of the rootball with your hands if it is tight.
- Put it in the hole, making sure the graft union stays 2 inches above the soil level.
- Backfill with the soil you dug out and/or mixed and tamp it down.
- Water well and mulch around the new rose.

SHRUBS

Whether you are planting a new shrub bed or replacing lost ones, consider these that are used too seldom:

All Zones

- Sweet mock orange (*Philadelphus coronarius*) is a big shrub with white, dogwood-like flowers and a pleasing aroma.
- Titi (*Cyrilla racemiflora*) forms a thicket with striking white flower whorls that seem to explode from every stem.
- Oakleaf hydrangea (*H. quercifolia*) has conical stacks of flowers and red fall color.
- Virginia sweetspire (*Itea virginica*) droops chains of flowers from a rounded shrub.
- Banana shrub (*Michelia figo*) brings its name-sake aroma in yellow cupped flowers on an evergreen with rare medium-green color.
- Florida anise (*Illicium floridanum*) grows into an aromatic large shrub/small tree with shiny green leaves dotted with 2-inch red or white flowers.

Zone 8 and Zone 7

- Beautyberry (*Callicarpa*) lines up its small flowers and big purple berries all along its arching stems. The leaves color up in some autumns to light up the shade.
- Fuzzy deutzia (*D. scabra*) is an old-fashioned favorite for puffy white flower clusters. Choose dwarf varieties like 'Pearls' (*D. gracilis*) for small gardens and containers.
- Sweetshrub (*Calycanthus floridus*), a slow grower, deserves attention because every part of this plant is aromatic, including its roots. And it is a beautiful native plant with deep maroon flowers.
- Weigela (*W. florida, W.* hybrids) impresses with cottage garden flair. It features widely spaced branches, loose flower heads, and

toothed leaves with great texture. With nearly 200 hybrids in existence, one will suit your garden style.

TREES

When you plant a tree, you grow a legacy because most trees mature slowly. You choose carefully, for color, trunk, and leaf quality, ultimate size, shape, and to create wildlife habitat. An important reason to grow native trees is their role as host trees for butterflies and moths. Nurture tiger and spicebush swallowtail butterflies with their host tree, tulip poplar (*Liriodendron tulipifera*). Invite zebra swallowtails with the paw paw tree (*Asimina triloba*) and eastern comma butterflies with elm trees (*Ulmus* spp.). With this approach, you may justify leaving at least one hackberry tree (*Celtis occidentalis*) in the weedy hedgerow to host emperor butterflies and a variety of moths.

VINES & GROUNDCOVERS

Planting groundcovers can be a tedious task, but pros and veteran gardeners have found ways to speed it along.

- Cover the area with weed barrier cloth, cut "X"s in the cloth, and plant through them. Fewer weeds will be able to sprout until the new plants can shade them out.

- Lay out a string grid or mark planting places with spray paint to keep proper spacing between plants. You'll find this strategy useful in large beds.

- Use a bulb planter or an electric drill to punch planting holes into the soil. This technique is especially helpful on large, sloped beds.

When a large area needs groundcover fast, on a budget, look for a solution at garden centers and home stores. Shop for overgrown flats and gallon pots of creeping fig (*Ficus pumila*) in Zone 9 and protected areas of Zone 8 or Asiatic jasmine (*Trachelospermum jasminoides*). Cell packs and flats of soil may have crowded or intertwined roots. Use a sharp knife to go around each cell as you might do a cake pan to loosen it and remove the plants. Slice through soil in flats to create small squares of

plants with roots attached. Gallon pots often have five or more plants in them that are easily divided once you unpot the rootball.

WATER GARDENS

Three kinds of plants establish harmony in the water garden, not only to the eye but also for cleaner water. If your water garden is missing any of the three types, plant them now.

- Underwater plants like anacharis stay submerged all the time and deplete algae's food sources.

- Floating plants such as water lettuce and butterfly fern cover the surface to reduce sunlight and limit algae growth.

- Floating islands and other plants that grow in water with their roots in soil or pots below the surface include some pitcher plants, hardy banana, water lilies, and lotus.

CARE

ANNUALS

Grooming annual plants can be a tedious, must-do chore or a welcome chance for healthy distraction. When you reach into a plant to pinch the stem of a faded flower or yellow leaf, you step away from the day's to-do list and the twenty-first-century world

■ *Annual plants can be more economical to buy as flats.*

■ *Get a head start on pruning—clip some flowering branches from the thickest part of your forsythia and enjoy them in a vase.*

of constant communication. When you concentrate on the task at hand, your brain can process the bigger issues in the background. Without grooming, most annual flowers will stop blooming and try to set seed, ending their season prematurely. Do it, and solutions can arise that you wouldn't have thought of consciously.

BULBS

Give a gift of potted Easter lilies in bloom with assurances of its future in the garden. Pinch off the yellow pollen tips that protrude from the milky white trumpets to keep both petals and nearby surfaces clean. After the holiday, take off the fancy wrappings and put the pot outside on the deck for a week or two in nice weather. Let it acclimate and then plant out in a sunny bed with well-drained soil.

EDIBLES

New seedlings and transplants attract critters looking for a fresh lunch. Corn and bean seedlings are bird favorites and tender transplants can bring in slugs, snails, and cutworms. Ripening fruit also brings in the birds, so you might invest in distraction devices to keep them away.

PERENNIALS & ORNAMENTAL GRASSES

Stake tall perennials like Joe-pye weed (*Eupatorium*) and others with heavy flower spikes to keep them from dropping into the dirt. Choose thin bamboo stakes and tie jute or cotton strips loosely as you would tomatoes. Or carefully guide growing stems into the wide loop atop a thin metal pole fashioned for peonies but useful for many flowers.

■ *Floating row covers can be laid directly on plants or suspended on hoops above plants, which allows for better air circulation.*

ROSES

Grafted plants join a hardy, disease-resistant rootstock with a different top growth chosen for its desirable blooms and, sometimes fruit or nuts. Modern roses are often grafted for healthy roots that produce the astounding stems and flowers of hybrid teas and others. Take a look at grafted plants to see the union and make sure it is above the ground and mulch to maintain good air circulation. If a graft union drips or oozes liquid, or if growth only comes out below the union, the graft has failed. Replace the plant now.

SHRUBS

Although there are few hard and fast rules in gardening, one applies most universally: if you prune flowering shrubs more than one month after they finish blooming, you are cutting off fast-forming flower buds. Nowhere is this rule easier seen than in azaleas, but it applies to other annual bloomers like Forsythia, flowering quince, and camellia. Trim off spent flowers and a few inches of stem to shape the shrubs. Or if you must rejuvenate, take away one-third of the shrub's overall size to stimulate the maximum amount of new growth.

TREES

Chaste trees (*Vitex agnus-castus*) dazzle with blue blooms every summer. A rapid grower and repeat bloomer if deadheaded, you can grow it as a multi-trunked, spreading tree or as a thicket. To gain control and shape yours, remove any growth that does not leaf out and then top the stems to

■ *Begin the process of controlling poison ivy now.*

thicken them. New sprouts will be more prolific with high-nitrogen fertilizers.

VINES & GROUNDCOVERS

Woody vines can cover fences and trees, sometimes too much, and a little maintenance now can direct their spread for months. Blanket mulch around the vines to suppress new growth and hoe, spray, or propagate them.

Dig up young vine sprouts from around coral honeysuckle and Carolina jessamine and pot them now while they are tender. Clip off a few inches, water with a root stimulator formula or compost tea, and grow outdoors in a shady place.

Poison ivy (*Toxicodendron radicans*) can be a pain, literally, and control becomes more difficult the longer you wait to do it. Where you saw its glorious red and yellow fall display climbing up trees or covering beds last year, count on the vines to sprout and multiply again. Cut the vines at ground level or mow the bed down now. New bright green leaves will appear in a few weeks and you can spray or paint them with a weed killer. By late March, temperatures are favorable and green leaves will yellow soon, indicating the demise of

■ *Plumleaf azalea under pine trees*

HERE'S HOW

TO MAINTAIN A WATER GARDEN FILTER

If your water garden holds less than 2,000 gallons and has (or could have) a waterfall feature, biofilters can enhance the environment for plants and fish. Depending on the size and shape of your garden, retail filter systems may be practical. For a custom fit and function, if none is available, build your own.

Gather these materials:

- 35-gallon plastic tub with a hole cut in the bottom to accommodate the pipe that you will divert from the pump into the filter.

- Plastic or vinyl grid cut to fit the tub bottom and PVC pipe pieces to act as its legs. Raise it an inch or so above the hole.

- Silicone glue and a bulkhead connector fitting to match your pipe and used to seal the pipe to the tub.

- Filter material to fill the rest of the tub that is porous enough to trap particulates, non-toxic, and able to sustain micro-life such as volcanic rock, packaged fiber mats, or even recycled pink sponge hair curlers.

Follow these steps:

- The hard part of this project comes first. Dig a hole big enough for the tub to sit right under or right behind the waterfall's high point.

- Guide the pipe that is used to go from the pump to the waterfall so it will run into the hole in the tub. Seal the entry to direct water into the tub first.

- Set in the PVC "feet" and secure the grid to them with another drop of glue.

- Fill the tub with filter material and turn on the water. It will flow up through the filter and onto the top of the waterfall as before. If it doesn't, cut a groove in the top of the tub to control the flow.

that particular sprout. The vines above will wither, and you can pull them down or let them rot in place. Keep the area mowed to further suppress the poison ivy. Caution: if you are very allergic to poison ivy, this is a job to bribe—or pay—someone else to do.

WATER GARDENS

Whether your water garden is a year-round feature or reopening this month, see to its needs now.

- Test all equipment, replace moving parts and skimmers if needed, and consider adding a UV filter to address ongoing water quality issues.

- Or revamp your system altogether with biofiltration behind a waterfall.

- Groom plants left in the pond all winter, check their basket pots for cracked or broken laths,

and repot if needed. Look for side shoots and baby plants to propagate.

- Treat and test water quality and temperature before adding or returning fish and introduce them gradually.

WATER

ANNUALS

When plant breeders work with annual flowers, they usually seek improved colors, longer bloom seasons, a self-cleaning habit that reduces the need for deadheading, and sometimes drought tolerance. In our states, we also need thunderstorm tolerance, and too few plants are so designated. As if torrential rain isn't enough, choosing the right supplemental watering method can be a challenge. Doing it right builds strong

Watering wands with gentle water breakers are the best tools for hand watering because they slow the flow of water hitting the ground and keep the soil from splattering. Count to ten while watering each plant.

stems and sustains flowers. Doing it wrong can thwart your best efforts, so choose wisely:

- Traditional watering cans with round, perforated heads (called roses) deliver water gently to new seedlings in beds and pots.

- Soaker hoses that leak water slowly are very efficient and can be used in almost any annual planting. They are especially useful under zinnias to keep leaves dry and help prevent leaf diseases.

- Find aboveground sprinklers with adjustable patterns to fit the shapes of your beds to conserve water and make sure every corner and curve gets its share.

- Run these sprinklers at the lowest flow rate that delivers water to the entire space to reduce its loss to evaporation in the air above the bed.

- Use a wide-pattern water breaker or fan nozzle to water beds and pots with a hose. The nozzle should break the stream into a gentle rain instead of a solid stream.

- Consider a simple drip system for container gardens to deliver ample water without wetting the deck or porch.

BULBS

In windy weather, tulip and daffodil petals can dry up too quickly. If the soil is dry, cut the flowers in bloom and soak the clumps to extend the chances that the remaining buds can open and last.

- Water pots of caladiums that you are starting for the summer and keep them warm even if it means a few nights on the kitchen floor.

- Dahlia tubers arrive dehydrated, and if they are shriveled, may be slow to sprout. Water newly potted dahlias very well and keep them consistently moist. But if they are badly shriveled, put the tubers into a bag of damp sand overnight or soak them in a shallow pan of water mixed with liquid rooting hormone for one hour before planting.

EDIBLES

If the month is dry, fruit development can be hindered. Use the index-finger test—when the soil feels dry up to your first knuckle, it's time to water. Be sure those that have bloomed and/or leafed out do not wilt. Soak the soil slowly, if needed, once a week. Add organic matter such as compost to the top inches of the soil under fruit plants if it is dusty and apply fresh mulch around each plant. The same basic watering strategies work for vegetable seedlings as for annual flowers.

Traditional garden rows have their advantages and are just about essential for vegetables like corn and melons that need lots of space and plenty of water. Keep a wheelbarrow full of garden soil near the plot and use it when needed to dam up the ends of the furrows. Capture the benefits when rain is expected or fill the furrows with water when none is in the forecast and the water will soak into every row.

LAWNS

Wait to irrigate the lawn until it begins to green up and then only if the weather is dry. Perhaps more than any other plant, we abuse lawn grass with improper watering or by letting it dry out excessively. If you water by hand or with hoses and sprinklers, resolve to water deeply but not too often.

Turn on the irrigation system in the lawn zone and observe. If runoff occurs while the system is running or after it stops, you're wasting water. Adjust the settings to flow more slowly for a longer time to allow the water to percolate into the soil.

ROSES

It's good advice to keep rose leaves as dry as possible to reduce disease outbreaks and preserve the flowers. To do that, irrigation heads can be set low, soaker hoses can wind through the rose bed, and drip systems can be placed at the base of each plant. But there is much to be gained from watering each plant by hand with a hose and nozzle. You can vary water amounts to suit the size and age of the rose, adjust the flow to prevent runoff as you go, and examine each plant up close for the presence of good insects and pests. It's a good practice, and if the weather is very dry, take a minute to wash the leaves as a gentle rain would do.

SHRUBS AND PERENNIALS & ORNAMENTAL GRASSES

Slopes need soil to hold them in place around plants in these categories. Channel rainfall away and control additional irrigation by using a drip system on sloped beds. Flexible hoses make quick work of snaking around the plants to place little drip heads where they will do the most good—at the base of each plant.

Excess water can doom drought-loving perennial plants. Check on vulnerable new plantings this year and raise them if water is collecting in their crown. Lift the edge of the clump with a fork and add garden soil underneath. Repeat on all sides and reset the grass so it will stay just above ground level.

TREES

Young and newly transplanted trees may need water this month. Check on tree reservoir bags to refill them and test the drip rate. Check the low dams around young trees and repair any that have washed away.

VINES & GROUNDCOVERS

Watering vines, especially those growing in pots, can be frustrating when no amount of water seems enough to keep up with their fast growth rate. Water the pot completely early in the day, and if it wilts again before nightfall, consider adding water-holding

polymers to the top of the pot. The polymers and an inch of ground bark mulch on top of the soil in the pot can help to moderate water loss.

WATER GARDENS

You have only to keep an eye on the water level in the water feature and maintain it this month. If you are planning for a fish family, learn about treating the water for them.

FERTILIZE

ALL

Annual flowers and vegetables are particularly affected by excessive amounts of nitrogen in the soil, but all plant groups are subject to its overstimulation. Too much nitrogen produces an overgrowth of leaves, often at the expense of flowers and fruits. When too much nitrogen is present, you will see symptoms like these:

- Zinnias have small flowers and weak stems that cannot support their big leaves.

- Tomato plants grow exuberantly with dark green leaves and no flowers.

- Stokes' asters produce thick clumps of leaves and small flowers on very short stems.

- Reblooming hydrangeas and azaleas don't put on new flower buds.

- Trees grow dense canopies but do not thicken in girth.

Some legume plants—edibles including beans and peas as well as flowering vines such as hyacinth bean (*Lablab purpureus*) and corkscrew flower (*Vigna caracalla*)—are able to obtain (fix) nitrogen from the air. Be aware of this trait and fertilize them sparingly, if at all.

ANNUALS

Some people think that if a little of something is good, a lot must be better. This is seldom true and certainly not for fertilizer amounts used on annual plants. Mix or distribute amounts *as indicated on the label* or use slightly less and apply the fertilizer a bit more often. For example, if you are to mix 1 tablespoon in a gallon of water and use it monthly, you can choose to mix half that amount and use it every three weeks.

Consider adding a slow-release pelletized fertilizer to large pots of annuals. Available as a balanced formula or one made for flowering plants, these nutrients are applied at the soil surface and become active when

water reaches them. Think of it as insurance against forgetfulness and heavy rain that can wash soluble fertilizers right out of the root zone.

For the first weeks after transplant, use a balanced formula fertilizer to encourage healthy roots, leaves, and to set the first flower buds. Once the plants have reached their expected size, excess nitrogen can be counterproductive. You can shift

---

Ready to Use **1**

FERTIFEED
All Purpose Plant Food

12-4-8 **2**

FertiFeed Ready To Use All-Purpose Plant Food
Net Weight 4lb. 12oz. (2.15kg)

GUARANTEED ANALYSIS **3**

Total Nitrogen (N)..12%

    10.2% Urea Nitrogen*

    1.8% Ammoniacal Nitrogen

Available Phosphate (P_2O_5)...4%

Soluble Potash (K_2O)..8%

5 Sulfur (S)...2%

    2% free Sulfur (S)

Manganese (Mn)...0.05%

    0.05% Chelated Manganese (Mn)

Zinc (Zn) 0.05%

    0.05% Chelated Zinc (Zn)

6 Inert Ingredients...76%

4 *Derived from urea, isobutylidene diurea, ammonium phosphate, and potassium sulfate. Potential acidity 0 lbs. calcium carbonate equivalent per ton.*

*Contains 6.8% water-insoluble isobutylidene diurea.

Information regarding the contents and levels of metals in this product is available on the Internet at http://www.regulatory-info-sc.com

KEEP OUT OF REACH OF CHILDREN

---

1 **The fertilizer brand name**
There are different brands of fertilizer, just like there are different brands of clothes.

2 **Fertilizer analysis or grade**
All fertilizers are labeled with three numbers that indicate the guaranteed analysis, or fertilizer grade. These three numbers give the percentage by weight of nitrogen (N), phosphate (P_2O_5) and potash (K_2O) as listed in the "Guaranteed Analysis." Often, to simplify matters, these numbers are said to represent the primary plant minerals (or "nutrients") nitrogen, phosphorus, and potassium, or N-P-K. This 4-pound 12-ounce (76-ounce) bag of 12-4-8 fertilizer contains 9 ounces of nitrogen, 3 ounces of phosphate, and 6 ounces of potash.

3 **Guaranteed Analysis**
The guaranteed analysis, or grade, lists the percentages of nutrients in the fertilizer and their sources.

4 **Derived from**
The label tells you the inorganic or organic sources that were used to manufacture this fertilizer.

5 **Nutrients other than N-P-K**
These are micronutrients, other nutrients that plants need in smaller amounts than nitrogen, phosphorus, and potassium. Besides the primary elements, the fertilizer may contain secondary minerals—such as calcium, magnesium, and sulfur—and trace elements—such as manganese, zinc, copper, iron and molybdenum.

6 **Other ingredients**
Other ingredients make the fertilizer easier to spread. Inert ingredients, also called filler or carrier, make the fertilizer easier to spread.

to a flowering formula at that point if leaves are outpacing flowers.

BULBS

After daffodils bloom for the first time and when you transplant amaryllis bulbs to the garden, fertilize them to promote deep rooting. Next year's flowers depend on this year's leaves, and there may not be enough of them without adequate nutrition. Use a general purpose, balanced formula (10-10-10 or its equivalent) to encourage leafy growth now.

EDIBLES

Sidedressing vegetable plants with fertilizer puts nutrients where growing roots can get at them, and it can be done in pots, raised beds, or traditional rows. Most gardeners add fertilizer when working up the soil and use a root stimulator or compost tea that has nutrients in it to prevent transplant shock. Six weeks in, most vegetables need more fertilizer, and sidedressing provides it without disturbing tender roots. Use a general garden fertilizer or one made for vegetables (5-10-5, usually) and put it a few inches away from the base of the plant. Open a space for the fertilizer, drop it in, and let the soil

fall back in to cover it. A rule of thumb is to use a heaping tablespoon of fertilizer per young plant.

Organic fertilizers have lower NPK numbers than chemical fertilizers, and the two should not be compared when considering their worth. Organics benefit micro-life in the soil and benefit their symbiosis with plant roots. That means an organic formula may work more slowly but also last longer in its nutrient effects. Apply organic fertilizers more often than chemicals to maintain consistent growth in vegetables.

LAWNS

Caring for lawn grass fills volumes, and most agree that you are wise to let the lawn green up slowly. Fertilizing at this point may work fine or it can be useless if it washes away before the grass can absorb it. Worse, excess nitrogen may push tender growth that can be damaged in a late freeze.

Fertilize healthy lawns after greenup with a formula made for your kind of turf to insure the proper balance of nutrients. This is especially true for centipede grass that can easily be overfed with

---

HERE'S HOW

TO USE A SPREADER

Read the fertilizer bag to learn its proper rate of spreading.

- Pour fertilizer into the spreader with an inch of clearance below the top.

- Find the name of your spreader on the bag and set it to apply your fertilizer.

- Roll the spreader to the edge of the lawn without engaging its drop feature.

- Grip the drop handle and walk across the lawn, pushing the spreader ahead of you at an even pace.

- If you stop and to turn around after each pass, let go of the drop handle.

- Watch where you have just been to keep the paths just overlapping.

- Pour any leftover fertilizer back into the bag, close it, and store dry.

- Rinse out the spreader and hang it upside down to dry.

■ *Successfully fertilizing with dry fertilizer means exacting measurements and a thorough watering to ensure the nutrients reach the grass roots.*

phosphorus. Indeed, many formulas for centipede grass are 15-0-15 and contain no phosphorus at all. Apply granular fertilizers with a spreader to be sure fertilizer is distributed evenly.

PERENNIALS & ORNAMENTAL GRASSES

As spring- and summer-blooming perennials begin their growth, they can quickly deplete available nutrients. To grow steadily, gain in size each season, and bloom their best, fertilize the clumps now. Choose a balanced formula for plants that did not grow well last year to boost their leaves as well as their roots and flowers. Select a formula made for flowering plants with less nitrogen and so a lower first number on the label for healthy, established clumps. Organic and conventional products with appropriate formulas are widely available. If you use conventional fertilizers exclusively, add extra organic matter—½-inch blanket of composted manure—to the bed annually.

ROSES

Roses are generally considered heavy feeders; that is, they will use about as much fertilizer as they can get. Exceptions to this rule include aggressive ramblers and some well-established climbers, but even they benefit from a fertilizer application now. When a rose is first planted, fertilize it monthly during the growing season for two years. After that, assess its behavior and fertilize accordingly.

Liquid fertilizers can be easier for young roses to absorb, but they often do not last as long in our humid soils as granular formulas with similar analysis. Weather permitting, you would be wise to use them in tandem, like having fertilizer insurance for the young rose. Work a general-purpose garden fertilizer into the soil around each rose bush monthly or as directed and use the liquid rose formula monthly.

SHRUBS

After you prune flowering shrubs, get them ready for the long growing season with fertilizer and mulch. If you didn't do it last month, begin with a blanket of composted manure to put organic matter into the soil around the shrubs. Spread ½ inch between the base of the shrub and its drip line

and work it into the top layers of soil. Add 1 to 2 inches of organic mulch and, two weeks later, use your favorite shrub fertilizer as usual.

TREES

Some trees have long taproots and secondary roots that are important to its stability, while others have wide root systems that spread as wide as its branches. Put fertilizers where they can be used: 2 to 3 feet from the trunk of taproot trees such as conifers, and for those with widespread roots, circle the drip line and make another ring halfway in between that line and the trunk. Drilling holes at regular intervals around the tree to accept fertilizer granules is traditional and effective. If that sounds like too much work, look for tree formulas made to be worked into the soil or applied as liquids instead.

VINES & GROUNDCOVERS

Beds of clumping groundcovers that you pruned earlier this year should be growing steadily by now. If they are not or if you have never fertilized the liriope or mondo grass, do it now.

You need a go-to fertilizer for general purposes like feeding beds of groundcover. Choose a balanced formula such as 10-10-10 that is complete with amounts of both NPK and trace elements listed on the label. Look at the nitrogen description and select one that has both immediate and slow-release forms.

WATER GARDENS

Plants that live in water naturally take their nutrition from the soil at the bottom and from the water itself. Plastic liners and concrete ponds do not have much soil in them, unless there's a problem, and water garden plants live in small pots with limited soil too.

Floating plants get most of what they need from the water, but submerged and potted plants need more than is available. Highly soluble fertilizer products that release their nitrogen very slowly have been developed in liquid, granular, and tablet forms. Use these water garden fertilizers on hardy plants when nighttime temperatures reach 50 degrees Fahrenheit. Wait until daytimes hover at 70 degrees Fahrenheit or above to fertilize tropical plants like night-blooming water lilies.

PROBLEM-SOLVE

ALL

Tender green growth is the favored food of slugs and snails, whether it comes from hostas, tuberoses, bean seedlings, or petunia transplants. Slugs and snails may seem worse in a wet spring, but they can be a problem anywhere that meets their basic needs. Baits and ground level controls of copper products or diatomaceous earth can keep them away from your plants, but go beyond the obvious. Think "dark and damp" to find their lairs, like undisturbed leaf piles, stacked rocks, and random boards or logs lying about. Turn the piles and lift the obstructions. There's nothing like a little sunshine to spoil the day for these pests.

Birds are beautiful when they pluck caterpillars off your plants, but when they snatch seedlings out of the ground or poke into fruit, they're pests. Keep them away.

ANNUALS

It happens to everyone. You arrive home with a few flats of plants and take advantage of Daylight Saving Time to plant the lot before dark. Then you discover a freeze is predicted in the coming nights.

■ *Harden off young plants so they can better survive their new environment.*

If annuals are stunted by exposure to cold temperatures at this growth stage, their growth may not be optimal and their vulnerability to pests will increase.

You can solve this problem by planning for a few days outside to harden off young plants and checking the long-term weather forecast before planting. But in the short term, take one of the steps on page 74 to protect tender transplants.

HERE'S HOW

TO KEEP BIRDS AWAY FROM EDIBLES

- Set up a bird feeding station far away from the edibles and include a water source such as an automated mister, sprinkler, soaker, or a pan you fill daily.

- Plastic owls and snakes will work for a while, sometimes long enough for the corn to thicken up and be less appetizing.

- Lean a mirror at the base of fruit trees or hang strings of mirrors on bamboo stakes over the plantings. The reflective surfaces can make the area less enticing.

- If you use black plastic mulch to warm the soil, spray silver stripes on it for a similar reflective effect.

- Spray seedlings or sprinkle red pepper on them to ruin their flavor for birds.

- Spread floating row cover over the vulnerable plants to protect them from birds (and egg-laying moths too).

■ *Motion-activated sprinklers are an effective and humane way to keep animals out of your vegetables.*

BULBS

When you await the reward of planting tulips, their failure to bloom can turn you off of them permanently. One of these reasons is likely to blame and can be easily remedied next year:

- Inadequate chilling before planting or worse, riding around in the back seat for a few weeks between the garden center and the refrigerator. Chill for eight to twelve weeks.

- Planting tulips deeper than twice their height can suppress flowering.

- Short stems and short-lived flowers are usually the result of temperatures warmer than tulips can stand, often the wide fluctuations that mark a mild winter.

EDIBLES

When okra and lima bean seeds fail to sprout, you dig some up and find they are rotten. You suspect a pathogen has gotten them and drench the bed with fungicide before replanting. But the second sowing happens after the soil warms up, and the first sowing simply rotted because the soil was cold when they tried to take up water from it. If you wonder whether the soil is warm enough to plant, get a soil thermometer so you can check it weekly. References are readily available for the vegetable varieties you choose, but as an example, most lettuce seeds will sprout in soil that is nearly freezing but put on their best stands in 45 to 50 degree Fahrenheit soils outdoors. The ideal soil temperature range for transplanting tomatoes begins at 60 degrees Fahrenheit and it is 70 degrees Fahrenheit for okra seeds. Exposed rows, raised beds, and containers in the same vicinity warm up at different rates and a soil thermometer also can be very helpful to test them.

LAWNS

Winter weeds—from chickweed and henbit to dollar weed and wild garlic—can make a still-dormant lawn look green. Even if they are not a serious encroachment yet, they will return and take over if left entirely unchecked. Once the weeds bloom, seeds soon follow, clumps increase in size, and before long you have a serious problem. Whether you never spray anything or have the lawn on a regular program of pre- and post-emergent herbicides, mow or use a string trimmer to cut off the flower heads on weeds now.

ROSES

When rosebuds do not open or try to unfurl their petals only to stop halfway, twisted and ruined, you can blame one common pest for the problem—thrips. To confirm their presence, slice open one of the buds and look for comma-shaped insects among the petals. Think back to last year to remember if petals were streaked brown in places, a common symptom of thrip infestation later in the year. Get a grip on thrips now to prevent their damage to the next rose buds.

HERE'S HOW

TO PROTECT TENDER TRANSPLANTS

- Drape plastic over the plants before the sun sets. If possible, support it with wire fencing or blocks at each end of the bed and cover both plants and supports.

- When freezing temperatures are predicted at night, set up a sprinkler and coat them with water as temperatures fall. This strategy protects strawberries in Florida and will insulate your plants too.

- Cover the plants with a cotton sheet, if you don't remember until the last minute.

- Be sure to remove these temporary covers as soon as possible or at least open an end for ventilation during the day. If poor conditions persist, consider individual cloches as described for planting edibles (page 58) where their use is feasible.

TO CONTROL THRIPS

- Practice good rose-bed sanitation by pruning off thrip-damaged stems and removing them from the garden.

- Put on fresh organic mulch such as ground bark and keep the rose bed weed free to remove hiding places for thrips and other insects.

- Water without wetting the leaves whenever possible.

- Hang sticky traps in the roses to monitor and control thrips.

- Conduct a spray program using permethrin or spinosad three times at eight-day intervals to break up the thrips' life cycle.

- Consider a systemic insecticide if the problem persists and/or remove the worst infested rose bushes.

SHRUBS

Evergreen azaleas can go overlooked most of the year but take center stage with their biggest flower show this month. That's when you really look at them and notice off-color leaves or yellowing that looks really unhealthy. This pest problem didn't start yesterday and it will not be fixed tomorrow. Wait until blooms are finished and pruning is done to begin control of the azalea lacebugs that are causing leaf damage.

Identify the presence of lacebugs by turning azalea leaves over. If there are small black things stuck to the undersurface, you've found the evidence of this common pest and will need to control them this season.

TREES

Your pear tree, either edible or ornamental, has a wilted branch that quickly turns red and brown. The most common description of this spring malady is that the branch looks like you took a blowtorch to it and burned the green material badly. Not rare at all, fireblight fungus attacks pears and their relatives to varying degrees. It is a terminal disease combated by heavy pruning to remove the infected parts.

To prune seriously diseased limbs and to prevent spreading disease among plants, dip blades, shears, snips, and saws in a solution of one part chlorine bleach mixed in ten parts water after each cut. Make cuts into healthy wood several inches below any sign of disease.

VINES & GROUNDCOVERS

More than any other herbicide, glyphosate is used to effectively control an assortment of weeds. If you are an organic gardener, alternatives are admittedly few. Sprays of full-strength household vinegar are especially effective in full sun but usually must be reapplied to be effective. Results with corn gluten products have shown good results in suppressing some weeds, but their effect is diminished in wet weather.

WATER GARDENS

A coat of algae across the surface of a water garden spoils its appearance and water quality. A beautiful water feature can be a balancing act to maintain, and success lies in the plants you choose, as much as the maintenance you do. An essential component to algae prevention is floating plants designed to cover close to half the water surface. You can handle this problem now while plants are available and look forward to fewer algae issues.

*Now is the time to savor the garden with morning coffee, because April can be the last sweet month of spring. Your garden, the neighbor's garden, even commercial plantings glow with late-blooming azaleas, the first Japanese hawthorns, roses, and Virginia sweetspire. Weigela and sweet bay magnolia (*M. **virginiana***), peonies (***Paeonia***), and poppies (***Papaver***) join the first lilies (***Lilium***) as the color riot explodes weekly with new flowers.*

In Zone 9, you see full bins at the farmers' markets and backyard gardens are full of beans, literally, and by the end of the month you may be digging potatoes. Farther north, you test the screw hooks, yank on old chains, and hang up the ferns and baskets of tender annuals. It's time to take the houseplants outside to shady spots before the transition to more sun. Still farther north, racks of beautiful containers call your name, some already planted, but some just waiting for your imagination.

Confidence soars this month. You know you can make it happen, whatever "it" is in your garden. You vow to really keep up with it all, to walk the garden daily, and turn the compost too. But the results can be mixed, because there's so much to enjoy in April and the weather is so unpredictable. This is the time when pleasant days lift the spirits and cool evenings make you believe everything is possible. Hopeless romantics steal away to smell the roses, and gardeners dig up space for more bushes. But some days you just have to plant something, sure that hot weather and its doldrums will get here too soon.

The sense of getting ahead can lead to frantic planting, especially if March was chilly and wet. Projects big and small get under your skin this month too. You might build a potting shed or cover an old swing set in trellising to grow a hyacinth bean (*Dolichos lablab*) tent, finally get those flagstone paths, or choreograph a symphony of colorful pots on the patio. April is the "get ahead to keep ahead" month in garden maintenance. Attention to tasks like mulching, edging, weed control, and pest prevention now will pay off big time in the summer. Prioritize and proceed.

PLAN

ALL

Statistically, April brings the most tornadoes of the year to our states, and while they are unpredictable, planning can help mitigate the damage to your property and perhaps save your life. The primary threats during less-than-completely-devastating tornados and strong storms with straight-line winds are falling trees and ordinary objects that become airborne projectiles. Make an appointment with a tree professional if you have large trees that could fall on the house or other structures. Sometimes pruning can lighten their weight and lessen the threat, but if the trees must be removed, plan for it. The work is expensive and the change to your garden may be dramatic, but not as much as if you let them fall without a thought.

Survey the furniture and other ornaments in your garden and plan where they can be stored or laid down when high winds are predicted. For example, the shepherd's hook that holds a hanging basket will be most unwelcome if it crashes through your window. Make a list if there will be much to do, such as a note to lay the hook in the flowerbed and bring the baskets indoors. If an old fence might fall onto the roses or a rickety gate could fly apart, plan to brace them. There is a reason meteorologists practice saying, "Strong spring storms." You can avoid compounding these potential disasters with an action plan. Make yours now and be sure to include the garden.

Plan before you shop to be sure you have enough mulch to finish a project. Calculate how much mulch you need with these steps. Find the area (length x width) and multiply that by the depth of mulch you want, to know how many cubic feet to buy. For example, a bed 10-foot long and 4-foot wide has 10x4 or 40 square feet of space. To mulch 3 inches deep, understand that 3 inches = ¼ cubic foot = 0.25. Multiply 0.25 x 40 square feet = 10 cubic feet of mulch. Most bagged mulches are sold in 3-cubic-foot bags and for larger projects, truckloads are available at many garden centers.

ANNUALS

Some flowers bloom almost from the day they're planted, while others require months of growth to

■ *Plant candlestick* Cassia alata *seeds now for beautiful flowers in the fall.*

put on buds. One such spectacular fall-blooming annual is candelabra or candlestick plant (*Cassia alata*). A long-lived tree in the tropics, where it is native, candelabra is a perennial in parts of Zone 9 but must be started from seed each year elsewhere. Because seed and young plants can be hard to find, plan your search now. Few annuals are as well-named as the candlestick tree. Its leaves spread to form a beautiful green base with golden stacks of flowers standing straight up like, well, candles.

BULBS

Plan for more daffodils next year by watching the shaded borders of your lawn this month. You may notice the grass is slower to green up and grow in these shaded areas, as trees and tall shrubs grow and lower light conditions encroach. Instead of waiting for those areas to die out, plan to mow them close to make a place for more daffodils next fall.

EDIBLES

The spring garden is well under way and summer planting starts soon where it hasn't already. Vegetables and herbs need full sun to do their best, and shade from a tall plant can limit how well shorter ones grow. Watch how the sun moves over the edibles area and what shade, if any, passes over it during the day. In general, you will want to plant so the tall plants cast their shade outside the garden. For example, plan for squash, bush beans, and other shorter crops on the east or north side of the sunny patch with tall tomatoes, pole lima beans, and okra along the west or south sides.

LAWNS

After the lawn greens up, it's time to assess its condition and make needed improvements. Look for areas that are not starting to grow as expected, for exposed soil that looks hard, where weeds have invaded, or places even weeds won't grow. If you have a mixed lawn, the mow-what-grows kind with

a variety of grasses and broadleaf weeds, plan to enhance it or convert it to only turf grass.

- Mixed lawns look better if they are fertilized with slow-release nitrogen in May. They will stay greener and walk easier if mowed slightly higher all summer than you would mow turf grass alone.

- To convert a mixed lawn to turf, determine whether you have a majority of one kind of grass. If so, plan a series of sprays to get rid of everything else. If nothing predominates, plan to spray the entire lawn and prepare the soil before sodding.

PERENNIALS & ORNAMENTAL GRASSES

The difference between a garden bed and a garden border is that while a bed may be viewed from one or more sides, a border is meant to be seen from one long view. Planning a border takes time and contemplation, not to mention construction and shopping because of the many elements

■ *Orient lower-growing plants so that they are not shaded by taller-growing plants as the sun moves overhead.*

involved—plant size and exposure, soil preparation, hardscape, color, and seasonal interest, among others. This project deserves graph paper for practical measuring plus garden tours and magazines for inspiration.

Dense shade creates a gap in the garden view that can benefit from interesting plants. They must tolerate the low light and often dry conditions there, yet hold their good looks. Cast iron plant (*Aspidistra elatior*) takes the shade and keeps on growing with big, dark green leaves that maintain their erect sword shapes.

ROSES

Hybrid tea rose growers maintain a careful schedule and often-scrupulous records of flower and stem size, maintenance, and products. Those who grow the roses called variously shrub, landscape, antique, or old roses seldom do maintain careful schedules but should think about doing so. Not nearly enough is written about these types, and as their popularity endures, local observations are important. Plan to note when the roses bloom, fertilizers used, the dates you deadhead them, and when they rebloom, if they do. Anything that catches your eye can be valuable to you but also to others who grow your kinds of roses.

SHRUBS

Flowering shrubs pop out from everywhere in spring, and if you want the colorful show to continue, plan to add summer's best.

- Sweet pepperbush, called summersweet (*Clethra alnifolia*) grows slowly to 4 feet x 3 feet or larger. It is nearly covered in fragrant, fancy white flower spikes from July until frost and has good fall color, too. The native is a fine butterfly plant that tolerates heavy soil and blooms well in part shade. 'Ruby Spice' has lovely pink flowers.

- Oleander (*Nerium oleander*) is a fast-growing evergreen shrub that can suffer cold damage and return to full blooming glory in the same year. Its flowers range from dark and light pinks through apricots to yellow and white. In hardy areas, plan for a row of dwarf oleander where the standard varieties will be too imposing.

■ *Oleander* (Nerium oleander) *explodes with flower clusters from every branch. Hardy in the southern zones and reliably perennial further north where it will return from established roots and bloom that summer.*

VINES & GROUNDCOVERS

The single biggest mistake you can make with spring-flowering clematis is to prune it too soon. Bare stems are not necessarily dead, even when the rest of the vine starts to leaf out and flower. Before you prune, plan to see what happens for a few weeks after the first flowers appear. The same is true for other well-behaved spring-bloomers like chocolate vine (*Akebia quinata*).

WATER GARDENS

If weeds grow thick on the bottom of ponds, filters can clog and water quality can suffer. Pulling or cutting may not work, but before you consider sprays and other measures, plan to get advice from a professional pond service or your county agent. It may be necessary to drain the pond and start over but it may not. The type of weed, extent of the problem, and implications of treatment determine your course, and all need studying to plan for long-term control.

PLANT

ANNUALS

Plant different flowering annuals together to attract more attention—and butterflies—to your flowerbeds and containers. Mix heights, colors, and flower shapes between and within families. Combinations that work include:

- An upright form like *Begonia* 'Dragon Wing' surrounded by trailing Supertunia (*Petunia* × *hybrida*) or million bells

- Spiky angelonia to contrast with rounder zinnias or periwinkle (*Catharanthus roseus*)

- Bold sunflowers and equally bold Mexican sunflower (*Tithonia rotundifolia*)

Plant a clock garden: moonflowers and morning glory for flowers night and day, plus four o'clocks (*Mirabilis jalapa*) to make time between the flowering of the vines.

Morning glory, moonflower, and their relatives like exotic love (*Mina lobata*) have hard seed coats that can take weeks to break down to allow sprouting. Start by cutting a small nick into the seed coat with your pocketknife and then speed the process with water that is *warm*, not hot or cold. The water temperature can make a difference, as when you soak seeds to facilitate sprouting. Drop the seeds into that warm water and swirl them around for several minutes. Pour the water out and replace it with fresh warm water and let the seeds sit for several hours before planting. At least the nick will widen as it soaks up water, and, more likely, the coat will split a bit.

BULBS

Plant more dahlias for their complex flowers, big impact, and amazing color range. Transplant any you have started and plant tubers in well-drained, rich soil along with their stakes or other supports. They'll need both—dinner plate dahlias grow rapidly and bloom at eye level in sunny beds.

■ *Stakes work best for plants with one to seven tall main stems. Leave a little "breathing room" between the stake and the stem when you tie the stakes.*

When white spider lilies (*Hymenocallis coronaria*) bloom, their wild and crazy flower explosions win your heart, but it's usually too late to find any to plant. Transplant conditions aren't great for these big bulbs, either, so plant them now. Like many "swamp" plants, these spiders do not need to grow in water and can be grown in garden beds that are irrigated regularly. A particular white spider lily native to Alabama is named for its water source, the Cahaba river, and is known as the Cahaba lily.

When you cut gladiola stems for the vase, several inches of stem remain that are not attractive. Plant a row of annuals in front of the glads that will hide the stems as they die down. And you'll get more flowers to cut in the process.

EDIBLES

When you plant herbs, know how they grow to choose the best spot for them. Basil (*Ocimum basilicum*) is a fast-growing annual herb, *Rosemary officinalis* is a drought-tolerant perennial, and both thrive in good garden soil but not usually together. Basil can use as much water and fertilizer as a tomato plant, while rosemary prefers little of either. Heavy soils and frequent rainfall challenge the Mediterranean herbs like sages, thymes, and oregano, yet the same conditions are fine for the wide array of mints grown in our states. Plant sage (*Salvia officinalis*), thyme (*Thymus vulgaris*), oregano (*Origanum vulgare*), and real tarragon (*Artemisia dracunculus*) in containers, preferably clay pots, for faster growth, cleaner leaves, and longer life than in most garden beds.

Each year more basils tempt you to grow and cook with them, and they're lovely even if you don't eat them. Four to know:

- Pesto or Genovese basil, the classic peppery, sweet herb used in Italian cooking

- African blue basil, sweet tasting purple leaves turn green as they age

- Thai basil, licorice-flavored but sweet and pungent

- Holy basil, used in Thai cuisine for its earthy, clove flavor

■ *Basil is a fast-growing annual herb.*

Purple- and red-leafed basils are quite strong in their taste and their impact on garden beds and pots.

Seed these directly in the garden, raised beds, or containers as the month progresses:

- Beans, green first and later limas, both bush and pole types (*Phaseolus*)

- Summer squashes—yellow, patty pan, and zucchini (*Cucurbita pepo*)

- Melons (*Citrullus, Cucumis*), cucumbers (*Cucumis sativa*), and summer spinach or Malabar (*Basella alba* 'Rubra')

Transplant tomatoes (*Lycopersicon*), eggplants, and bell peppers (*Capsicum*).

LAWNS

The turf grass you plant this month will be there for years, and choosing the right one depends on where you live—both the zone and local conditions.

- Tall fescue (*Festuca*) makes a beautiful lawn in north Alabama and very north Mississippi where it's cool-season habits are less taxed than elsewhere. This bunching grass is dark green, medium textured, and easy to start from seed.

In fact, you are well-advised to sow additional fescue seed each fall to keep the stand thick through the summer.

- Centipede grass (*Eremochloa ophiuroides*) grows slowly and is a favorite of people who do not like to mow as often as other grasses require. Grown in our states since early in the twentieth century, centipede grass is lighter green in color, has specific fertilizer needs, and can be grown from seed or sod.

- Bermudagrass (*Cynodon*) stands up to children playing and requires frequent mowing to maintain its low profile. Fine textured, fast growing, and easy to start from seed, bermudagrass thrives in full sun.

- *Zoysia* grass grows at a moderate rate into a thick green lawn that can be mowed high for much of the summer. Its texture is coarser than bermuda but nowhere near the bold profile of St. Augustine grass.

- St. Augustine grass (*Stenotaphrum secundatum*) has slightly greater shade tolerance than other turfs but also less ability to stand the cold of upper Zone 8 and Zone 9. It is deep green, coarse texture makes a great walking surface for low-traffic areas.

PERENNIALS & ORNAMENTAL GRASSES

You'll find perennials both familiar and unknown until you meet them at garden centers, home stores, and plant swaps. Planting conditions for perennials are great now. Work up the soil, adding organic matter and granular fertilizer to each hole as you transplant. Water each clump well with a solution of rooting hormone, compost tea, or root-stimulator fertilizer.

For tropical tones in hardy perennial plants, you can't beat the lilies—calla (*Zantedeschia*), canna, and toad, plus butterfly ginger (*Hedychium*). These common names are misleading because none are true lilies, but all belong in the spring garden for their strappy leaves now and flowers later. Except for the callas, these "lilies" bloom in summer.

ROSES, SHRUBS, AND TREES

Continue planting woody plants that have been grown in containers. Prune at transplant and water to prevent wilted leaves and withered tips that are signs of dehydration. Night temperatures above 65 degrees Fahrenheit with days above 75 degrees Fahrenheit will be more stressful, but with a little extra TLC, including mulch, they'll be fine.

Organic mulches like pine straw, and pine and hardwood barks, are plentiful and available; each has a best use. Pine straw is attractive and lasts at least a year before it turns dark. When you turn it over, white mycelium is often visible in aged pine straw. At this stage the straw becomes a water trap and should be removed, perhaps to line a foot path. It is still ages from proper rot, but it cannot be turned into the soil or added to compost. Bales of wheat straw are used for newly seeded lawns, strawberry beds, and huge vines, such as pumpkins, and are also very slow to decompose. Barks are sometimes shredded, but are more often chipped into 2-inch nuggets or pieces that average 1 inch or less.

SHRUBS

Groups of shrubs so thick they seem to choke the tree above reveal poor planning that happened years ago. If there is no air circulation around the trunk or if tree roots are pushing the shrubs out of the soil, pruning may help, but is not a long-term solution to this problem. Move the shrubs farther out from the trunk or take them out entirely. When you site beds around trees, start at least 5 feet out from the tree trunk on all sides.

VINES & GROUNDCOVERS

Passionflowers (*Passiflora*) are hard to resist and both native and exotic selections are abundantly available. The Southeast native maypop or wild passionflower (*P. incarnata*) brings a strong sense of place wherever it is grown and is particularly well suited to cottage gardens. Tropical passionflower (*Passiflora* species and hybrids) instantly transports you with bold shades of deep reds and purples in contrast to the native's more subtle purple and white. All are vigorous climbers that thrive in full sun or mostly so. Put up a trellis when you plant—these are fast growers.

■ *We grow 2 kinds of passionflowers* (Passiflora *species and hybrids). Native maypop opens with spidery purple blossoms followed by yellow fruits; the plants reseed or become perennial. Tropical passionflowers offer starry flowers in red and orange shades on a more compact vine.*

WATER GARDENS

Add marginal plants, those that grow around the edges of your water garden. Include sword shapes like flag and Louisiana iris, statement plants such as Abyssinian banana, and rice paper plant (*Tetrapanex papyrifer*), and still have room for night blooming jasmine (*Cestrum nocturnum*) to draw you out into the night garden this summer.

Plantings in and around water features can look one-dimensional when the size and color are similar. The addition of one dramatic clump, such as dwarf papyrus (*P. isocladus*) changes all that. The designation "dwarf" is misleading because the canes average 30 inches tall with radiating tufts of thin green leaves at each end that turn bronze in September. When the canes grow heavy, they fall over and start new plants in a charming display.

CARE

ALL

Your garden can be a sanctuary where water gurgles, flowers bloom, and a busy day turns blessedly tranquil when you step through the gate. Or it can buzz with energy as you bustle about doing what it takes to maintain that oasis mood. April makes light of garden chores, and you can weed a sunny bed without much sweat. If you don't already have one, it's time to establish a routine that takes you into the garden daily for an hour now. You'll get plenty done for the plants and condition your body for the summer's heat so you can keep with the routine in the coming months. Each plant group has specific challenges that present themselves, but your good care can meet them all. Spend an hour so you don't miss the good, or especially the bad and ugly signs of pest damage in time to identify the intruders and control them with the least long-term effect on the garden.

Take care of *yourself* with sunscreen, insect repellant, garden gloves, and a straw hat.

And put one more thing on your list, this time in the spiritual care department—sit down at the end of that hour and enjoy the view.

ANNUALS

Take advantage of a good price on a flat of annuals even if it's too soon to plant in your area. Unless the plants are grossly overgrown, you can keep them growing for several weeks at home. Put the flats outside in shade and elevated on bricks or a

TO PREVENT TRANSPLANT SHOCK

- Transplant to sunny areas in the late afternoon.

- If soils are very dry, water well the day before transplanting.

- Mark planting spots and amend their soil if needed before you unpot the plants.

- If rootballs do not slide out easily, squeeze the sides of plastic cells or pots to release them.

- Dig a hole, drop in the plant so it sits at ground level, and press soil around it.

- Water in well and mulch around the plants.

bench for good air circulation and to keep the slugs at bay. Grab an empty flat and separate the cells or pots for more space around each one. Water daily and fertilize lightly each week.

Should you pick or not pick the first flowers off of young annual plants? Some say yes, it's important to pick while others say it's no big deal. Roots are the first priority at transplant time, and healthy roots mean flowers, but your good care can prevent transplant shock and a few flowers can make the move without difficulty.

Fast-growing annuals can grow straight up with few flowers, but you can redirect them. Pinch leggy annuals like coleus (*Solenostemon scutellarioides*) to keep them bushy and prevent flowering. Use your thumb and forefinger to remove the pair of leaves at the top or more, if needed. Each pinch will create two growing points; pinch those when they put on two new sets of leaves to get four more, and so forth.

BULBS
Caladiums, elephant ears (*Alocasia*), taro (*Colocasia*), and other Arums grown for their leaves may send up blooms prematurely, even while still in their nursery pots. Remove them

immediately because flowering deters leaf production and can slow or stop desirable growth. When St. Joseph's lilies (*Hippeastrum* × *johnsonii*) finish flowering, their red and white flowers will soon form seedpods unless you cut them. If yours did not bloom this year, they may have sunk or become too crowded and need to be dug up, separated, and replanted.

EDIBLES
Keep the weeds pulled and let tomato flowers be your cue to shake the plants gently to aid in pollination. Continue routine sprays of fruit trees to protect this year's fruit and keep the trees healthy. If only one sex blooms first on squash, batter and fry them. More of both sexes will follow, but if only one male flower is surrounded by ladies, you can be the bee—use a cotton swab or small paintbrush to move pollen.

Squash vine borer moths lay egg clusters of ¼-inch amber orbs on young squash stems. Look for and scrape off those egg masses now, or one summer day you'll find the plants collapsed and dying.

■ *Coleus is a popular annual plant with brightly colored leaves. Pinch off coleus flower stalks when they sprout so that the plant stays neat and tidy. If coleus gets too large, just cut off the top half of the plant stems. They will resprout.*

■ *Thin crowded branches of immature fruit so fewer—but larger— fruits develop.*

Plant recommended varieties of tomatoes in well-drained, full sun beds with plenty of water and fertilizer. There are many fruits, but none gets as large as advertised, so you may be disappointed. Some varieties are bred to grow larger fruit and you should seek them out. But you may also want to use some ideas from gardeners who compete to grow the biggest tomatoes. They thin the fruits to take off half (or more) and then fry or pickle the green tomatoes. Some take off all but one fruit and remove leaves from the lower half of the plant to direct more water to the ripening fruit. Still others add a constant feed nutrition approach by adding soluble tomato fertilizer with every watering.

Young fruit trees may start more plums, pears, or apples than they can possibly finish. For the first two crops and any others that weigh branches down so they must be supported, you must thin the fruit. When a tree cannot ripen its crop, it will drop every one, a real cause for tears. Now, while fruits are small and their stems pliable, pluck every other one off so the rest can ripen.

LAWNS
Mow your lawn often enough that you cut about one-third of each grass blade each time and maintain it in the recommended height range.

- Fescue–3 to 4 inches

- St. Augustine–2½ to 3½ inches

- Centipede–1½ to 2 inches

- Zoysia–1 to 2 inches

- Bermuda–½ to 1½ inches

For example, to maintain zoysia at 2 inches, let it grow to 3 inches before you mow one-third off. No matter what height you choose, leave ½ inch at the top range now with plans to raise the mowing height by one notch in July.

PERENNIALS & ORNAMENTAL GRASSES.
Clip off spent flowers as they fade.

For most perennials, their potential to rebloom can be seen in the flower stem. Stems that have true leaves behind flowers may put on another bud if you will cut off the old flower with only a little stem. But when stems are leafless or have only modified leaves behind the flower, they are unlikely to rebloom. Trim them to right above the perennial crown.

Fall-blooming flowers like 'Clara Curtis' mums (*Chrysanthemum rubellum*), boneset, and Joe-pye weed (*Eupatorium*), perennial sunflower (*Helianthus*), and false asters (*Boltonia asteroides*) grow tall and fall over by the time they bloom.

■ *Depending on the model and age of your mower, setting the wheel height adjustment on a push mower can be a difficult, strength-testing feat. To make it easier with any mower, use a scrap 4×4 or the sidewalk curb to prop the deck up so that the back wheels are off the ground (this only works with rear-wheel height-adjustment models), then change the height adjustment. It should require far less pressure to make the change.*

The flowers either lie on top of each other and their bedmates or disappear from view altogether. Keep the flowers visible and clean by pinching a few inches off of each stem now and monthly through June to control their height without compromising flowers.

SHRUBS

Heavenly bamboo (*Nandina domestica*) has been grown for years, and increases its stand by sprouting new canes each year, or trying to. When old hedges or individual shrubs grow thick, young, new canes can be suppressed. Allow a few new canes to grow by cutting the oldest down at ground level.

If any particular shrub's flowers and pollen set you to sneezing, waxleaf ligustrum or any of the privets (*Ligustrum*) are likely to do it. When the culprits are common and variegated littleleaf privets, you should remove them because they are invasive. The slightly more demure waxleafs make excellent hedges and screens, but are equally sneezy. Shear off the flower clusters before they can bloom and aggravate you further.

TREES

Weedy trees like mimosa (*Albizia julibrissin*) can be beautiful, but their fallen seedpods and tendency to sprout usually relegates them to backyards and alleys. Unlike other situations, this one calls for 3 inches of thick mulch, such as compost gin moat or leaf mold. Lay the mulch on thick and forget about fertilizing mimosas—enough nutrients will leach from the mulch to sustain them.

VINES & GROUNDCOVERS

Vines like poison ivy (*Toxicodendron radicans*) and Japanese honeysuckle (*Lonicera japonica*) can develop woody stems quickly that are difficult to treat with herbicides. To gain control, cut such pests down to the ground now and treat the new, more vulnerable growth when it sprouts.

WATER GARDENS

If your water feature is small enough to skim by hand, get in that habit now. Yes, leaves will fall in and rot nicely, but too many leaves is no help for water quality or filtration. Larger ponds usually require a motorized skimmer to limit leaf drop.

WATER

ALL

The Deep South may not be a monsoon climate, but it can seem so when April showers dominate the forecast. To know just how much rain has fallen, set up a rain gauge or several, depending on your property size and the microclimates within it. Also known as an ombrometer and other designations depending on application, these devices measure rain or irrigation water applied in a specific period of time. The simplest ones look like tubes stuck to a stick with a ruler painted on the side and they are surprisingly reliable. All you have to do is set them up and remember to monitor, note the results, and empty the gauges.

High water costs and devotion to sustainability marry well when you collect rainwater for future use. Aboveground systems can be simple barrels on blocks or cisterns that collect all the water that flows through gutters. Underground installations vary from small and simply filtered and then pumped out to those that collect, recycle, and treat all that runs off of a property. Consult an experienced landscape architect about the underground projects and remember these points about aboveground water collection:

- Keep screens intact to prevent leaves and other trash from falling in.

- Remember that standing water is a breeding ground for mosquitoes, so keep tanks covered when not collecting or install an aerator.

- Check on the water level after heavy rains and drain or shut off to prevent overtopping.

- Use clear plastic tubing to siphon water from the tank to garden and keep it clean.

Traditional advice says that garden plants need 1 inch of water weekly. This is perhaps the most common "average of all averages" cited in gardening because plants and conditions can contradict it. Now that you know what most plants want, use a rain gauge to be sure they get it. For example, beds under trees will be drier than the lawn and beds outside the canopy, but how much more you should water will be unknown unless you measure it first.

When plants have grown to fill a pot, you'll need to water daily.

ANNUALS

Watering plants in pots can make the difference in their performance.

- Combination pots of annual plants should be based on the compatibility of its occupants. When one plant in a potted group wilts the day before the others, you have two options. Remove and replace it with another plant or leave it to be the wilt meter—when it sags, you know it is almost time to water the others.

- Houseplants moved outdoors in spring soon begin to grow more rapidly and need water more often than they did indoors. If they dry out overnight, however, their need for water may indicate it is time to repot. This is especially true if water rushes through the pot and out the drain holes without time to percolate into the soil.

BULBS

When clumps of daffodils have turned half brown, they are ready to be moved or separated. Water them deeply and slowly the day before you want to dig and lift entire groups out with a shovel to lessen the chance of damage to the bulbs. Cut off the browned leaves to reduce dehydration during transplanting or storage.

Caladiums that you started in pots may be getting crowded as they wait to be transplanted into the garden as soils warm up. Water them often enough to prevent wilting that can stress them at transplant time.

EDIBLES

Wilted leaves are *not* your friends, especially in rapidly growing vegetables and ripening fruits. Mulch helps, but very regular watering is *essential*. Water new transplants and seedlings by hand and shift to soaker hoses or sprinklers after about one month. How often you water depends on soil and weather conditions, but repeat the slow, deep soaking when the top of the soil feels just dry to the touch. Once edibles have begun growing, put their irrigation schedule on a timer for convenient, reliable watering.

LAWNS

April can be a mix of hot, dry, cool, and wet weather as when Jackson, Mississippi, and much of Zone 8 receives an average of nearly 6 inches of rain. In-ground irrigation systems can keep up with the changes if you monitor them. Be sure that timers work reliably and that rain sensors prevent that neighborhood embarrassment, sprinkler systems spewing in the rain.

PERENNIALS & ORNAMENTAL GRASSES

If you built low dams around ornamental grasses when you planted their divisions during the winter, knock them down now. To encourage deep rooting of other young perennial plants, water each one deeply by hand, mulch around and between the plants. Mobile, Alabama, (Zone 9) averages more than 5 inches of rain each April and that may be plenty—poke your finger into the soil around the newbies to see if they need water or bailing out. Be aware of particular plants' abilities to tolerate lots of water or very little of it but know that none likes a soggy crown.

ROSES

On very windy days, some rose leaves can wilt, although their soil has ample moisture. Go against conventional wisdom and wet the leaves. The added water will evaporate quickly without contributing to disease concerns but also reduce the stress of wilting.

SHRUBS AND TREES

Healthy, mature shrubs and trees should not need water more than once a week when summer drought sets in. They seldom need additional water this month, and you should adjust watering practices or irrigation zones to avoid overwatering if the averages hold true. For example, Tupelo, Mississippi, in Zone 7 can expect almost 5 inches of rain in April.

VINES & GROUNDCOVERS

If established clumps of groundcovers just sit there, get down to their level for closer inspection. No new growth and hard, dry soil indicate near drought conditions, but no growth and soggy soil is just as bad. Moderate these extreme water conditions to kick-start the clumps: rake mulch away from plants in waterlogged soil or open a temporary ditch if necessary. Lay soaker hoses in "S" patterns around the clumps during prolonged dry spells to water the soil deeply and efficiently.

WATER GARDENS

With averages that promise plenty of April showers to bring May flowers, your water garden can be awash in fresh water. When water features spill over, your natural instinct is to grab the excess to water containers and plants nearby. Naturally occurring true pond water may need to be treated with potassium permanganate to kill waterborne diseases, but the water in tightly lined water features does not.

FERTILIZE

ANNUALS AND PERENNIALS

Broadcast flowering formula granular fertilizer over beds of annuals and perennials if they are full. Otherwise use your trowel or hoe to circle each clump or plant, drop the fertilizer in, and cover it. By placing the fertilizer instead of broadcasting it, you avoid encouraging weeds below the surface to sprout.

BULBS

Even if you use liquid fertilizers regularly, get a slow-release formula that is released with watering and use it around caladiums. Competition can be stiff for nutrition, especially when they are planted with annuals like impatiens. Place the slow-release fertilizer near the caladium but not on top of it.

EDIBLES

When picking is done, fertilize new and established asparagus beds with a balanced formula that has

equal numbers for N, P, and K such as 10-10-10. Organic gardeners can use any organic product that has all three elements.

LAWNS

If you have not fertilized the lawn yet, do so now unless greenup has been delayed. Use a product with slow-release action on healthy, established lawns to keep them that way. You may pay a little more for a bag of slow-release lawn food but get back time in lower maintenance during the summer. Some of the other fertilizer products that are used in April include:

- Weed and feeds are combination products designed to control existing weeds and then deliver fertilizer to the lawn.

- New lawn starters provide plenty of nutrients to recent sod installations to emphasize root development and maintain good green color at the same time.

PERENNIALS & ORNAMENTAL GRASSES

When you replant divided perennials and use a rooting formula, its effects last a few weeks. That time is critical to new root formation, but a month after planting it is time to fertilize with a balanced formula that includes major and minor elements.

ROSES

You will hear about the great roses (and bell peppers) grown with Epsom salts sprays (1 to 2 tablespoons/gallon of water) but may not know why they can work. Magnesium and sulfur are two elemental nutrients in the salts that plants need, and if they are not available, growth suffers. The presence of magnesium makes phosphorus and nitrogen more rapidly accessible and sulfur, an ingredient in chlorophyll, is important in photosynthesis. Our old soils can be deficient in magnesium, and if organic matter is lacking, so is sulfur. Users swear they have more roses with better color and petal retention and thicker-walled bell peppers too.

SHRUBS

Not every plant needs fertilizer every year, particularly mature shrubs and those prone to overgrowth, especially if they should flower but do not. Those happy shrubs are making the most of the available nutrients, including those in aging organic mulches. Work the rotted mulch into the soil when you replace it with fresh material, step back, and smile.

TREES

Young trees (and shrubs) as well as those of any age that need new growth will respond to fertilizer now followed by regular watering. Consult package labels for how much to use per plant, which is usually based on the diameter (or caliper) of trunks. Know what you are buying: some tree fertilizers are meant to be worked into the soil; others must be deposited into holes you drill under the tree's canopy.

VINES & GROUNDCOVERS

After annual vines sprout and grow 4 to 6 inches, they are ready for additional fertilizer. Mix up a soluble formula such as 20-20-20 and use the gentle sprinkle from a watering can to drench each one. In this way, you put the fertilizer right where it is needed without knocking over the little plants.

WATER GARDENS

Some fertilizer is good, but too much can cause rapid growth of algae in water gardens. Use slow-release nitrogen fertilizers made for water gardens on the plants around water features to lessen the chance the nutrients will make their way into the water. Fertilize plants living in water with appropriate aquatics fertilizers, but do not overuse them.

PROBLEM-SOLVE

LAWNS

Dark-colored mold forms on grass blades and looks awful. To solve this problem, turn off sprinklers in the area and try to blast the mold off with a stream of water from the hose. If that doesn't work, let it dry again and sweep it off with a broom.

A more serious problem for bermudagrass is spring deadspot (SDS), a pathogen that attacks the roots and shows up in spring as large and small dead circles. Aerate the soil if needed to reduce

compaction and break up the fungus, improve drainage if it is an issue, and dethatch if the layer is more than an inch deep. Consider fungicide applications in fall and spring for very difficult cases of SDS.

PERENNIALS & ORNAMENTAL GRASSES

Yellow-orange dots on daylily leaves are rust fungi. Remove damaged leaves immediately and spray the remaining plants with fungicide.

ROSES

Holes in rose leaves appear almost overnight as almost perfectly round or with neatly scalloped edges. Any of a number of caterpillars feed on roses as they chew their way across the garden toward maturity. Dusts and sprays work equally well to control caterpillars, but both may need to be reapplied.

- Dipel dust and Thuricide spray are trade names for *Bacillus thuringiensis (Bt)*, a predatory organism that feasts on caterpillars of moths and butterflies (*Lepidoptera* insects). They are effective natural controls but work slowly—apply them late in the day at the first sign of damage.

- Pyrethrin and rotenone, two naturally derived insecticides that are often combined in products, are more effective together than alone. They go to work right away and have little residual effect.

- Hot pepper wax sprays work externally and are effective almost immediately, with some continuing effect. Neem also has some residual effects on insects, mites, and fungi.

- Sevin dust (carbaryl) is effective but should be reserved for seriously large populations of caterpillars because it is highly toxic to bees as well as your target insects.

Clusters of pinheads on rosebuds and other flowers are aphids. Blast them off with a stream of water and keep watching. If more appear, spray the plants with insecticidal soap, pyrethrin, or another contact insecticide labeled for aphid control.

TREES

Trees that have fewer leaves each year or areas that do not leaf out at all can ruin the view. The problem may be caused by transplanting, storms, construction, or age, and time is not on your side to return them to active growth. When your efforts to prune, water, and feed the trees have not worked, the trouble may be deeper in the ground. In that case, you will want to consult a tree professional who focuses on soil compaction, root feeding, and disease prevention.

Mature trees can be home to an assortment of wildlife without issue, but you should be aware of their true pests so you can plan their control at the earliest stage possible. Symptoms to watch for include:

- Webs high up in trees get attention in the fall, but wise gardeners watch for them beginning in summer. Tent caterpillars are the culprits and they begin work much sooner. Watch and plan for their control early, before the damage is done.

- Cocoons on evergreens are often bagworms that are harmful. Keep an eye out for them to begin forming and pick or snip them off immediately or plan to spray.

- Leaf drop in large numbers out of season and/or black sooty mold on leaves can indicate

■ *Tent caterpillars create "webs" and eat the foliage of young trees.*

pests are feeding above. Plan to control the pests at the first sign of trouble and the tree will leaf out again.

- Significant early leaf drop can also be the result of fungus disease that began in early spring. Plan to keep the leaves raked up and to spray next spring as the new leaves emerge.

Usually fatal symptoms include:

- Browned areas in conifers, especially pine trees, can be the result of boring insects that inflict fatal damage.

- Oozing trunks tell you that the tree is seriously compromised. Clean it up and spray the trunks with a combination of insecticide and fungicide but be aware that this may be a futile effort.

VINES & GROUNDCOVERS

Perennial vines and vining groundcovers such as Asiatic jasmine drop leaves and may look pale or wilted. Woody plants draw on all available water to support new stems and leaves and to mature the growth started last year. Groundcovers and vines can get left out when trees and shrubs with more extensive root systems deplete the water and nutrients available. Water separately and apply soluble fertilizers as a spray to the leaves to target the losers in this natural race.

■ *Uncontrolled aphids multiply every 8 days.*

May

Every garden—large, small, new, and old—looks good in the optimistic month of May. Daisies and daylilies are not hard to grow, and everyone does, so there are plenty to pick. Pots as different as spirea and bell pepper grow side by side on the sunny deck and jasmine takes over trellises with fragrance. Lizard families climb the porch and ladybird beetles get busy on the tomatoes, eating aphids.

In May you can hike the woods and come home resolved to add native ferns and Indian pink to shady beds. A walk at the beach reminds you that gaillardia (*G. pulchella*) and lanceleaf tickseed (*Coreopsis lanceolata*) , also known as sand coreopsis, are not only wildflowers but also great garden plants. Or you sit on the back porch in search of the first fireflies and hear the crickets sing. But they aren't the only noisy critters around now. You will surely pick up the drone of the cicadas in May and sometimes next month, depending on the location and year.

For the first time this year, attention turns to the other end of the thermometer when warm nights and days become the norm everywhere. It's the time of year when zone lines fade, when Huntsville, Alabama, in Zone 7 averages 78 degrees Fahrenheit in the daytime and 57 degrees Fahrenheit at night. Those days are only 3 degrees cooler than Kosciusko, Mississippi, in Zone 8, and a mere 6 degrees cooler than Houma, Louisiana, deep in Zone 9. The nights are not as far apart, but these are only average temperatures. For example, cooler microclimates in north Mississippi can grow lily of the valley and a rainbow of peonies. A few miles away at lower elevations, you'd need bags of ice to bloom the lilies and the only successful peony is the heat-tolerant 'Festiva Maxima'. The differences are great enough between the extreme ends of our states that while standard zinnias are blooming in Biloxi, gardeners in Decatur are just planting seeds outdoors.

PLAN

ALL

May lets you hit the reset button on those less-successful garden projects, especially vegetables and new plantings that take time to plan. Look over the hedge you planted in March and the new lawn repairs made last month. If such projects are not green and growing, figure out what's wrong and plan to fix it.

ANNUALS

Brush up on the symptoms of heat stress so you can recognize and deal with any symptoms that show up this summer. When all has been going well with annuals planted this spring and suddenly they aren't doing well, watch for:

- Pale or burnished leaves even though the plants are adequately fertilized

- Wilting at a faster rate than the week before even though you watered

- Flowers that dry up one day after opening or do not open at all

- Plants that collapse overnight with their roots intact on the sunnier end of a bed

BULBS

Plan a new cutting garden with bulbs as anchor plants and you may not need other plants. For a start, sketch a 3 foot by 6 foot bed—it might become a section of a larger bed, but stay small while you're evaluating your options. Think about triangles of tall tiger lilies and knee-high Easter lilies, rows of gladiolas, centerpiece space for dinnerplate dahlias, and daffodils all around the edges.

EDIBLES

It's not too early to plan the fall garden because tomato seeds will need planting next month. Choose seeds for heat-tolerant tomatoes and other fall favorites, such as broccoli, that are best transplanted to the garden, rather than seeded directly. Plan to change the location in the garden or to replace container-growing soil for the fall crop of tomatoes to avoid nematodes.

■ *Order garlic now so you'll have it when it's time to plant in September.*

Garlic can taste too bland or too spicy because too few varieties are grown commercially. A second issue arises when you try to order exotic garlics for fall planting and can find none. Order now from online suppliers and purchase fresh garlic locally; store both of them yourself in paper bags in a cool, dark place until September. Asparagus can also be difficult to find in the very early spring, which is the best time to plant a new bed in the Deep South. Our soils are usually too acidic and the farther south you go, temperatures and humidity conspire against the spears at times. Secure new clumps whenever they are available and go the extra mile to get them started, even this late in the year.

LAWNS

If St. Augustine grass or zoysia has grown thin in some areas or was damaged by disease, plan to fill in grass gaps with rooted sprigs you grow yourself. Sometime this month the healthy parts of the lawn will try to grow into flowerbeds and driveways and you'll let them. In a few weeks you'll be able to clip a bunch to root for homegrown sprigs in a flat of soil.

PERENNIALS & ORNAMENTAL GRASSES

When perennials flourish, it's time to think about a new bed for them. Even if you won't work on this project until the fall, choose its site now and plan to forego fertilizer on the grass there. Decide what you will do with the grass and when will be the best time to either kill or transplant it. If the new site will be away from water sources, address that issue in your plan.

ROSES

Potpourri does not happen overnight, and when you want to give a fragrant, homemade gift, it's too late to start collecting materials. Plan now to collect fragrant roses and the shattered petals that fall out of vases in your house. It's okay to ask friends to save petals for you, and they'll admire your foresight when you return a jar of potpourri as a birthday gift. Set up a tray with a piece of window screen on top, separate the petals, and let them dry indoors away from the sunlight. Once a batch dries, store them in a screw-top jar. Red roses, in particular, develop richly dark colors that hold when you dry and store them with proper care.

SHRUBS

When planning a new property, plant with your eyes first, long before you dig any holes. May is a

■ *Live oak tree*

TO DESIGN FOUNDATION PLANTINGS

- Know the style of your house and work with it. For example, symmetrical arrangements of windows flanking the front door will look out of sync if the plantings on each side are wildly different. But doors on porches and off-center entrances need focal-point plants to direct traffic to them.

- Show off your house. Choose plants that will mature in balance with its size to put the entire scene in perspective. At extreme ends of this issue are small houses shrouded by huge shrubs and houses that look hugely out of place because the foundation plantings are too small.

- Plan for interesting plant features across the year, such as a spring-flowering tree, summer perennial or annual flowers, fall berries, and evergreens.

- Use restraint but do include garden ornaments in foundation plantings.

great time to see what you like now, while many shrubs are at the peak of spring growth. Look at mature growth for overall effect in the garden and notice differences in new growth, such as color changes. Foundation plantings take special planning because passersby will see this part of your garden every day. You want it to look good even when you're busy with other things, so plan for low maintenance.

TREES

Take a look at trees now to appreciate their leafy and full canopies. Smile because they look so good, but if major branches looked weighed down, they probably are. Plan to consult an arborist later in the summer about thinning the canopy to reduce the weight and inquire about cabling in serious situations. The cabling process can prevent the damage caused when large limbs separate from trunks.

VINES & GROUNDCOVERS

Grapevine wreaths are naturally attractive decorations that can be customized for any holiday or season. If you have grapes, good, but other vines also can be cut in summer while they are supple. Fashion them into circles, fasten the vines together

HERE'S HOW

TO CREATE A CONTAINER WATER GARDEN

- Find a large, handsome pot with no drainage. Go for a big ceramic one that holds at least 5 gallons of water.

- Add a dwarf water lily (*Nymphaea leibergii*) and water lettuce (*Pistia stratoites*) plants. The lettuce will float and the lily will live at the bottom of the pot and float on top. If the lily doesn't have a pot, you'll need:

  > A basket made for an aquatic plant that will accommodate the small lily and fit in the pot you choose

  > Aquatic compost/gravel mix—one small bag will do, available where water garden plants are sold

with clothespins, and hang in a dark, ventilated place. The vines will drop their leaves, retain the form you have created, and be dry and ready to use in time for the fall holidays.

WATER GARDENS

No father needs another tie, so plan to put together a one-pot water garden for the June honoree this year. You'll need a few items that can be put together ahead of time (or at the last minute).

PLANT

ANNUALS

Sunlight is strong enough this month to prickle your skin at noon, and that means the soil is warm enough to transplant and sow seed for the boldest annuals of the year. How much space you use matters less than the combination of heights and flower shapes you choose. Good examples include:

- Low-growing annuals for edges of pots and beds—moss rose, Madagascar periwinkle

- Knee-high—'Sparkler' celosia, standard coleus, dwarf cleome

- Waist-high (grow these from seed)—African marigold, 'Firecracker' sunflower

BULBS

May gives the green light to plant caladium tubers directly in the ground in Zones 7 and 8 without fear of rot. There are sun-tolerant varieties of caladium; most are red shades and are shaped more like arrows than the traditional shade-loving, heart-shaped leaves. Most caladiums are nearly solid with bold veination or wild patterns in shades of red, green, pink, and white.

EDIBLES

Summer vegetables will really grow now that the soils have warmed up. Start sweet potatoes from slips, plant peanuts, and sow an assortment of seeds in May: okra, pumpkins, cushaw, southern peas, and luffas (Chinese okra).

Read the seed packets to calculate planting times. Know your limits when it comes to the last dates to plant vegetables that take more than two months to produce. For example, southern peas need about ninety days to mature, but jack-o-lantern pumpkins planted in June will just make it in time for Halloween, about four months.

LAWNS

There's no time like May to start a lawn from seed. A popular practice used to be to sow carpet grass seed (*Axonopus fissifolius*) along with the bermudagrass because the carpet will sprout first and

---

HERE'S HOW

TO SEED A LAWN

1. With the soil prepared, spread the seed. Set the drop spreader to the setting listed on the seed bag, test the dispersal rate on a driveway or sidewalk, and begin seeding.

2. Rake the seed into the surface of the soil. Drag a leaf rake upside down over the surface to rake in the seeds. Rake gently to prevent dispersing the seeds too much.

3. Roll the surface of the lawn with an empty drum roller. The goal is to press the seeds firmly into the soil without crushing them.

4. Water the surface immediately. Protect the newly seeded lawn with ropes or tape to keep dogs and cats off the surface. Cover the lawn with clean straw or degradable garden fabric to help ensure germination and retain moisture. Spun bonded poly mesh will also protect the seeds against birds, but it is not readily degradable.

the bermudagrass will overrun it later. Carpet grass is better suited to slightly shadier, moister areas of your property and forms clumps, but not a true lawn.

Buffalograss (*Buchloe dactyloides*) can be grown in microclimates closer to its native prairie conditions than our states' average humidity and rainfall affords. But there are notable exceptions, especially in parts of Louisiana where this turf grass has gained attention for its bluish hue, soft texture, and ability to grow long leaves that fall over into each other.

PERENNIALS & ORNAMENTAL GRASSES

Sun or shade, dwarf mondo grass (*Ophiopogon japonicus nanus*) is regaining popularity because it is beautifully neat, grows fairly fast, and meets your needs for a low-growing, low-maintenance groundcover. Topping out at 4 inches, this small member of the lily turf family thrives in the dry shade between trees and the deep shade under eaves on the north side of your house. Where a taller mondo will work, go for black mondo grass (*O. planiscapus* 'Niger'). Plant sprigs or clumps this month and water weekly for two months to

■ *Angel Trumpet*

encourage deep rooting now and drought tolerance later.

The fabulous angel trumpet (*Brugmansia*) flowers hang down from their branch tips with an umbrella of fat green leaves overhead. By contrast, the stunning trumpets of nightshade, known as devil's trumpet (*Datura*) rest on top of their fat green leaves. Both are essential for bold texture and floral extravagance in the summer garden.

ROSES

Miniature roses get too little respect from gardeners for their precious little flowers most often seen on plants about 2 feet tall. Those big pots deserve a prominent place on your balcony or the deck out back. Plant the miniature rose in a 1:1 mix of potting soil and ground bark, water well with a starter solution, and protect it from direct sun for two weeks. Pair one with a particularly nice pot for your cousin and deliver it before the weeding next month, after the chance of transplant shock is over. Roses are a sentimental plant, so express yourself with sweet rose names:

- 'Absolutely' apricot

- 'Ice Crystal' double white

- 'Sweet Sue' pure pink

- 'Velvet Cloak' stunning red

SHRUBS

Sometimes you see a shrub in bloom in a nursery and simply have to have one right away in your own garden. Gardenias (*Gardenia jasminoides*) are that kind of shrub, a worthwhile impulse purchase that works well with every garden style. Give them morning sun and late afternoon shade for best flowering.

- Cape jasmines are the 4- to 6-foot (or taller) gardenias that bloom heavily once or twice and sporadically the rest of the summer. 'August Beauty' is a vigorous cape jasmine gardenia.

- Hardy gardenias are smaller, with smaller, single flowers and good cold tolerance. 'Daisy' and 'Kleim' mature and are easily maintained as 3-foot mounds of flowers.

- Dwarf or groundcover gardenia is a different species with equal fragrance and smaller leaves. It can reach 2 feet in height unless a hard freeze hurts it.

Oleanders, especially dwarf varieties, grab your eye at the garden center now, for beds and pots everywhere. If an oleander dies back, it will return like a woody perennial plant; the dwarfs rebound and bloom weeks sooner than tall, standard oleanders. Prized for long thin leaves with lighter midribs, some variegated with creamy yellow and flower bunches, oleander flowers are its crown jewels that set a sultry, tropical style. Born in clusters at the stem tips, each flower has five jaunty petals so close together they almost overlap in colors from white to reds, pinks, and salmon.

TREES

Planting instructions for trees urge you to water regularly until established, but that condition can be hard to define. Trees planted anytime this year or last, but especially those you plant now, require more consistent attention than those that have been in the ground longer. Soak new plantings deeply and weekly unless there is plenty of rainfall. Use root stimulator fertilizer or compost tea regularly through the summer.

VINES & GROUNDCOVERS

Gourds (*Cucurbita pepo*) that you grow for decorating and natural scrubbers, dishrag gourds (*Luffa*), are not considered edibles and do not need to be grown with them. The vines of birdhouse, dipper, apple, swan, and other cleverly named gourds can cover a pergola in two months and soon grow heavy with fruits. If you have an old-fashioned clothesline, you have a gourd growing area—sun, support, and a clothesline to grow on. Plant seeds in slightly raised hills of soil at the foot of the structure and position a water reservoir next to them.

Recycle a gallon jug into a reservoir by poking a few small holes in the bottom of the side wall where it becomes the bottom. Bury about two-thirds of the jug in the side of the hill so it can leak into the root zone. Keep it filled with water and soluble fertilizer to create a constant-feed system and leave the cap on to reduce evaporation.

WATER GARDENS

You still get credit for planting even if the new plants float. These beautiful plants use up the nitrogen so the algae can't use it. They are natural filters and their shade moderates water temperatures. Not all are welcome everywhere—consult local regulations—but look for them in paper cups at plant sales if they are not available commercially. Because they are tropicals and to avoid overgrowth, put some in a pond pot and compost the rest each fall.

- Frogbit (*Hydrocharis morsus-ranae*) Rosettes of nickel-size leaves shaped like little lily pads float on tiny air-filled natural bladders.

- Fairy moss (*Azolla* sp.) Tiny, fast growing ferny leaves that turn red in fall.

HERE'S HOW

TO MIX A ROOT-STIMULATOR TEA

- Fill a 5-gallon bucket half full of compost, your own or a store-bought product.

- Add water to the top, cover, and steep for four days.

- Strain the mixture through cheesecloth into another bucket.

- Put the solid leftovers directly into a shrub bed or leaf pile.

- Add water to the mixture until it looks lighter than good sweet tea.

- Use as a starter solution for transplants and cuttings.

- Drench or spray plants at any stage for nutrient and organic matter benefits.

CARE

ALL

Time spent to care for your garden can go straight down the tubes when your pets dig holes and shred plants. Repellants work as long as you keep them in place and work by aversion—your pet smells the ingredients and moves on. Untreated plants and areas remain vulnerable whether you use a bagged product or a homemade recipe. You have to keep at it until your pets get the message. The practical strategy may be to fence or ban them if their destructive habits cost you precious garden time. If the situation becomes dire and you must rework or replant entire beds, lay chicken wire over the areas as a temporary physical barrier. Clearly, training the pets we love is the best way to have them in the garden.

Pollen can be a huge problem. Sometimes pollen comes from the shrubs in your garden, other days it comes from grasses or trees. You cannot control the entire environment, but when you use fans to draw in cool breezes you may be importing the very pollen you try to avoid outdoors. Serious allergy sufferers clip off flower clusters as soon as they are formed to avert the problem. Even though such effort has limited effect, at least you'll be able to take refuge indoors without sneezing.

ANNUALS

Keep an eye on geraniums for reddening leaves or other stress signs as heat builds. Clip off old flowers and move their pots into less sun for the summer. Weed pots and beds that grew Johnny jump-ups this year if seedlings sprout and you do not want them. Get in the habit of deadheading annual flowers weekly and you will be rewarded with new flower buds almost as often.

Hollyhocks (*Alcea rosea*) can be confusing. They are often sold as annuals, but they are actually biennials that bloom, set seed, and die in the second year. After they bloom, cut off the flowers to prolong the life of their attractive clump.

BULBS

Be careful! When digging new planting holes and lifting out underground weed parts, remember that red spider lilies are dormant under there. Bulbs may also be bigger than you know, so dig with care around clivia, crinum, elephant ears, true lilies, St. Joseph's lilies, and other big boys.

EDIBLES

Tomato suckers are green stems that form in the crotch where main stems sprout branches. Remove them if you want bigger fruit; leave them if they shade those ripening.

■ Hollyhock (Alcea rosea) *makes a stately show when planted in rows or in a bed with other cottage garden favorites like old roses and daylilies. Usually a biennial, it blooms the year after you plant it.*

LAWNS

Do not mow over fire ant mounds in an attempt to suppress them. The mounds you see are only part of the colony, and the majority of ants will hide or pack up and move. Because more than one queen may be involved, mowing can multiply the mounds. Fire ants will cling onto your pants as they evacuate and sting your ankles or worse.

PERENNIALS & ORNAMENTAL GRASSES

Iris flowers left on their plants will set seed in heavy pods that can be very attractive for decorating and flower arrangements. If you do not want seed or ornaments, cut them off with their stems.

ROSES

When you cut roses for the vase, do it to promote more buds and shape future growth. Look behind the flower to find the first leaflet with five leaves on it and cut there or below on the stem. Take care to cut just above a five-finger leaflet oriented away from the center of the rose to direct the new stem and flowers.

SHRUBS

Check on shrubs you rejuvenated with heavy pruning in early spring. Evergreens such as ligustrum and hollies should be growing again by now and can be lightly trimmed and fertilized again this month. Give azaleas and other spring flowering shrubs a fertilizer made for them but do not prune them anymore this year.

VINES & GROUNDCOVERS.

Not all vines are created equal when it comes to natural twining. Some grab and go while others need help to climb and stay attached to their trellises. Pick your method to secure the stragglers loosely so you don't damage the vines.

- Wire and plastic-coated wire must be used very carefully because they can cut through vines, both green stems and woodies.

- Adhesive pads with plastic clips stick to walls for training espaliered vines.

- Jute string can be cut to your specific needs and lasts about a year.

- Preformed plastic vine clips grab well, last forever, and are inexpensive.

- Recycled t-shirt and ladies' hosiery materials can be cut to length and last a year.

The popular flowering liriope groundcover forms clumps less than a foot tall that bloom reliably each spring. The berries that follow the blooms dampen our enthusiasm for this low-maintenance plant when they stain concrete and brick with purple juice that must be scrubbed off every year. Deadhead the flowers as they fade or replant the bed with a different edging groundcover.

WATER GARDENS

One of the finest reasons to have a water garden is the opportunity to watch toads, dragonflies, lizards, and butterflies enjoy it. Give them a place to sun by incorporating a flat rock into the scene. Place it to peek out from a clump of plants with most of its surface completely exposed to the warm sun.

WATER

ANNUALS

Vary the way you water pots of annuals. Alternate using these methods:

- Water from the bottom to encourage deep rooting by filling saucers.

- Put a water breaker on the garden hose to gently fill the headspace without washing soil.

- Set up a sprinkler or do it by hand, but water from overhead occasionally to keep leaves clean.

BULBS

You can take it for granted that bulbs need less additional irrigation than other plant categories. One exception is clumps that have been divided and/or moved within the past year. Make it a point to include them in your watering regime every few weeks.

EDIBLES

Shield seedlings from excess water when they're fresh out of the ground. Tender shoots can get pounded by storms, flattened by a strong stream of water from the hose and sprinklers intended for other, taller plants nearby. Water the youngsters separately and cover seedlings, such as cucumber and squash, with an empty pot while you water the rest of the garden. Rows of newly sprouted southern peas can be avoided or baffled temporarily for protection from rain.

LAWNS

Allow the lawn to dry out after watering before using mowers and other equipment to cut it. After a few hours, the grass has absorbed all it needs and stands tall for a proper cut. Excess water evaporates at the same time so your shoes stay dry too.

PERENNIALS & ORNAMENTAL GRASSES

Perennial clumps, including grasses, depend on their crown to survive from year to year. That structure gives rise to both stems and roots and can be compromised if it sinks or soaks under mulch. Bog and water plants need to stay consistently moist, but others in this group depend on your good water management to thrive over the long haul.

ROSE

Extremes are not good for roses when it comes to water. You amend their soil so it drains well because their roots die in constantly wet soil. But shallow watering in good soil discourages root growth. If you are watering roses every day, either the soil is too lightweight and needs reworking to add organic matter to it, or you are doing it wrong. Keep mulch around the rose bushes and soak them slowly and deeply once a week from now until fall.

SHRUBS, TREES, AND VINES & GROUNDCOVERS

When you set irrigation zones in underground systems, pay attention to beds of established plants in these categories. If you are routinely giving them as much water as the lawn and edibles, it's likely you are wasting water and money. Established plants need water less often than young ones, shaded areas may need less or more water depending on competition, and excess water in the bed gives more

moisture to the weeds. Dial back the rate and/or frequency and keep the beds mulched.

WATER GARDENS

You test the water quality regularly to keep it balanced for your fish. But it is also a very good idea to check its amount as you add fish and as they grow. When fish become crowded, they are vulnerable to many diseases and can create too much organic matter, clouding the water garden. For example, a goldfish smaller than your hand requires roughly 10 gallons of water and 1 square foot of surface area to thrive. Check the volume of water this month and again in August.

FERTILIZE

ALL

Except for water, which is critical for existence at every level, nutrition in the form of fertilizer is the best thing for plants facing summer in our states. In August, the difference between two adjoining homes with many of the same plants often comes down to fertilizing done this month. Pale leaves, few flowers, even wilted beds and crunchy lawns—these are some sad summer signs you can avoid by fertilizing now.

ANNUALS

This month give annual flowers in beds and pots some fertilizer insurance by adding a slow-release three-month formula made for flowering plants. Continue any other fertilizer program you have been doing, confident they'll be covered when you go on vacation.

When replacing spring annuals like pansies with summer's periwinkles, pull out the pansy (or whatever spring annual you planted) and shake the soil off its roots into the hole. Add a tablespoon of granular general-purpose fertilizer to the soil and work it in with your trowel before planting the summer flowers.

BULBS

Easter lilies moved to the garden recently have dropped their flowers and may be dying back for

HERE'S HOW

TO FERTILIZE EASTER LILIES

- Pull back the mulch for 6 inches around lilies that were growing in 6-inch pots.

- Use a three-tined hand cultivator at the circle's outer edge to work up 1-inch deep and 1-inch wide all the way around.

- Sprinkle 3 tablespoons of bulb food evenly in the cultivated circle and work it in.

- Water well and replace the mulch.

the year. However they look just now, they'll come back stronger next year if you fertilize them with bulb food.

EDIBLES

Except for new transplants and seedlings, change to a vegetable garden fertilizer now with a formula such as 5-10-10. Once the vegetable plant has plenty of leaves, it needs more phosphorus and potassium to flower and set. When the first tomato fruit or other vegetables are formed and growing, reduce fertilizer by half until they are picked.

Beans and peas are legumes, plants able to take nitrogen from the air or "fix" it into their leaves. The process sounds magical, and understanding it takes none of the mystery from this all-too-rare ability. In practical terms, it means that while you may work fertilizer in before planting beans and peas, you do not want to add more once the plants are growing.

■ *Beans will not need fertilizing while they are growing and producing fruits.*

LAWNS

Organic lawn fertilizing depends on organic matter in the root zone to promote root exudates that feed microorganisms, which in turn decompose into more organic matter for the roots to use. It's a powerful natural cycle that works, but not quickly and not without your help. To fertilize your lawn organically, repeat the compost/manure blanket used on all lawns earlier this spring: put an inch of material over the entire lawn and use a garden rake to shake it into the thatch.

PERENNIALS & ORNAMENTAL GRASSES

Choose solubles or granular fertilizers, depending on how often you want to feed perennial plants. Hose-end sprayers filled with a fertilizer solution should be applied to leaves and soil at the same time. Depending on the formula, you may need to feed more than twice a month. If the bed is large or if your time is limited, longer-lasting granulars may be more practical. Fertilize this group now and repeat as required by your product.

ROSES

If you amended the rose bed with organic composts last fall or this spring, pay attention to their leaves. You will still fertilize after each flush of flowers and at midsummer if they do not rebloom. But if rose leaves are thick and large, it is time to back off on the nitrogen. Use a rose or flower formula that has a lower first number.

Rose fertilizers are often packaged as combination products with insecticides. Read the label to learn about the insects targeted by the product, and if they are a common problem on your roses, consider their use. Be aware that these are not selective insecticides; bees and other pollinators will be injured if they happen to visit the rose. If insects are not usually a big problem in your roses, choose a standalone fertilizer for regular use. Watch for signs of insects and deal with them if and when they arise.

SHRUBS

Every rule of thumb has its nuances to account for special situations. You are always told not to overfertilize plants because more is not helpful and might burn their leaves. This is true *except* when rejuvenating old shrubs, a process that takes growth to accomplish. Get more new growth by fertilizing these patients now and again in July as part of the effort to regrow shrubs that have to be heavily pruned. One of the great boons of using organic fertilizers is that, because of their ingredients, they are very unlikely to burn plants. Use them often in rejuvenation projects.

TREES

Don't depend on lawn food to nourish trees with relatively shallow roots. For example, the best-looking flowering trees are fertilized after bloom each year regardless of whether they are ever pruned. Classic dogwood and star magnolia, but also flowering cherry and plum, grancy greybeard (*Chionanthus virginicus*)—trees in this large group have more and better flowers when you fertilize them separately from the lawn. These showy trees deserve a formula made to promote long life and plentiful flowers.

VINES & GROUNDCOVERS

Beds of groundcovers planted last fall and this spring should show new leaves by now and vining types might be starting to spread. At this stage, put slow-release fertilizer around each plant to promote steady growth this summer. Older groundcover beds can use a formula with both quick- and slow-release nitrogen, such as is found in many lawn foods. When the fertilizer fits, use it—regardless of the name on the product, its label will detail ingredients and alternative uses.

WATER GARDENS

Mature water lilies, lotuses, and other plants that grow in baskets underwater will keep their green color and steady growth rate with fertilizer made for use in water. Tablet-form products take the hassle out of this task—no measuring, mixing, or wondering where liquids go once you pour them on the roots. Lift the basket to the surface and nestle the tablet into the plant. Depending on the product, your work may be done for the year.

ALL

Hoe, pull, or spray them, but get weeds under control now or they will compete with your plants—and probably win. That's a problem. Another dilemma is the question of what sprayer to use for what purpose. When using an incorrect sprayer or nozzle, sprays can go everywhere except where you are aiming. When herbicides are involved and sprays go in the wrong direction, plants can die. Pick the right sprayer for the job.

You can't change the weather, so change your schedule. Tackle chores rained out last month, such as sealing the deck and painting benches, to lengthen their life. With cleaning and applications, be sure to allow enough time for drying before more rain is forecast.

EDIBLES

Watch for pests, especially tomato hornworms, which first appear as inch-long green worms this month. Turn over leaves, inspect stems, and stomp any worms you see, but don't let down

■ *Watch out for tomato hornworms, which can devastate all parts of tomato plants.*

TO SELECT A SPRAYER

- Hose-end sprayers cover a large area in a short time and are usually used for applying fertilizer, not weedkillers.

- Hand pump sprayers are useful but limited in weed control because their nozzles have two settings at most. It is easy to spray a larger area than you intend.

- Pump up pressure sprayers have twist nozzles that are more adjustable than hand pumps. Better models have more flexibility in nozzle settings that put you in control of where the spray goes.

- Get two sprayers and mark one clearly for use with herbicides. Even a well-cleaned spray head can retain some chemicals and you want to avoid that problem.

your guard. Almost overnight they will strip the leaves in a voracious feeding frenzy and grow as big as your little finger before they're done. After you remove all you see, spray or dust the plants from top to bottom with a product labeled to control hornworms.

Tomato hornworms pupate in the soil, and their presence is another good reason to rotate tomato plants. Do not grow tomatoes (or their close relatives, potatoes and eggplants) in the same place twice in one season or two years in a row. Rotate to reduce this pest population and also nematodes, microscopic worms that form devastating knots on tomato roots. You won't notice them the first year, but replanting in the same garden or container soil gives them time to give you trouble with plants that fail to thrive.

One way to confuse insects is to separate their favorite food plants. Instead of planting all the tomatoes in a row, flank each one with basil and alternate those three with pole beans. Choose diverse combinations based on their height and spread, but most importantly for water management. For example, the same amount of water that tomatoes and beans need would ruin herbs other than basils, which lose their flavor when they're overwatered.

LAWNS

Fairy rings are unsightly circles that form on the lawn, usually caused by fungi growing on old tree roots deep below. Fertilize the lawn regularly and mow it high to mask the rings or disturb them manually. Use a soil probe or other slim metal rod to poke holes in the fairy ring at 3-inch intervals all the way around. Mix up soapy water so it is sudsy and pour it into the holes. This process essentially drives water into the ring in hopes of pushing more grass growth to overcome the fungi. The "poke 'em and soak 'em" approach takes repeated treatments to have any effect.

Older lawns and those sodded with less care can have dips and low spots that make it hard to mow. Fill them in with sand and plant sprigs, plugs, or grass seeds in the problem areas.

Attack those pesky lawn weeds by applying the second half of the herbicide you chose earlier in the year. After each mowing, rinse the mower deck and blade and empty the grass catcher away from the lawn so weed seeds and plant parts do not get a free ride to other parts of your lawn and flowerbeds.

PERENNIALS & ORNAMENTAL GRASSES

Hosta and other shallow-rooted plants that grow in loose soil or mulch seem to fall over and their roots are chewed. The culprits are likely voles, rodents about 2 inches long that roam through loose soil in

Fairy ring often proves a stubborn foe in the lawn but you can reduce its impact by using lower nitrogen fertilizers.

search of food. Unfortunately, they favor roots and savor hostas. Move the hostas to containers on a shady deck or try to run the voles off with repellants, but the most effective control is a cat or dog that likes to chase them.

If you grow most varieties of tall, bright pink phlox, powdery mildew will start low on the stem. Watch for it and pluck off any that develop a gray coating, then spray the stems with a fungicide to stop its progress before it can spoil the flowers. Maintain space around phlox plants by transplanting some to other parts of the garden and choose mildew-resistant varieties such as *Phlox paniculata* 'Robert Poore'.

ROSES
Perfectly healthy roses are covered with flowers and buds one evening, but they disappear by breakfast. If nothing else is damaged, suspect deer. Many plants make their list to browse but few are as selectively eaten as rose flowers. Tall fencing is the obvious solution where it is practical; elsewhere this is a case for deer repellant sprays. Homegrown efforts to keep deer out of the garden can sound comical or impossible, yet lots of gardeners swear by these:

- Motion activated lights and loud music can work well but may also disrupt your sleep and your neighbor's.

- Soap on a rope approaches are said to repel deer. Drill a hole through the bar of soap and tie it to a piece of jute or nylon cord. Hang them like ornaments on vulnerable plants.

- Bleach and baby diapers made of cotton work on the same repellant principle. The cloth is dipped daily and rehung on wires suspended above low fences around gardens. Like the soap, this approach is unattractive and requires daily monitoring.

- Larger mammals, such as men, can be called on for the age-old practice of marking territory to drive away intruders like deer. For example, the composted elephant poop that the local zoo markets repels smaller mammals

and fertilizes too. In this case, think about the large plots of southern peas that the deer want as much as you do, and send Pop out to "water."

TREES
Gray lichen looks like old-fashioned gathered lace growing on tree and shrub branches. It is unsightly and causes worry when it appears. While lichen is no threat to woody plants, it is an opportunistic growth that takes hold in declining plant parts. That is, the tree is not growing as actively as it should be and therefore the lichen is able grow. Prune out the lichen and shape the branches to compensate. Put the tree on a regular program of water and fertilizer to restart its growth.

Powdery mildew shows up on crepe myrtles in late spring as grayish white patches. It can be triggered by cool, wet weather, but it is much more of a problem on older varieties. At the first sign, clip off the affected parts to let them regrow in warmer, drier weather. Fungicides can be used to suppress further development with routine sprays when outbreaks are severe.

VINES & GROUNDCOVERS
Japanese honeysuckle (*Lonicera japonica*) teaches children how sweet nectar tastes when they dissect the flowers. But this plant is not sweet at all and has invaded our states, spreading rampantly with few natural predators. Gaining control is not a simple matter of slash and burn because the vines grow over desirable shrubs and into trees. Cut Japanese honeysuckle vines at ground level now, and when the first two leaves sprout from the base, spray or paint them with herbicide.

WATER GARDENS
Scum forms on the surface of water gardens on the first hot day even though the pump is turned on. The water looks dark and, while not oily, something is wrong. If you didn't clean the water feature well earlier this spring and have overlooked grooming the marginal plants, too much organic matter builds up and scum forms. Skim off what you can, turn up the pump rate, and clean the filter. If the scum continues, drain and clean the pond to clear it of the leaf buildup on the bottom.

June

*Change is in the wind this month. The jet stream retreats north to block all but a few cool nights, and the Gulf of Mexico warms rapidly, pumps humidity and fuels storms. Spring lingers in north Mississippi and Alabama, but the mild days are fleeting. Gardens everywhere, though, are jumping! Crepe myrtles, St. John's wort (**Hypericum***), and summersweet start blooming; you smell a gardenia and see visions of childhood sundresses and picnics.*

We pick the last of the true spring vegetables in the north this month, and the first hot peppers ripen on the Gulf Coast; in between, the microclimates decide what's growing and going to the compost. But blueberries are ripe everywhere, and those smart enough to grow a hedge are picking every day.

French hydrangeas fill the garden with periwinkle blue balls, flower heads of papery bracts that have a clean if unusual smell up close. Gardeners in the northern tier of our states enjoy rhododendrons just as those in the south welcome the oleanders that bloom most in the summer months. Ours is a wild variety you can see with just a day's drive.

Wildlife in the garden changes now too. Lizards that were thumb size now sprawl on the walls and clamber over plants in search of insects to eat. Our favorite insect, the firefly, provides a great reason to linger after dark in the garden to be amazed by their flickering lights. Even urban gardens sometimes hear, but don't see, raccoons and possums on a nighttime shopping expedition. The critters soon learn who has trash cans without tops and who leaves dog food outside. Unfortunately, fire ants and tomato worms also ramp up their populations this month and, like the roving mammals, must be handled wisely and with care.

The garden drone rises to a hearty pitch this month. Crickets and cicadas sing the blues until they get a date, gnats and mosquitoes buzz in angry outbursts like fans hissing the umpire's call. Add in lawn mowers, string trimmers, edgers, and blowers, and you've got a symphony.

PLAN

ANNUALS

Fall garden mums look better for longer when you start them from small plants. Doing so takes planning. Visit the local garden center to see how soon you can get plants, or if they can order flats of young plants for you in advance of planting next month.

BULBS

A cottage garden staple, tiger lily (*Lilium tigrinum*) flares its spotted petals back as if in an elegant snort. At 4 feet tall on average, this tiger towers over its smaller, sweeter mates in the bed. When tiger and other true lilies bloom, everyone wants some in their garden, but summer is not the best time to plant them in most places. Plan for more now by taking pictures of ones you like and search for them through local and mail order sources.

EDIBLES

Successful backyard food gardening is admittedly a combination of wise planning and dumb luck. In truth, serious folks plan at least one growing season ahead, and often more. Start by planning for succession, the practice of following one vegetable with another that thrives in the following season. For example, in our north you might transplant cucumbers as you begin taking out lettuce plants in late spring. When the cucumbers finish in the fall, you plant Brussels sprouts. Farther south, summer squash might replace lettuce earlier and then give way to okra or another squash planting. The idea is to keep a desirable plant in the space almost continuously. As a side benefit, you grow more food (and fewer weeds) by planning in succession.

More planning and probably more space than you imagine will be needed to grow bunch or scuppernong grapes (*Vitis*) or hops (*Humulus lupulus*). If you see winemaking or brewing as a future hobby, plan for it now. Learn about suitable microclimates and varieties as well as how many bottles you'll need.

■ *Asiatic hybrid lilies* (Lilium)

LAWNS

It happens every year. As soon as lawngrass really gets going, it spreads under edging, over other

HERE'S HOW

TO GROW YOUR OWN GRASS CLUMPS

- Reuse open-weave or perforated plastic flats for this project. Line each with newspaper.

- Prepare a mix of garden soil and ground bark and set it aside.

- Use a pointed trowel to dig up the grass clumps. Start on the side nearest the lawn so you can cut the clumps away without ripping the grass.

- Set the clumps close to, but not touching, each other in the flats.

- Fill in the gaps with the mix you made and water the flats.

- Put the flats in the shade and water regularly with a root stimulator, compost tea, or dilute fertilizer solution.

plants, and into garden beds at its edge. Plan to use the new plants to fill in gaps elsewhere.

PERENNIALS & ORNAMENTAL GRASSES

If the idea of a long, lush border enchants you, make a list of the plants you want and plan how you can get them. Some are growing in your garden now, others you can buy, and some you will want to trade with a neighbor to obtain. However you acquire them, plan to propagate what you can to have plenty for planting.

ROSES

Plan for a succession of low-growing plants that will be a living groundcover under hybrid tea rose bushes. Good companions to hug the ground and moderate water conditions might include annuals like purslane (*Portulaca oleracea*) followed by sweet alyssum and anemone bulbs. Or you could choose low-growing sedums or dwarf mondo grass for a more evergreen, perennial cover.

SHRUBS

Pool and patio areas may look great in summer but draw yawns once the colorful tropicals are done blooming. Plan now to add bold, year-round shades in variegated shrubs. Gold dust acuba can be a backdrop along the fence, while variegated shell ginger paints pots and beds with striped delights.

TREES

If you don't have shade on the west or south of your best outdoor sitting area, plan now to establish some shade this summer. Hedges and trees will be best for the long term, but temporary baffles will get the job done while they grow. You might use pots of hedge plants along the patio, put up bamboo or wicker curtains, or stand willow fencing between the edge of the deck and the sun.

VINES & GROUNDCOVERS

If you want to add a vine or two, plan for their mature sizes and shop for trellises now. A 4-foot obelisk may be enough to support delicate vines for a while, but most vines will soon swallow them

and keep on going. Instead of fighting with vines, go with a larger trellis than you think is necessary.

WATER GARDENS

Every hour or less, water should completely circulate through pumps and filters and back into your water feature. Regardless of its size, the health of your garden will be compromised if the system does not work properly or is inadequate for the situation. Plan now to make changes and repairs before hot weather puts more stress on the situation.

PLANT

ANNUALS

Sunflowers of all sorts, including Mexican sunflowers, African marigolds, cleomes, and other large heat lovers can be added to the flower garden this month without missing a beat. Look for plants in all kinds of retail locations (grocery stores as well as nurseries) or seed them in southern areas where you can count on longer growing seasons.

■ *Make room for an easy-to-grow annual, Mexican sunflower* (Tithonia). *Big and bold, its orange color pops in the summer garden.*

BULBS

Plant the bulbs, tubers, corms, and rhizomes you bought or swapped but are still in their packages. Time is not your friend here—these storage organs are alive but may dry up or turn to mush if left out of the soil too long. When researching plants in this category, it's helpful to know a bit more about how they store energy underground:

- True bulbs have five parts. Roots grow from the basal plate under the fleshy storage scales, which are covered by a papery tunic. The shoot and lateral buds complete a true bulb, also called a tunicate bulb, such as tulip, daffodil, and onion.

- Lilies are almost true bulbs, except that they are undressed. They have no tunic layer and so have a shorter shelf life out of the ground.

- Corms are modified stems that swell into the structure we know as gladiolus and crocus bulbs. If you cut a bulb in half crosswise and see no rings, it might be a corm.

- Tubers have no tunics and no basal plate, either. Growing points, or eyes, dot the surface to sprout roots or shoots on tubers of caladium, anemone, and potatoes.

- Tuberous roots store nutrients in modified stems and roots, examples include dahlia, gloxinia, begonia, and sweet potato.

- Rhizomes are sometimes called rootstalks, but are actually underground stems that store energy and have growing points, or nodes. Roots and shoots emerge from rhizomes that

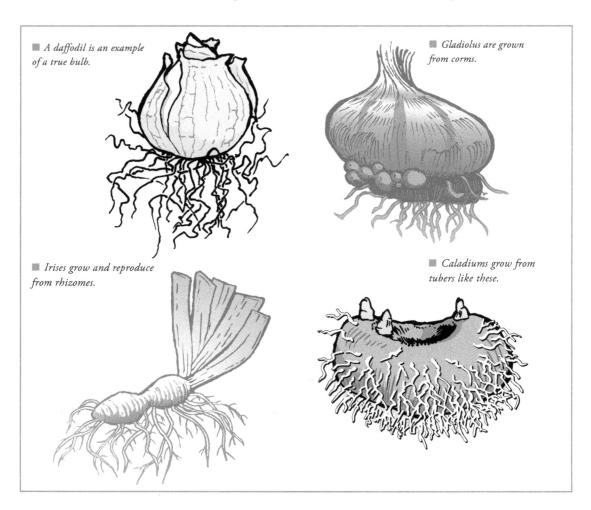

■ *A daffodil is an example of a true bulb.*

■ *Gladiolus are grown from corms.*

■ *Irises grow and reproduce from rhizomes.*

■ *Caladiums grow from tubers like these.*

may continue underground or spread to the surface and grow there.

- Fleshy roots describe peony and daylily storage organs. Their roots are distorted by storage but are otherwise no different from other roots. Because they have crowns but also fleshy roots, plants like these two are categorized as bulbs and perennials interchangeably.

Crinum won't bloom anymore and it looks like increasing shade is to blame. Because these bulbs can bloom for years with no attention, it comes as a surprise when they stop. Usually overcrowding is to blame, along with less sunlight over time. Dividing them takes time and strength to accomplish without cutting into the bulbs. Set up a sprinkler and run it slowly all day to deeply soak the ground around the clump. Dig all the way around with a shovel to create a 6-inch-deep trench at the outside edge of the leaves. Use your shovel to push into the trench and under the bulbs all the way around before you lift out soil and bulbs. Replant immediately.

EDIBLES

Pumpkins and gourds need lots of sun, water, fertilizer, and room for vines that can spread more than 15 feet in several directions. Jack-o-lantern-sized pumpkins and large gourds, such as dipper and birdhouse types grow best on the ground, but go vertical for mini pumpkins and smaller decorative gourds. Set up a trellis as you would for cucumber vines or put that old clothesline to good use. Pull up a hill of well-drained soil at each end, make a slight indention in the top and plant several seeds there. With a little guidance, the vines will go up the poles and across the clothesline. The mini pumpkins and little gourds will hang from the lines or rest on top of the leafy arbor.

Harvest garlic bulbs when the leaves fall over. Dig up the garlic with leaves attached, brush off the dirt, and lay them out to cure on newspapers in a cool, dark, dry place for a month. Then cut off the tops and clean up the bulbs. Now your garlic is ready for the kitchen, but be sure to save some for fall planting.

LAWNS

Buy squares of sod to match your lawn grass and cut your own plugs to replant areas that didn't rebound

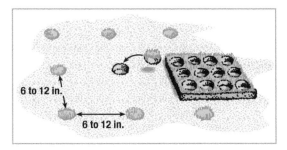

■ *Grass plug placement*

well this spring. (You can find sod for sale in garden centers, home-improvement stores, and sod dealers.) Work up the area, add compost, and cut a 2-inch plug right before you plant it to prevent it from drying out. Use a starter solution and keep the areas watered well until they begin growing.

PERENNIALS & ORNAMENTAL GRASSES

Filling in any empty space in perennial beds and borders with plants will add both flowers and texture to the summer garden. Make the most of reblooming daylilies—use them to carry vibrant color and noble trumpet-shape flowers through summer and fall. Add beeblossom (*Guara lindheimeri*) for fine texture and old-fashioned white yarrow (*Achillea millefolium*) for flat flower heads and ferny leaves.

Stokes' aster (*Stokesia laevis*) bridges the bloom gap from spring to summer with fringed, daisy-shaped flowers that are blue, pink, or white. You can remove the spent flowers to encourage rebloom, but let a few go to seed. Stokes clumps will increase in size with more flowers each year until they become crowded. New seedlings can be dug up or left in place to thicken the planting faster.

ROSES

The cuttings you rooted earlier this year should be large enough to move up into gallon pots. To get them ready for the garden next fall or spring, grow rose babies in dappled shade or bright light this summer.

SHRUBS

Most shrubs (including many roses) will now have stems that can be rooted. Bend the tip of a stem to test for semi-hard wood. If the stem easily bends around your finger or snaps right away with the effort, the wood is too green or too hard. In most cases, you want wood that is in between these two extremes. Take 6-inch tip cuttings, strip the leaves off the lower half, and stick the cuttings into moist, well-drained rooting mix such as potting soil mixed with equal parts of ground bark. Put the pots in the shade to root and keep the soil moist.

To make the most successful cuttings, use a single bladed knife to make a slanted cut to expose more stem area to the rooting mix. It may seem like a small difference, but more surface area on the cutting gives it more potential rooting space.

TREES

If Uncle Dell wants you to plant trees this month, do it—as long as he agrees to check them daily for signs of transplant shock and call you. With careful planting, well-prepared soil, mulch, and ready access to water, trees planted now will be fine. Shock is not always readily apparent in trees, and the damage it can cause is preventable! Signs to watch for include:

- Leaves in the process of emerging do not actually unfurl and may drop off.

- Leaves wilt and do not recover after watering.

- Intact leaves at the tips of branches fall off and when you scratch the bark there, it is brown instead of healthy green.

- In the long run, trees that suffer transplant shock will grow more slowly and may fail to thrive.

Take immediate action to remedy transplant shock.

- Water the tree slowly and deeply to soak the root zone or dig a swale if the tree is in a puddle.

- Prune several inches off of each branch.

- If the trunk is small and the canopy thick, take some of the branches off entirely but maintain the general shape.

Morning glory

VINES & GROUNDCOVERS

There's plenty of time to get moonflowers and morning glories going for lush vines and flowers for months. No trellis? No problem. Put a row of nails or hooks 3 inches apart along an eave and tie a string to each one that extends several inches onto the ground below. When seeds come up, guide each new vine onto its string.

WATER GARDENS

The problem with poring over magazines for ideas is that reality seldom matches the perfection of a photo. Look at your water feature and bring it closer to ideal—fill in gaps in water feature plantings with underwater, floating, surface, and marginal plants. Use smaller water features to show off miniature versions of favorite water garden plants. Like hardy water lilies, the teacup lilies are available in a range of colors, but these grow in almost any amount of water. It only takes one of them or a blue tropical mini to make a big show.

Louisiana iris quickly form large clumps and spill out of their space. Lift and divide the clumps after bloom; replant and/or spread them around. Versatile Louisiana iris can grow in water, as marginal plants, in a wash or swale that sometimes fills with water, or in garden beds that are watered regularly.

CARE

ANNUALS

Move pots of geraniums out of full sun to a spot that is shaded most of the day. They will continue growing and may bloom again, but if you can keep them fairly healthy all summer, they will return with panache in the fall.

Use a three-prong cultivator with a short or long handle depending on whether you prefer to work sitting or standing. Just don't stoop! Cultivate around annuals now to loosen crusty soil and get rid of weeds.

BULBS

Let the weather guide you to a good day for digging Easter (*Lilium longifolium*) and St. Joseph's lily (*Hippeastrum* x *johnsonii*) bulbs that have grown crowded. If the season is hot already, gardeners in the southern half of our states should wait until fall to work on these bulbs. Most years, now is the time to dig, separate, and replant these bulbs in most of Zone 8 and north.

EDIBLES

Mosaic virus on summer squash leaves shows up as a mottled light/dark green pattern on the leaf. Insects like aphids and beetles carry the virus to the plant and deliver it when they feed. The infection spreads through the plant's vascular system (its pipes) to disable it with varying results. There is no remedy for mosaic virus except to control the insects. Because you do not always see them, consider growing squash under floating row covers and spraying the plants with a contact insecticide as a preventative. White, porous fabric, floating row covers let in sunlight and water but camouflage the plants underneath. A double layer over lettuce plants can shade them just enough to prolong the harvest.

After you pick all their fruit, it's time to prune berries—both black and blue.

LAWNS

Proper mowing includes the clean up after cutting is done. Keep an outdoor broom handy to sweep clippings off pathways, driveways, and porches so surfaces don't get slippery or stained. Tilt the mower up and hose it off every time it's used, especially if brown patch fungus has been a problem. Dump the grass catcher and hang it upside down after each use for cleaner, longer life.

If you have a thick lawn and use a mulching mower, catch the clippings a few times this summer to prevent excessive buildup in the thatch. Dump the clippings into the compost.

HERE'S HOW

TO PRUNE BERRY BUSHES

- Blackberry canes bear very well one year, well the next, and not so great after that. You can create a productive cycle that lasts for years.

- Prune out the weaker canes in the first three years after planting to build the bramble.

- Prune out the oldest canes each year after that and allow new ones to grow.

- Blueberry bushes can be left unpruned, but shape and encourage thicker growth by tip pruning annually until the plants are as tall as you can easily reach to pick. After that, prune to maintain that size even if it means taking off several inches of stem.

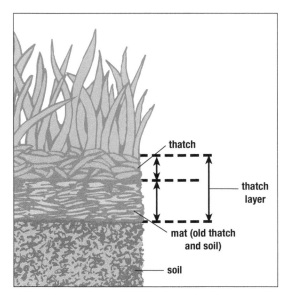

■ *Grass with thatch layer*

PERENNIALS & ORNAMENTAL GRASSES

Large and vigorous perennials can be bullies if you let them. For example, some lantanas (*Lantana montevidensis* and hybrids) and verbenas (*Verbena bonariensis* and hybrids) bloom and grow simultaneously at a fast pace, shading out the plants around them. You can clip individual stems if you have the time or shear these plants to deadhead spent flowers, shape them, and keep them in check. Other vigorous perennials should only be grown where their rampant spread can be controlled. For example, in a small space defined by concrete such as you'd find between the sidewalk and the steps to the back stoop, you'll want to put dooryard plant (*Ruellia brittoniana*) and Mexican hydrangea (*Clerodendrum bungei*). In well-cultivated garden beds, these plants, like 'Homestead Purple' verbena, will make you wonder why you ever planted them.

ROSES

Prune out old canes that did not flower this year on once-blooming roses to make room for new ones to emerge. If space is tight, limit the number of new canes by selecting the strongest, well-spaced ones and pruning out the rest. With regular water and fertilizer plus room to grow, they'll bloom next year.

SHRUBS

Continue shrub rejuvenation with a light shearing to stimulate more growth. Lay on another ½-inch blanket of compost/manure now and fertilize again in two weeks. French hydrangeas (*Hydrangea macrophylla*) usually have blue flowerheads in our states because they get plenty of aluminum from our old, acidic, low pH soils. If you plant hydrangeas with pink flowers in garden soil, they will turn purple or blue in a year or two unless you work on the pH to limit the uptake of aluminum. You can do it, but the best pink hydrangeas are grown in big containers where you can control their soil conditions.

VINES & GROUNDCOVERS

Retrain woody vines while new growth is firming up but before it is too stiff to bend your way. Shear

Blue hydrangea

HERE'S HOW

TO CHANGE HYDRANGEA COLOR

Every soil has a chemical reaction depending on its native components. That reaction is measured as pH on a scale of zero to fourteen. Above seven, soils are alkaline and often chalky. Seven is neutral, and lower numbers indicate fewer hydrogen ions and thus an acid state, like most of our native soils.

- To keep blue hydrangeas blue or to deepen their shade, add aluminum sulfate to the soil around mature shrubs three times each year (1 tablespoon per gallon of water). Use fertilizer that is low in phosphorus and high in potassium.

- To maintain pink shades or at least keep a tinge of pink in them, add dolomitic lime three times a year to help raise the pH and tie up aluminum in the soil. Use fertilizer with high levels of phosphorus or supply it as an additional nutrient when you lime.

and slope the edges of groundcover beds to lower their height to meet the lawn or driveway on its flank and aide in water flow off of the bed. Cut back autumn clematis to control its rampant growth now and bring on the flowers. This vine is too often considered a weed because people do not catch its sweet-smelling stars by pruning now.

No annual vine covers a chainlink fence faster with finer texture than cypress vine (*Ipomoea quamoclit*). Also known as cardinal vine for its brilliant red tubular flowers that flare to welcome hummingbirds, grow it in full sun for fast cover and color. It does not need to be deadheaded, but do so to prevent rampant reseeding if you do not want more.

You plant Asiatic jasmine (*Trachelospermum asiaticum*) under trees and star jasmine (*T. jasminoides*) on a dooryard arbor for fragrance. Some is thin, some thick enough in which to lose a basketball. Trailing groundcovers like jasmines and hardy vinca (*V. major*) will respond to pruning now with plenty of new growth to even out the bed and arbor. Cut back the thick parts a bit more than the thin, but shear the entire planting and fertilize it lightly.

WATER GARDENS

Lift draping leaves at the pond's edge and check for tiny snails hiding in the cool damp darkness. They nest where there is too much thick cover or too much mulch and will find their way to the rest of your garden. Thin out the dense leaves and rake back some of the mulch to ruin their happy home.

'King Tut' and other papyrus plants will send up more handsome stems with whirligig toppers if you cut off any that turn brown. Use them for a textural accent in arrangements.

WATER

ALL

You can prevail on a gardening friend or hire a professional, but arrange for someone to water your plants when you go on vacation. It may involve nothing more than watering a few pots and having the phone number to call if the irrigation system suddenly breaks. Make a list of your

Direct water from a watering wand into the soil next to the plant.

particular needs and see that it gets done so your garden doesn't lose ground while you're away.

When you will be away overnight, most potted plants will be fine. For those that need daily watering or, just to simplify your life, use ice. Six ice cubes in a big potted fern will take hours to melt slowly and water the plant thoroughly.

ANNUALS

One way to ensure that potted plants make it through your vacation is to set up a kiddie pool in the shade. The day you leave town, put every pot in the pool filled with several inches of water. Small containers will need separate attention, but medium and large pots can take up just what they need without being overwatered. And the friend who comes to water will be glad too.

BULBS

The most successful beds under and around trees are those with a dedicated water supply such as their own sprinkler heads or a soaker hose. There is competition from the tree, of course, but achimenes and caladiums must be watered regularly. If not, the former will stop flowering altogether and the latter will bloom at the expense of continued leaf production.

EDIBLES

Warm soil and warm air combine to create conditions for fast growth in sunny vegetable beds. Water drives the process, and the lack of water stalls the steady growth rate vegetable plants need to be productive. Well-drained, fertile soil in beds and pots will need water twice weekly unless there is a deluge and you are building an ark. A brief afternoon rain does not count towards the 1 to 2 inches per week necessary to grow vegetables.

LAWNS

Healthy grass can outgrow its weeds, and regular irrigation promotes healthy grass. Therefore, watering the lawn actually is one important part of weed control. Do it weekly if nature doesn't.

PERENNIALS & ORNAMENTAL GRASSES

If rainfall and irrigation water run between perennial clumps, two things are happening that work against your efforts: the plants are not getting watered and soil is washing away from between them. Mix a 5-gallon bucket of equal parts ground bark and garden soil. Fill in the gaps, tamp down the mix, and water it well. Put fresh mulch on top and keep an eye on the situation.

ROSES

Fence rose is an old name for the thorny ramblers that can cover a fence in a year. These and other roses in remote parts of the garden can depend primarily on rainfall alone and need your help in dry times if they are to bloom well. Use a stiff rake to pull up some soil and mulch near the base of these roses to trap rainfall when it happens.

SHRUBS

The importance of regular water for shrubs you are rejuvenating is almost equal to that of new plantings. Water each of the patients deeply, weekly to speed their recovery if there have been less than several hours of rain that week. The relationship between water and fertilizer is mutually beneficial—each does its job better when they are employed together.

TREES

When watering options are limited or nonexistent, reservoir bags can be helpful for young trees but mature ones need a different approach. Because their most active roots are usually far from the trunk, mulch from the trunk out to the drip line and try to get water there. Rake up a low dam there to direct rainfall to the inside of the drip line.

VINES & GROUNDCOVERS

Native vines and established groundcover beds are well-adapted plants that need water only after weeks of drought. Rainfall and mulch should be enough for them. Keep a close eye on non-native vines and new groundcover plantings to be sure they get the minimum inch per week needed for most garden plantings.

WATER GARDENS

Add water as needed in dry weather to compensate for evaporation, but be aware that water loss can also indicate a leaking pond liner. How fast water evaporates naturally relates to the size of the water feature, the surface area and depth of the water, but any loss that seems excessive should be investigated.

FERTILIZE

ANNUALS

Lower leaves turn yellow when the younger, upper parts of a plant lack nitrogen. The older leaves give up, wither, and die. If this happens to your annuals, you have forgotten to fertilize or didn't put in a slow-release formula for insurance or heavy rain has diluted it all. Act quickly to relieve the stress—use a fast-acting soluble fertilizer that can also be sprayed onto the leaves.

BULBS

When flowers on favorite bulbs are smaller than you remember, June is the time to fertilize them so that they can make and store energy for next year. This rule applies to bulbs that do not usually crowd themselves such as grape hyacinth, autumn daffodil, and well-behaved crocosmias. These include 'Lucifer', 'Ember Glow', and 'Alborado', not the weedy orange-flowered rogue called montbretia. It is a prize elsewhere but not in our states.

EDIBLES

When you have finished picking blueberries, blackberries, figs, and plums, use a general garden fertilizer or one made for fruit trees. The number and quality of leaves can determine next year's fruit crop, and these plants will continue active growth for months after harvest.

Heavy applications of fertilizer made when edibles are forming may cause the fruit or vegetable to fall off as the plant struggles, usually with nitrogen overload. But plants can deplete most available nutrients during ripening and need more to continue producing. Wait until vegetables such as eggplant and pepper are beginning to ripen and use a fertilizer with a lower first number (5-10-10).

LAWNS

When you put in a new lawn, the question of how to fertilize it is made simpler with specialty formulas. If good soil preparation was done before the new sod or seeded lawn went in, it will get started just fine and after six to eight weeks, it's time to use new lawn starter formulas. They are higher in nutrients used for rooting but still have enough nitrogen to keep blades green and growing. Do not use herbicides or lawn food containing weedkillers on new lawns during the first year.

PERENNIALS & ORNAMENTAL GRASSES

It takes a healthy perennial crown to constantly put out roots, leaves, and flowers, and to multiply the clump. Fertilize crowns that you divided and replanted this spring or last fall to keep them growing through the summer. If you feed regularly with water-soluble formulas, change to a longer-acting granular formula for summer feeding.

ROSES

If you feed tea roses monthly, you need only to put it in your calendar to know when to fertilize. Fertilize the rest of your roses now as well to promote new, thrifty growth.

Thrifty growth means that a plant adds new stems, leaves, and other plant parts steadily at the rate you expect. Overuse of fertilizers or a complete lack of nutrients seldom produces thrifty growth. For example, a rosebush with no fertilizer at all will have small leaves and small or no flowers. Too much fertilizer and the rose sends up tall, wild canes that do nothing for the overall form of the plant and may make flowers that shatter too easily.

SHRUBS

Spireas, glossy abelia, and other shrubs that form thickets of thin stems use roughly equivalent

Spireas are staples of Deep South gardens – spring and summer bloomers, some with brilliant fall color. The rosy fuchsia flowers of Anthony Waterer spirea appear in late spring and sporadically at other times.

amounts of fertilizer elements. Use a complete, balanced formula that includes minor elements too. A shrub 3 feet by 3 feet usually requires about a cup of fertilizer spread around its base at the drip line, but consult product labels for complete directions.

TREES

Water first and then fertilize young trees (those less than three years in the ground) and any older ones that you are rejuvenating this season. However, resist the urge to fertilize trees where there is no access to water except rainfall. At best your labor will be wasted or simply used to feed the weeds; at worst it will be rained on just enough to burn fragile roots.

VINES & GROUNDCOVERS

Sweet autumn clematis (*C. paniculata*) and other fall-blooming clematis bloom on the current year's new growth and can be fertilized now with a flowering formula. Broadcast general-purpose garden food into beds of bugle flower (*Ajuga*) and coral bells (*Heuchera*). Rinse fertilizer granules off of leaves to prevent burning.

WATER GARDENS

If you did not fertilize the plants around and in the water garden this spring, do so now. And if you did fertilize, but some plants look wimpy or pale, fertilize around each clump or in each pot. By locating aquatic fertilizers where they can dissolve slowly exactly where they are needed, you avoid the pitfalls of overgrowth and overfertilization.

PROBLEM-SOLVE

EDIBLES

Tomatoes look great until the bottom of the fruit turns black. The issue is blossom end rot caused by a basic watering issue. No matter where tomatoes grow, if they wilt, their ability to move water is compromised even after you water. If this happens often enough at any time during the growing season, the cells at the bottom of the fruit—the blossom end—collapse. It's best to pick affected

■ *Brown patch*

fruit and cook the good parts, and then pay more attention to watering. Sometimes soils are at issue, but regular irrigation usually solves it.

Calcium sprays can be used to prevent blossom end rot by spraying the flowers to strengthen their cell walls. While it is true that additional calcium helps tomatoes set, it will not work if you have poor watering practices.

LAWNS

When parts of centipede grass or St. Augustine lawns turn yellowish and then die, you treat for the common lawn disease, brown patch, because you had it before and recognize the early symptoms. Then the yellow areas die and you discover a worse lawn disease, take-all root rot. Fungicides are seldom as effective as these cultural controls:

- Mow at the height recommended for your grass and often enough to maintain it.

- Test the soil and maintain the pH between 5.5 and 6.0.

- Avoid nitrate fertilizers; instead choose slow-release ureas.

- Do not overfertilize with potassium and do not use herbicides that work through roots.

■ *Low calcium levels in the soil and uneven soil moisture both cause blossom end rot in peppers and tomatoes. To correct this problem in new fruits (you can't fix tomatoes that already have the problem), use soaker hoses around plants to keep the soil evenly moist.*

PERENNIALS & ORNAMENTAL GRASSES

Phlox, peony, daylily, and some other perennials have brown leaves that look burned up even though the bed gets water twice weekly. Summer dormancy or heat and drought stress (or both) may be at work here, and unless you know some things about your plants, it's confusing. Peony, early phlox (*P. subulata*), bleeding heart (*Dicentra spectabilis*), and some other spring-flowering perennials finish their season and turn brown as they go dormant. Others, such as daylilies (*Hemerocallis*), may be dry under the mulch. Check right after watering, and if the soil is still dry, water more slowly and for longer each time to remedy the situation. Browned leaves on hostas can be caused by drought but can also be the result of voles chewing their roots. Repellant products are effective and useful in deterring voles, but once they are present, a cat or small dog that likes to chase and hunt them can be the best control.

ROSES

Rosebushes that are supposed to resist blackspot disease get it anyway. You're not one to spray anything and worry the roses will die. Roses are considered resistant to blackspot because they are able to live with it when they cannot avoid it entirely. A few yellowed leaves with black spots should be removed and destroyed. When more than half the leaves are affected, it's time to remove them but also to cut back the rose and spray it with a fungicide.

SHRUBS

A black mold forms on shrubs in one part of the garden but not everywhere. You can rub it off with your thumb, and the leaf looks okay. When conditions are right, the ever-present sooty mold fungus can grow on plants, patio furniture cushions, and anywhere else outside. Wash off the mold with soapy water and find the source of this problem. Shake the bushes to see if whiteflies are present and spray to control them. Stand nearby if the shrubs are under trees. If it feels like tiny drops of rain are falling on you, the insects are feeding in the trees above and dropping what they cannot digest onto everything below. You should consider systemic insecticides if the trees are too large to spray.

TREES

Some years the big old river birch (*Betula nigra*) tree drops a lot of leaves in summer but not always. The reason for this sporadic problem is that birch leaf blight begins in cool, wet springs. Its first symptoms are easy to miss—small brown dots on the leaves that develop yellow halos. The disease is seldom more than ugly, but you are wise to reduce its impact. Rake up the leaves and do not compost them. Do a soil test to see if fall feeding will be beneficial to fortify potassium and phosphorus levels. It is wise to treat young trees with lime-sulfur sprays in winter or fungicide sprays on new growth, but that is usually impractical for large trees.

Monitor crepe myrtle, river birch, and other deciduous trees for signs of insects feeding on their lush canopy. Trees may just not "look right"—pale leaves, thin areas, or flowers fail to open. But more often you'll feel the dripping honeydew on your arm, the sugary excrement that the insects could not digest. Soon you may see black sooty mold on leaves below the insect buffet. Control the insects with sprays or drenches of water to stop the feast.

HERE'S HOW

TO MAKE YOUR OWN FUNGICIDE

Commercial fungicides can be sourced from either organic or conventional sources. If you do not use either, consider making your own spray to deter black spot fungus. Clean up the roses and spray weekly with 1 teaspoon baking soda plus 2 drops liquid dish detergent mixed into 2 cups water plus 2 cups fat-free milk.

July

Fireworks and flags, beach days and shady glades, harvest baskets and bins full of bounty at farmers markets—July delivers as promised. Everybody has a favorite summer memory—a first kiss, the pranks you got away with, an overturned canoe, or disastrous road trip that seems funny in retrospect. Most of us have a favorite summer plant too.

Perennial ferns such as southern shield are knee high, romantic althea blooms in every color but orange, and its cousins, the tropical hibiscus, take care of that with their glorious orange blossoms. The most popular summer vegetable is tomatoes, grown by more people than any other edible and often the subject of competition—witness weigh-ins at the library and bragging rights over the backyard fence.

They say, "It's not the heat, it's the humidity," and July has both in abundance. You can find respite in beach breezes or plan a trip to Mount Cheaha, the highest point in Alabama at 2,411 feet above sea level, or 2,419 feet above New Orleans (which is 8 feet under sea level). The gurgling sounds of a water join frogs croaking a throaty tune, and trees are twice as sweet when you're sitting in their summer shade. They signify the joys of July. A wise gardener determines a way to get a fan into the garden and dons the "traditional" fragrance of summer—insect repellant combined with the scent of sunscreen. It may be "too hot to breathe," but July is perfect for the ladies that bloom at night—jasmine and cereus.

This month can call on the optimism of gardening when a month-long drought breaks into a tropical storm, insects multiply overnight, and sticker weeds in your lawn become barefoot hazards. July is statistically the hottest month on the calendar, and nights can be too warm to set tomatoes but fine for growing sweet potatoes, gourds, pumpkins, and another hibiscus, okra. This is the time that sets you apart from the neighbor whose garden is a weedy mess because it's too hot and they didn't stay ahead of the inevitable situations. Your garden is yours to enjoy now because you keep at it all year long. And now it's time to start the fall vegetable and flower garden!

PLAN

ANNUALS

Imagine cutting bunches of your favorite annual flowers for tailgate parties this fall, so plan a cutting row. Find space anywhere it's sunny that you can water, decide if it needs digging, and locate seeds to start or sow directly next month. Plan for love lies bleeding (*Amaranthus caudatus*), Amazon celosia (*C. argentea*), mid-sized sunflowers such as 'Valentine' (*Helianthus annuus*), and tall zinnias 'Pacific Giants' and 'Raggedy Anne' with quilled flowers (*Z. elegans*).

BULBS

It is a smart investment of time to make a storage plan for caladiums and dahlias well ahead of fall. The big idea is to hold them in a dry, well-ventilated space that will not let them freeze but is not warm enough for them to sprout. An enclosed garage or potting shed might do. Start collecting cardboard flats or mesh bags, such as the ones onions are sold in; locate sawdust or cedar shavings; and a bag of powdered sulfur.

EDIBLES

Get to know the cole crops you can plant soon, which are members of the mustard family (Cruciferae). Because they do not ship well, some great vegetables are hard to find fresh but easy to grow.

■ *Use an old cardboard box to store bulbs in.*

■ *The swollen stem of the kohlrabi is the edible part.*

- Rapini, or Chinese broccoli (*Brassica rapa*), has slender stems, tender leaves, and loose heads of flower buds. It is more closely related to turnips than true broccoli and has a nutty, pungent flavor long popular in Italian and Chinese cuisines. Look for 'Quarantina' and others for their 40-day harvest.

- Kohlrabi (*B. oleracea*) has everything but good press. Its stem swells to form a delicious orb just above ground level. Crisp like an apple when eaten raw, and sweet like a turnip in stir-fry, kohlrabi can be purple or light green. Look for 'Crispy Colors Duo' and 'Grand Duke'.

- Brussels sprouts (*B. oleracea*) are well worth the space and time they need for their tender, fresh taste. Their intriguing habit of forming what looks like little cabbages along thick stems keeps your interest. 'Diablo' has good cold tolerance.

Even the popular broccoli, cabbage, turnips, collards, and mustard are better when you grow them yourself because you have access to so many more varieties.

LAWNS

If you have a new property and will be building next fall, put a lawn in your plan. Both budget and timing should be considered on the front end, not as an afterthought. The issue of slope and drainage must be addressed early on. You may be looking at new sod or limited to perennial ryegrass at first, but the way to know what will work in your area is to plan.

PERENNIALS & ORNAMENTAL GRASSES

If you think about it, wildflowers are primarily native perennial plants, and the best can be started from seed in the fall. Plan now to give some space to coneflowers, cosmos, coreopsis, black-eyed Susans, and more by deciding which seeds to buy and which to save from your own garden. Mark the nicest flower stems and let them go to seed when you cut back others to encourage rebloom.

ROSES

Take a hard look at shrub and groundcover roses this month to assess their garden future. Make a note of the ones you want to replace and those you might move this fall to improve their growing conditions.

SHRUBS AND TREES

Plan to do soil preparation this summer for shrub and tree planting in the coming months. Maybe you need a new focal point or a hedge to block new neighbors. Perhaps you see a visual dead zone that could be enhanced with variegated forms of shrubs like holly, hydrangea and Japanese mock orange (*Pittosporum tobira*). Each has varieties with white or yellow edges and/or markings.

HERE'S HOW

TO GRADE A LAWN

1. Drive a stake into the soil at the base of the foundation and another at least 8 ft. out into the yard along a straight line from the first stake. Attach a string fitted with a line level to the stakes and level it. Measure and flag the string with tape at 1-ft. intervals. Measure down from the string at the tape flags, recording your measurements to use as guidelines for adding or removing soil to create a correct grade.

2. Working away from the base of the house, add soil to low areas until they reach the desired height. Using a garden rake, evenly distribute the soil over a small area. Measure down from the 1-ft. markings as you work to make sure that you are creating a ¾" per 1 ft. pitch. Add and remove soil as needed until soil is evenly sloped, then move on to the next area and repeat the process.

3. Use a hand tamp or a roller to lightly compact the soil. Don't overtamp the soil or it could become too dense to grow a healthy lawn or plants. Add a little more soil after tamping as a seed bed for the grass seed or sod.

4. Use a grading rake to remove any rocks or clumps. Starting at the foundation, pull the rake in a straight line down the slope. Dispose of any rocks or construction debris. Repeat the process, working on one section at a time until the entire area around the house is graded.

VINES & GROUNDCOVERS

One of summer's worst tasks is coping with slopes where grass and weeds mix. Decisions about such areas usually boil down to the degree of slope and how much sun it gets. More of both makes lawn grass tough to maintain and may call for groundcover or other perennial plant alternatives. To prevent erosion, you'll want to have plants, seeds, and/or mulch on hand at the same time you take out the weeds. Like most onerous chores in the garden, you can lighten or eliminate this one if you plan before acting.

WATER GARDENS

Whether you have a new garden or one that needs updating, it can be frustrating to wait for plants to grow. When you decide to put in a water feature, though, you will feel its impact as soon as it is installed. Start planning your new water garden: watch how the sun moves across your property, figure which pump and filter will meet your needs, investigate plants, benches, and path materials, and get excited.

PLANT

ANNUALS

Take advantage of lush growth on tropical plants to start cuttings for the fall garden and/or to grow in pots. Coleus and calico plant (*Alternanthera dentata*) are good candidates, and you will find many more. Take tip cuttings 4 to 6 inches long and root in a loose mix.

Later this month, plant your own pansy seeds to get the latest releases or your favorite colors and mixes. Or go for the panola, a hybrid of pansy and viola, and sterile hybrids of Johnny jump-ups that won't seed all over the garden.

In areas where plants will be scarce, also start seeds for nasturtium, stock, English daisies, and Canterbury bells to grow over the winter.

BULBS

You'll find full pots of caladiums with plenty of brightly painted leaves at garden centers now. They can be transplanted to the garden or, better yet, grown in containers alone or in mixed pots with dwarf canna lilies, dwarf 'Cavendish', or 'Truly Tiny' bananas (*Musa*).

EDIBLES

Fall garden edibles are planted earlier in the north and later in the South during the months of July, August, and September. July brings the last opportunity to plant southern peas, but don't stop with black-eyed and crowder peas. Plant cream, lady, and pink eye purple hull peas too. Get okra planted from seeds or plants by July 15.

HERE'S HOW

TO GROW TOMATOES IN A GARBAGE CAN

1. Drill six holes, ½-inch in size, at the bottom of the garbage can and, four holes on the sides near the bottom edge of the can.

2. Add 1 cup dolomite lime and 2 cups slow-release fertilizer pellets to 30 gallons of soilless potting mix.

3. Put the can on top of four bricks in the sun near a water source.

4. Fill the can with mix leaving 2 inches of space between the top of the soil and the top of the pot.

5. Plant two disease-resistant tomato varieties in the mix. This is not the place for most heirloom varieties—go with 'Better Boy', 'Goliath', or a grafted variety. Water well.

6. Put an 8-foot section of galvanized wire around the pot with enough to make a 6-inch overlap. Place the hogwire around the outside of the can and use the overlap to make a hinge. Close the wire.

7. Pound three steel stakes (made to hold chicken wire or something similar) into the ground around the can and secure the wire to them.

8. Water the soil, not the leaves, whenever possible, and fertilize weekly with a formula made for tomatoes.

Start planting seeds at mid-month, including:

- Bush and pole lima beans

- Pole snap beans

- Vining cucumber

Start transplants at mid-month, including:

- Tomatoes

- Hot and bell peppers

- Eggplants

The biggest tomato plant you might ever see is one you grow in a 30-gallon garbage can.

LAWNS

Hydroseeding is a process that mixes grass seed with mulch in a slurry to be sprayed onto prepared lawn sites. Sites without water available, slopes, and bare ground around new construction can be mud holes for months, or dry up, blow away, and create dusty conditions. Hydroseeding is usually more expensive than seeding but not as pricey as sod and can be done during the summer in those difficult areas.

PERENNIALS & ORNAMENTAL GRASSES

Too many gardeners shy away from garden center perennial racks in July because of concerns about planting in hot weather. But there are bargains and sought-after plants to be found that you shouldn't miss.

ROSES

The roses you layered (propagated) back in February or last fall should have new sprouts by now, indicating they have rooted. Dig the layer up by first severing its ties. Cut between where you buried the cane and the mother plant, and then dig up the root ball. Whether you plant it in the garden or pot it up, get rose layers planted this month.

SHRUBS

A wise gardener once noted, there's nothing you can't do in the summer garden if you garden in the shade. That includes planting dwarf shrubs in beds under trees and along partly shady paths. The dwarf shrubs that mature at 3 to 4 feet tall and respond well to pruning:

- 'Little Henry' itea

- 'Moon Bay', 'Wood's Dwarf' nandina

- Littleleaf boxwood (*Buxus microphylla*)

HERE'S HOW

TO TRANSPLANT DURING THE SUMMER

- Water soil and plants well before transplanting.

- Transplant in late afternoon, preferably on a cloudy day.

- Dig one hole at a time and work some compost/manure into a spot slightly larger than the rootball. There is seldom a need to work up large areas in existing plantings unless old roots get in the way.

- Spread roots into the hole if possible. Rough up or prune roots if they are crowded for added stability.

- Water in first, then water again with a starter solution. Apply fresh mulch around the plant but not over the crown.

- Check daily and water as needed. Fertilize in two weeks and remove the first flower buds if they appear on woody plants this summer.

In more sun:

- 'Little Richard' abelia (*Abelia grandiflora*)

- 'Cherry Dazzle' crepe myrtle (*Lagerstroemia indica*)

TREES

Tender, tropical Norfolk Island pine trees can grow for years in containers and even be a living Christmas tree in the living room. The tree will be badly damaged by temperatures below 40 degrees Fahrenheit but adjusts well to summers outdoors in the shade and winters in a bright, warm room.

Large trees can be a challenge to repot. Do it to encourage growth by repotting annually into a slightly larger container each year. Once the plant reaches the desired size, repot it every third year. Take the plant out of its pot, prune an inch off its roots, and repot it in the same pot with fresh soil.

VINES & GROUNDCOVERS

Layer vigorous vines and vining groundcovers to propagate them this month while they are actively growing. Cherokee rose (*Rosa laevigata*), English and Algerian ivies (*Hedera helix, H. canariensis*), goldflame honeysuckle (*Lonicera heckrotti*), little periwinkle and hardy periwinkle (*Vinca minor, V. major*) are good candidates for layering this month. Simply bury a section of vine in a trench with the tip exposed. Cover the trench with soil and weigh it down if necessary with a brick.

WATER GARDENS

Babies abound now, especially in patches of floating plants such as water lettuce. Leave enough to cover half to two-thirds of the surface and scoop the rest out. Plant the babies in pond pots to grow on or share. Change the water weekly or drop in an aerator stone to prevent mosquitoes.

When nothing is in bloom, the water garden area can look very green. Adding plants with raucous leaves sets a bright mood, especially when you opt for versatile striped canna lilies. They're at home at the pond's edge or in the water, allowing you to plant a cascade of 'Bengal Tiger' (*C. generalis*) for green leaves with striking gold stripes and orange flowers. Red stripe canna (*C. indica* 'Purpurea') brings green leaves with deep red stripes and midrib and showy red flowers.

CARE

ALL

Many of the to-do tasks this month can be considered investments—time spent now will pay off in the fall. July is hot and humid, and generations have adjusted by tending their gardens early in the day or near its end. These days we still avoid the noonday sun, but concerns about skin cancer and mosquito-borne illnesses like West Nile virus have made us wiser yet.

Keep a bucket by the door to the garden filled with twenty-first-century necessities: sunscreen, mosquito repellant, sunglasses, gloves, and a hat. These items should be as big a part of your gardening repertoire as water and mulch. Stay safe from the preventable problems associated with sun exposure and mosquitos—use these items every time you work in the garden.

■ *Goldflame honeysuckle*

ANNUALS

Restart beds and pots of annuals such as impatiens, which can get leggy in the heat. Cut the plants back by as much as half their size if needed. Just be sure some leaves remain to continue photosynthesis. Add an inch of mulch to pots if you have not done so to help with moderation and soil temperature. Fertilize after pruning with a flower garden formula or one made for general garden use.

BULBS

Lots of your favorite tropical plants are Aroids (arums), monocots that belong to the Araceae family. Some, like caladiums, grow from bulbs and all send up a spathe or cupped shield around an exposed flower stalk. Except for those grown for this showy spathe, such as flamingo flower (*Anthurium* hybrids), it is wise to remove the spathe so the plant's energies remain devoted to making leaves.

EDIBLES

There are two good ways to get fall tomatoes—plant new ones or rehabilitate the ones you already have. You can start seeds this month to plant out six weeks from now, in mid-August on the Gulf Coast, or shop for them this month farther north. Both of these means of acquisition can be more challenging, but if spring tomatoes have healthy leaves, keep them going.

Gourds, melons, and other long vines need a balance of water and fertilizer that keeps them growing steadily. Don't miss a week or the crop can be compromised.

Once bush beans finish, dig them into the soil below to provide organic matter and nutrients.

HERE'S HOW

TO MAINTAIN
SPRING-PLANTED TOMATOES

1. Assess their condition. Blighted or insect-riddled plants must be discarded, but a few yellow leaves or broken stems will be fine. The failure to fruit when night temperatures stay above 70 degrees Fahrenheit does not disqualify the plant, either.

2. Groom the plants very well and cover any exposed roots with soil. This particularly is a problem in unmulched pots of tomatoes.

3. Prune each stem by at least a few inches to stimulate new growth and root some of the trimmings if they are healthy.

4. Continue a very regular schedule of water and fertilizer even though the plants are not blooming or making tomatoes.

5. Look for new flowers when night temperatures allow for them.

LAWNS

By July, most lawns have been mowed at least eight times and grass blade tips may be split from recutting at the same level. No matter what kind of lawn you grow, raise your mower height by one notch now to change the cut slightly.

Sometimes the lawn just won't grow in places even though you fertilize, water, and mow it properly. If shade is not looming over the area, note whether the poor growth corresponds to a slope, a driveway or sidewalk, or a footpath.

- Slopes and drop-offs can drain much faster than the rest of the lawn, so water and fertilizer applications are less effective. Provide extra water to those areas and blanket them with one-half of compost/manure each spring and summer.

- Poor growth near paved surfaces can indicate that white grubs may be nesting below ground. Dig around with a trowel to check for grubs and if you find them, treat the lawn.

- Lawn grass that is constantly walked on can become compacted, limiting growth. Redirect the traffic, install steppingstones, or aerate the area to rejuvenate the grass.

PERENNIALS & ORNAMENTAL GRASSES

Good garden sanitation keeps the garden looking neat but underneath those good looks are important strategies for pest control.

- Groom and clean up around perennial clumps to maintain good air circulation and reduce their vulnerability to diseases.

- For the same reason, lift new plants around the edges of crowded clumps.

- Deadhead old flowers (unless you are saving their seeds) to prevent mold.

- Blow leaves out of the mulch and inspect them for insect damage or the sooty mold that can follow feeding.

- Keep the weeds pulled so they do not compete with your plants and cannot harbor insects. Weed the beds and that patch behind the garage, too, where weedy grasses pop up under the garbage cans.

ROSES

Prune all roses to bring on fall flowers except those that blossom only once in the spring and climbers that are currently in bloom. Treat hybrid teas as you did in February, but cut vigorous ones even shorter, to 18-inch canes. Prune shrub roses to remove no more than one third of their overall size. Root tip cuttings if the cane still bends slightly but does not snap easily.

SHRUBS

Voluptuous and aggressive shrubs such as loropetalum can be pruned to shape and control their growth after each flowering. Shape gardenias after their first flush of blooms, too, and remove spent flowers to prevent diseases that can grow on petals.

TREES

Shade in wooded areas can grow so dense that groundcovers cannot grow and roots can become overly exposed. Make selections now while the canopy is thick and cut out unnecessary and weedy trees. If you remove large trees because they are not as healthy as younger ones nearby, leave a tall stump (15 to 20 feet) for the woodpeckers to enjoy.

VINES & GROUNDCOVERS

Trumpet vine (*Campsis radicans*) that bloomed in the spring has long seedpods now. Wait for the pods to ripen and turn brown, then cut them off the vine and place in a cardboard flat or similarly shaped vessel. When the brown pods dry completely, they split and the seeds roll out. By capturing the seed this way, rainy weather cannot spoil the drying process.

Use a leaf rake to pull fallen leaves and other plant debris out of groundcover beds to improve air circulation around the plants, deter some pests, and keep it neat.

WATER GARDENS

Hardy water lilies send up leaves that get larger as warm weather sets in. Each lasts a month and then yellows. Remove the yellow leaves to encourage the next round. Do the same for their flowers. Most open and close for three to four days and slowly shrink down as their stem retracts. Pick them out to promote more flowers.

WATER

ANNUALS

Keep seeded beds consistently damp until new seedlings have at least two sets of true leaves and then back off slightly, but do not let them dry out. Keep a watering can handy for zinnia, sunflower, cypress vine, and other annual flower seeds starting in the garden now. Use the same basic strategy for annuals you're starting in peat cups for the fall garden.

BULBS

If the summer is very dry, it may take an almost daily soak to fill out dahlia flowers. Water early in the day so dahlias won't drop their flowers on a hot afternoon.

Water caladiums to prevent them from trying to flower.

EDIBLES

Tomato cracks happen because too much water gets to the plants when they are dry, usually when a thunderstorm follows a very dry period. Your watering practices can make it worse if you do not water thoroughly and slowly, each time. Some tomato varieties are more prone to cracking that disfigures the fruit, but the ugly fruit is still very edible once you pare away the damage. The cracks

Tomatoes that have cracked due to uneven watering can still be eaten.

are just that—skin that cracks around or down the sides because the fruit inside expands faster than the outside can handle. Pick right before a storm to prevent cracking.

Fruit and nut trees must have additional water every summer. To fill and mature, pecans, pears, persimmon, pomegranate, and others you hope to harvest in fall need slightly more than the classic 1 inch of water weekly during the growing season.

LAWNS

This month, it is especially important to water through new sod to the thatch and soil below. Set the sprinkler to slowly water and allow for good percolation, to be certain the blades, thatch, and roots are well irrigated. This strategy lets the new sod push roots down into the soil for a long lawn life.

PERENNIALS & ORNAMENTAL GRASSES

When preparing to fertilize or to divide perennials, water the bed very well the day before to facilitate the process. After you broadcast granular fertilizer, water again to be sure the product is rinsed off the leaves too.

ROSES

Irrigate in the afternoon and cut roses the next morning. Take a bucket of water with you when cutting roses (and other flowers). Cut the stem and strip the lowest leaves off, then put the stem in the bucket. Set up a sprinkler to use during dry weeks to shower rose leaves. This keeps them clean and hydrated, and may even knock a few insects off.

SHRUBS

We like evergreen shrubs in part because they are unfazed by extremes of weather. Whether in thunderstorms or dry heat, they stand tall, but you should dig under the mulch to check soil conditions. If it's soggy—pull away the mulch for a day or two. If it's crusted or dusty—change your watering practices to get more water deeper into the planting.

TREES

When your area is in drought but not under water restrictions, water mature trees every other week.

VINES & GROUNDCOVERS

Shady beds can be dry even if rainfall is average because trees absorb most of what falls. Woody groundcovers such as coral berry need water at least monthly to fill berries properly.

WATER GARDENS

Temperatures can rise rapidly, especially in shallow water gardens with only average circulation rates. If temporary shade seems appropriate, choose a roll of fencing made of bamboo or a similar material available at garden centers and home stores. Pound rebar stakes into the ground to support the fencing. Tie it to the stakes so you can take the fence down and roll it up for winter storage.

FERTILIZE

ANNUALS

Hyacinth bean and vines in the morning glory family can bloom for months but may try to set seed, which stops the show. The vines are hard to deadhead; instead, give them a steady supply of fertilizer to keep new leaves and flowers coming. A balanced, soluble formula such as 20-20-20 works well for this task, as do organic formulas with analysis such as 5-1-1.

■ *Colorful, tropical calla lilies* (Zantedeschia) *are usually stored over the winter.*

BULBS

Calla lilies (*Zantedeschia*) come in two types and both will benefit from a bulb food or general purpose garden fertilizer this month. In general, you can sprinkle 1 tablespoon of fertilizer in a 6-inch pot or ¼ cup in a 5-gallon-sized pot. Work the fertilizer into the soil and water the calla lilies well.

1. Aethiopicas (*Z. aethiopica*) have evergreen leaves, white flowers, and grow from rhizomes that make bulblets along their sides. Except in the warmest areas with very well-drained soil, they are best grown in containers and easily make the transition to the indoor garden in winter.

2. Mini callas with colorful flowers have tubers, are not evergreen, and must be stored like caladiums over the winter.

EDIBLES

You can fertilize blueberries in early spring, but many gardeners skip it in cold, wet weather. A second opportunity for fertilization presents this month and should not be missed. After harvest, blueberry bushes put on new growth, which will be thicker and more robust if you use an acid-forming fertilizer. Formulas made for azaleas and camellias work well for blueberries, as do most organic fertilizers.

LAWNS

When an established lawn never quite takes off with good green growth, you may be tempted to pour on the fertilizer and water. This may or may not be a good idea. Do a soil test and fertilize or lime as directed by the results to return the lawn to active growth. The lack of fertilizer may be indicated by pale green color and poor growth, but if the pH is too far out of line, nutrients you apply may not become available. Adding more fertilizer without adjusting the pH (usually with lime) may be a costly and useless endeavor.

PERENNIALS & ORNAMENTAL GRASSES

You might think that many of our favorite fall perennials are low-maintenance native plants, and you'd be correct. However, when we bring ornamental grasses such as *Muhlenbergia*, perennial sunflowers, Joe-pye weed, and false aster into our gardens, some attention is merited. Especially during the first two seasons, a light application of a complete formula fertilizer helps to build their clump and produce garden-quality flowers.

■ *Blueberries grow best in acidic soil.*

ROSES

Rose bushes not on a regular fertilizer program may have smaller leaves and flowers now because they have used up the available nutrients. Put them on your schedule for a rose food or flower garden fertilizer right after summer pruning this month.

SHRUBS

Plants use nutrients for more than just leaves and flowering shrubs especially need fertilizer now to bloom this fall. Specialty formulas provide the elements for bright colors, strong cell walls, and long-lasting flowers. Use it now on long-blooming summer shrubs such as abelia, loropetalum, and gardenia.

TREES

If you have not yet fertilized conifer trees such as pine, cedars, and juniper this year, use a tree food or general purpose garden formula now. Product labels indicate how much to use based on the tree size. Use the fertilizer as directed because more is not better for this task.

VINES & GROUNDCOVERS

Some groundcover beds can look ratty even though they are adding new leaves at their centers. Depending on the size of the bed, use scissors, hedge shears, or a string trimmer to get rid of damaged leaves. Fertilize the beds now to promote new growth. Fall-blooming native passionflowers will benefit from a complete fertilizer now.

WATER GARDENS

Fertilize pond pots in the "nursery" this month, as well as more sophisticated pond gardens. Use aquatic, slow-dissolving formulas to avoid root burn in the containers. Fertilize mosses and reeds at pondside with the same aquatic plant formula to put its nitrogen on the plants and not in the water, where it can promote algae.

PROBLEM-SOLVE

ALL

Solarization is a process that focuses the sun's rays to destroy plant material. It can solve several problems for uncultivated areas in your garden. That areas might be the vegetable patch you don't intend to replant because weeds consumed it. Or perhaps you want to start a new bed or border where a mix of plants has been a mow-what-grows green carpet. Solarization has been shown to control weed plants and seeds to depths greater than 12 inches.

ANNUALS

Pots of annual flowers and tropical plants grown for their leaves can develop coppery areas on their leaves. Dark green leaves may look burnished, leaf tips can turn crispy, and variegated leaves turn their light parts brown, even if the plants never wilt. Like you, many plants can sunburn, and you have to be their sunscreen. To prevent this leaf disorder, move pots so they get afternoon shade, unless you are growing true sun lovers.

BULBS

If you find small holes in iris rhizomes, iris borers have found you. Bearded irises are most susceptible, but it is not uncommon to find them in older clumps of Siberians and others. These fascinating larvae attack rhizomes and tubers, are reportedly cannibalistic, and spin zip lines to reach the irises. Cut out the damaged parts and discard them; dust the rhizomes before replanting with vegetable garden dust that contains both sulfur to prevent rot and an insecticide. Keep old leaves and spent flowers picked up and limit mulch around irises.

Caladiums sometimes develop brown spots on their leaves that you might attribute to stress, but other factors may be at work:

- Soil pH higher than neutral (above 7.0) is seldom to blame in our native soils, but garden soils are seldom entirely native. Do a soil test and amend as directed to acidify the soil if needed.

- Low levels of calcium and potassium in the soil can be solved by using a complete fertilizer or a flower formula that also contains trace elements.

HERE'S HOW

TO SOLARIZE A GARDEN BED

- Define the area to be solarized—full sun exposure works best, and green stemmed weeds are more readily controlled than those with woody stems.

- Dig a shallow trench around the area if you do not want to impact the space adjacent to it.

- Measure a piece of thick, 6 mil clear plastic to fit the space plus 1 inch longer and wider than the area to be solarized.

- Lay the plastic directly onto the ground and secure it tightly. Bury it in the trench or cover the edge with bricks, soil, wood, or whatever you have that will hold tightly in place.

- Check on the project and keep the cover tight— if water gets in, remove it immediately.

- Look for yellowing in a month and dead weeds in eight to ten weeks of hot summer sun.

- Remove the plastic, rake out the dead plants, and make your new bed.

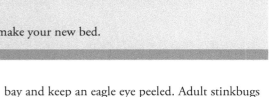

- Xanthomonas bacterial leaf spot disease is aggravated by wet leaves and poor air circulation around plants.

EDIBLES

Some insect pests, such as squash bugs, are named for the plant they eat, but stinkbugs carry no vegetable brand because they eat practically everything you do. They spend the early part of the year in clover, wheat, and seedling soybeans. By July, those crops have matured and stinkbug populations have built to levels that can do serious damage to tomatoes, butter beans, southern peas, and more, if left unchecked. Ruined peas and beans, tomatoes that won't ripen, and cow-horned okra (it curls from their sting), are just some evidence of their feeding. Few other problems require preventative sprays, but you can count on stinkbugs to find your summer garden. Use pyrethrin, permethrin, or Neem oil twice monthly in summer on susceptible crops to keep them at bay and keep an eagle eye peeled. Adult stinkbugs migrate in summer, so it is possible more can be on the way at any time.

Brown stinkbugs are more of a challenge than green stinkbugs (southern green stinkbugs). And yes, there are predatory stinkbugs that prey on the others. But they arrive in fewer numbers and cannot usually be depended upon to take care of this problem.

■ *Watch out for stinkbugs that can damage your entire garden.*

LAWNS

Dry patches can show up in zoysia and St. Augustine grasses, and you may think it's just hot weather. Sadly, it might be tiny chinch bugs sucking the life out of your lawn. To be sure, take the ends off of a metal can and sink it into the edge of the browned area with an inch above the ground. Fill it with water for 10 minutes and watch for bugs to float into view. The adults are black with white wings folded on their backs. Nymphs may be yellow, pink, or red with one white stripe.

PERENNIALS & ORNAMENTAL GRASSES

You plant hostas and if the deer don't eat them, the plants dry up in the heat before they can bloom. Deer repellants work, as long as you use them regularly. But hostas are a favorite browse for deer, and a serious fence may be the best choice for serious hosta growers. Where deer are not an issue, prepare a fertile, organic soil in the shade and choose hostas recommended for your zone. Remember that, in general, bluer hosta varieties will do better in the northern parts of our states than farther south.

Heat-tolerant August lily (*Hosta plantaginea*) brings two very important traits to the summer garden. This is the only fragrant hosta, and it can grow all the way to our coasts. The flowers rise on stems (called scapes) stiff enough to hold bold white bloom clusters that open late in the day and close in the morning. Luckily, the closed buds are quite attractive too.

ROSES

Rose buds look like they are about to open but don't and quickly develop fuzzy gray mold. Or they open, but some of the petals are browned when they unfurl. If it was earlier in the year, you'd suspect thrips, and they may be to blame. But the gray mold gets prolific on dying plant material; it does not cause the problem. Cut the damaged portions off the roses and get rid of the prunings. Spray the plants with a fungicide weekly until new leaves are fully open or the weather gets consistently dry and warm.

SHRUBS

Azalea lacebugs and spider mites are real problems but knotty galls that form on their stems are not problematic. In this case, pruning solves it.

Leaf galls on azaleas and camellias are unsightly. Remove them and do not compost or shred any material ruined by galls.

Carry a bucket or bag with you as you traverse the garden. When you pluck off a spent flower or clip a galled leaf and drop it on the ground, you set up a laboratory where pests can thrive. Practice good garden sanitation—pick up plant debris.

TREES

Watch out for webs in young trees that tell you webworms are in residence. These pests are not as dangerous to mature trees, but you should remove all you can reach. A truly high pressure water blast may be as effective as pesticide sprays, or you can go low tech—wrap cheesecloth around a broom and wrap the web around it, then pull it out of the tree.

VINES & GROUNDCOVERS

Carolina jasmine, trumpet vine, star jasmine, and wisteria can encroach on nearby plants and become beautiful nuisances. Keep after them by trimming errant vines if they cannot be twined around other parts of the plant or its supports.

Japanese honeysuckle and poison ivy can seem like they are under control only to sprout back suddenly this month. Spray the young leaves with herbicide while they are small and can readily absorb weed control products.

WATER GARDENS

An outbreak of snails can chew up water lily leaves and distract from the beauty of the flowers. Commercial products can control them, but to avoid disturbing the chemistry of the water garden, try this: Float a few lettuce leaves in the pond just before nightfall. The snails will gravitate to the lettuce—perhaps it tastes better that the lilies. Scoop both leaves and snails out the next day. Repeat as needed for several nights.

August

August seems to feel hotter as it wears on, yet plants sparkle this month, none more than the huge leaves of elephant ears, bananas, and rice paper plants, plus lotus and lily pads in water gardens. If you like colorful leaves and flower clusters as big as your head, bougainvilleas impress now as do yellow cestrum (C. aurantiacum), pink mandevilla (Dipladenia), and bright white, night blooming jasmine.

Container gardens rock the deck this month as plants such as blue butterfly (*Rotheca myricoides*), bleeding heart (*Clerodendrum thomsoniae*), fine lotus vine, and wildly painted sweet potato vines compete for attention. Pots of copperleaf, also called copper plant (*Acalypha wilkesiana*), and sanchezia (*S. speciosa*) fill the space behind huge pots of cherry tomatoes dripping with fruits. And every pot of peppers lights up with red, orange, yellow, and sometimes purple—just waiting to be picked and pickled. Smaller palms and bananas add more tropical flair to your patio, perfect companions and shade for a host of "houseplants" such as striped corn plant (*Dracaena fragrans*), colorful crotons (*Codiaeum*), and Chinese evergreens (*Aglaonema*).

The sharp heat you can feel is pleasant compared to the languid stickiness of building humidity that seems to hover right over you. Soon, the sky changes from sunny to cloud-soaked and gives way to blinding thunderstorms and sometimes, severe storms. When they end, the world looks and feels clean again and the slightest breeze cools you. Plants and people are tested in August, and both feel honor-bound to pass. There's plenty to do, especially if you are a vegetable gardener, and it's wise to split gardening time between early morning and late afternoon.

When you work outdoors, pace and good hydration are as important as knowing when dangerous heat is predicted so you can avoid it. Those are the days when we turn the traditional garden year on its head. We peruse seed catalogs and Internet sites now, not in January, in search of short-season vegetables and flower colors never seen before locally. Some days in August are made for lots of air conditioning, cool drinks, and time to plan next year's garden.

PLAN

ANNUALS

Make a plan to safely carry over your favorite summer annuals to next year. Some of these tropical natives will come back from their roots, others make great companions as houseplants, and another group is best propagated. For example, scarlet sage (*Salvia coccinea*) can become perennial but is also easily dug up and potted or propagated from cuttings.

Large coleus plants, however, do not make good indoor companions and freeze to their roots most winters but should be in your propagation plan. The best cuttings of coleus and many other green-stemmed plants come from pinching. This process uses your fingertips (or very small scissors) to clip out the tip of the stem and two to four sets of leaves. Each time you pinch at a point where leaves emerge from the stem, the growing points (the nodes) located there can be stimulated to sprout more leaves. One stem pinched becomes one stem that "breaks" and sends out two stems from that spot. This process gives you a cutting to root and produces a bushier plant in the garden.

■ *Sternbergia*

BULBS

Get serious about Holland bulb planning this year to light up your garden next spring with daffodils, hyacinths, grape hyacinths, crocus, and all the rest. Survey beds, borders, and pots to find space, locate gaps in current plantings, and use graph paper to diagram what's available. As a general guide, 1 square foot of space can be filled with:

- Two clumps of large daffodils or three small ones

- Four tulips and eight grape hyacinths

- Four hyacinths and six crocus

You would like more low-maintenance plants such as bulbs in the perennial border. Holland bulbs and local favorites for fall planting will be in garden centers soon, but you may have to order these old timey ones:

- Oxblood or schoolhouse lilies (*Rhodophiala bifida*) look like short, clustered amaryllis.

- Sternbergia (*S. lutea*) is called fall daffodil but looks like a yellow crocus.

- Siberian squilla (*Scilla siberica*), like Siberian iris, grows well here despite its name. With flowers bluer than the sky, the plants spread under trees.

EDIBLES

It's hot today, but soon you will want the vegetable season to go on and on. You can make that happen if you make plans now to add semi-permanent hoops to your raised beds. Visit the hardware or home store to look for supplies and make plans to get hoops ready.

LAWNS

Plan to do something about "mow-what-grows" lawns to improve their look and ability to cover the ground. Think about using a fall fertilizer formula and consider seeding fescue, carpet grass, or perennial ryegrass this fall.

You can get a head start on fall planting projects by doing the soil building this month. It seems too hot to transplant, but the sod you'll remove from the

HERE'S HOW

TO MAKE VEGETABLE BED HOOPS

1. Use ½-inch-diameter plastic pipe to make hoops.

2. Each one needs to be long enough to go up and over the bed to a height of 2 inches over the plants.

3. Measure from side to side of the bed, from the middle of the outside boards or to the ground if the bed has no sides and cut the pipes.

4. Pipe strapping can be attached to the bed sides to secure the hoops.

5. Ground-level pipes can slip over short pieces of rebar stuck into the ground beside the row or bed.

6. Use oversized clothespins covered in plastic to clip sheet plastic onto hoops.

Larger vegetable beds and large collections of pots can be protected in an unheated plastic house or hoophouse, as shown above. See notes about protecting tender plants outdoors in September, Care.

new bed site might work well in the backyard. You can hold sod squares—ones you cut out or any left over from patching projects—for up to eight weeks. Cut 1-foot squares with blades, thatch, and 2 inches of soil. Put them in open weave flats in the shade. Water well and add soluble fertilizer at half strength

weekly. Treat the sod as you would any other divided perennial plant—but remember that there are hundreds of individual plants in each square.

PERENNIALS & ORNAMENTAL GRASSES

Lush areas now can look barren later unless you plan for late fall and winter interest in the perennial border. Those that bloom in winter and early spring provide green leaves to brighten the bed after the rest have bloomed out or gone dormant. Consider these: sweet violet (*Viola odora*), bearsfoot hellebore (*Helleborus foetidus*), Lenten rose (*Helleborus orientalis*), candytuft (*Iberis sempervirens*), and sweet butternut (*Petasites fragrans*).

ROSES

Hybrid tea roses seldom perform at their best for more than a few years in our states for several reasons including heat, humidity, pest threats, and a fast growth rate. Note which roses rebloom best in your collection this fall and plan to replace the least successful with new releases next winter. Or go for old favorite hybrid teas that smell as sweet as they look: 'Radiant Perfume' (yellow), 'Double Delight' (bicolor red/yellow), 'Mr. Lincoln' (red), 'JFK' (white).

SHRUBS

If you don't seem to have your fair share of birds in the garden, plan to make it more accommodating to them. Determine how to provide water and places for birds to rest, nest, and eat, such as allowing some existing shrubs to become safe, dense thickets. Check out native berried shrubs for food sources such as arrowwood (*Viburnum dentatum*), beautyberry (*Callicarpa americana*), and chokecherry (*Aronia arbutifolia*).

TREES

Hanging branches called snags can be left as elements in wildlife garden habitats unless they can fall and injure people and plants below. Make the most of what can be an expensive job. Survey snags, squirrels' nests, big balls of mistletoe, and other elevated hazards to make a plan for their removal in one operation.

VINES & GROUNDCOVERS

Groundcover junipers get overlooked, yet their creeping habit adds color, texture, and living

■ *Supply water to attract birds to your garden.*

mulch. Plan for one of these to tame a slope or to reinforce the larger junipers elsewhere in the garden.

- Creeping juniper (*Juniperus horizontalis* cultivars)

- Dwarf juniper (*J. procumbens* 'Nana')

- Sargent juniper (*J. chinensis* 'Sargentii')

- Shore juniper (*J. conferta* cultivars)

Annual vines are fine for summer shade on fences but have to be planted each year. If you already have Carolina jessamine and chocolate vine, consider another perennial vine instead. Pick out a favorite or propagate one now so you will be ready when the annual vine plays out.

- In Zones 7 and 8, the native Dutchman's pipe (*Aristolochia durior*) twines rapidly to a bold,

■ *Trumpet creeper,* Campsis Radicans *'Minnesota Red'*

lush display of green heart-shaped leaves. Flowers are quaint, small, and have an unusual but not unpleasant aroma.

- In Zone 9, coral vine (*Antigonum leptopus*) has similar leaves to Dutchman's pipe but puts out bunches, called racemes, of bright pink flowers in summer. Root hardy in Zone 8, coral vine will come back if its top freezes.

- Cross vine (*Bignonia capreolata*) blooms with orange-red flared flower trumpets in spring, earliest in Zone 9 and a few weeks later as you go north. This Southeast native vine climbs rapidly to find the sun and attracts hummingbirds.

- Another beautiful native vine, trumpet creeper (*Campsis radicans*) is not a good choice to grow on painted structures. Its aerial roots stick with a strong adhesive that will ruin them. Elsewhere in the garden, it blooms all summer and attracts hummingbirds with loud flower trumpets.

WATER GARDENS

A new pond doesn't happen overnight. Look at magazines and visit other water features but plan to make it your own with a truly personal centerpiece fountain. Take time to think about, and budget for, a piece you will really want to look at every day. A three-tiered, curvy concrete fountain with a pineapple at the top sends a decidedly formal message. Another fountain with three rectangular concrete tiers that directs water off its edges is more contemporary. Freeform metal and wood sculptural fountains evoke different passions.

PLANT

ANNUALS

Shop early for fall garden mums and plant them right away because smaller plants with closed buds suffer less transplant shock than larger mums in bloom. Space the plants with an inch between their most outstretched leaves because the buds are set. Additional growth will be minimal and close planting works to quickly color up beds and containers. Put a

■ *Plant herbs in pots so they are easily accessible when you're ready to use them.*

teaspoon of flower garden fertilizer in the planting hole, cover it with a little soil, and plant on top. Water new mums in with a starter solution, add mulch, and water often enough to prevent wilt.

BULBS

Keep planting tubers of classic cemetery iris, crinum bulbs, and plants such as Powell's white and oxblood lilies.

EDIBLES

Herbs can be hard to get to while you are cooking and they're out in the garden. Besides, in wet weather their taste seems bland. You can put in a kitchen garden or plant herb bowls to grow close by the back door. Get pots wider than they are deep or shaped like salad bowls to gain control of the growing conditions and always have tasty herbs at hand. Group them by their habits:

- Thyme, sage, and oregano are perennial herbs that grow best in the dryer soil and make excellent companions in clay pots.

- Chives are reseeding bullies, but miniature basil will crowd them nicely in the warm months. Once the basil is done for the season, replace it with parsley to grow over winter. Grow in plastic to keep the soil warm and moist.

- Rosemary is usually too large to grow as a companion, but creeping rosemary will fall out of a pot nicely and tastes great. You won't have long canes to turn into skewers but clip creeping rosemary and add it to holiday wreaths for color, texture, and a bright, clean smell.

You can plant beets all this month at weekly intervals to stagger the harvest. If you want only one round, sow beet seeds immediately in north Mississippi and Alabama, by August 15 in north Louisiana, central Mississippi and Alabama, and by the end of the month farther south.

Finish planting by mid-month:

- Bush snap and pole beans

- Summer squashes

- Lima bush and pole beans

- Cucumber

- Tomato

- Pepper

- Eggplant

Transplant from August 1 to August 15. Temporary shade and a sprinkler shower can be keys to a successful fall garden and are usually not needed for more than a week. The shade may be no more than a short, leafy branch stuck in the row or pot between the tender seedling and the afternoon sun. Set up an arc sprinkler on a timer to gently rain on the seedlings at late morning.

- Broccoli

- Cabbage

- Oriental cabbage

- Cauliflower

- Brussels sprouts

- Kohlrabi

- Pak choi

- Bok choy

- Parsley

- Irish potatoes (from seed potatoes). If you must cut potatoes, cut big pieces with at least one eye. Lay them out for four days to heal over (callus) to prevent rot in warm soil.

Start planting August 15 from seeds:

- Kale

- Collards

- Lettuce

- Turnips

- Mustard

LAWNS
This month the neighbors notice who has centipede grass because that homeowner isn't outside mowing as often. This difference from other warm season grasses is like that between malts and shakes—if it matters to you, it matters. Centipede grass grows more slowly and inches its way over the soil by sending out short runners that arch like the namesake, as they grow. Other distinguishing characteristics include:

- Slower growth, slower recovery from stressors

- Different nutrient needs call for specialty formula fertilizers; organic fertilizer works, and may increase seed head formation

- Slightly lighter green color than zoysia or St. Augustine grass

- Less need for water than St. Augustine grass but more than bermudagrass

- The availability of sod and seed. Sod now through next month but seed only repair jobs now. New lawns grown from seed take three years to really establish and are best begun in June.

PERENNIALS & ORNAMENTAL GRASSES
Pot divisions that you make now and those you get as gifts and hold them in shade until good transplant conditions present. Wait for a cloudy day with temperatures below 85 degrees Fahrenheit, even if it's a month away. Mix good garden soil with ground bark to hold new divisions, water them with a root starter, and transplant with their soil mix. Or heal them into the leaf pile as a temporary holding bed.

ROSES
Take advantage of late summer's green canes to layer to propagate vigorous climbing roses such as 'Peggy Martin' and 'Mermaid'.

SHRUBS, TREES, AND VINES & GROUNDCOVERS

Woody plants crowded in their containers are better off in the ground than in their pots. Take advantage of late summer sales in these categories and plant with caution:

- Prune top growth by one-third before planting.

- Trim off crowded roots and cut through thick roots to encourage more growth.

- Use starter solution—root-stimulator fertilizer, compost tea, or liquid rooting hormone.

- Build a low dam of soil and mulch around the base to hold water; do not let new plantings dry out.

WATER GARDENS

Louisiana iris will put on new growth beginning next month; divide and replant clumps now at the edge of your water feature. Louisiana and flag iris are more versatile than their relatives. Both can grow in water, on the margins where they prevent bank erosion, and in garden beds that are watered regularly.

■ *Louisiana iris*

ANNUALS

Annual plantings may not be all the same plant, but there should be consistency in the quality of their colors, flowers, and growth. This month can reveal inconsistencies in planting depth. Unlike some other plant categories, annuals grow at ground level, and if their center sinks or sticks up, the stress will show this month. Fill in around the high growers with mulch and use it to lift the sinkers if possible. Use a planting fork to reach under the crown and raise it slightly as you press soil and mulch into the space created.

The most important task can be a hot bother, but well worth the sweat. Lots of annual flowers can keep on blooming if you stay ahead of deadheading this month. Keep the bucket handy and drop old flowers in as you move through the plants. Grooming also includes plucking off yellowed leaves and noting needs for more mulch, water, or fertilizer.

Trailing flowers like petunia, million bells, annual verbena, and many others drop leaves, try to set seed, or stop flowering this month. You can rejuvenate them with clippers or shears or even scissors. Leggy baskets lose energy trying to support that dying growth, so cut it off and promote rejuvenated growth and flowers with a constant-feed strategy. Water often enough to keep the soil just moist and add soluble fertilizer each time for three weeks to rejuvenate the baskets.

BULBS

Cut out and remove spent flower stalks from crinum, iris, perennial gladiolas, and other summer-flowering bulbs unless you want seeds to start more plants for the garden or backyard plant breeding. Seed heads can also be attractive dried in arrangements, but allowing them to develop will take nutrients and energy away from the clump. Remove flower stalks from reblooming daylilies to encourage more growth.

EDIBLES

Spinach (*Spinacia oleracea*) can be a challenge to grow in our states and the fall garden offers our

■ *Prepare soil now to plant spinach in the fall for the best results*

best opportunity. When it fails to grow in the fall, it is often because the soil is too acidic (low pH). Test the soil's pH, but if you have not limed the spinach bed, do so now. Some organic gardeners also prepare a weekly drench of crushed eggshells that they say benefits the spinach:

- Collect a dozen eggshells. Rinse each one and put them in a bowl in the refrigerator as you accumulate them.

- Crush the eggshells in the bottom of the bowl and pour in 2 to 3 cups of very warm water.

- Steep the mixture overnight on the kitchen counter and strain it into a watering can.

- This mix will drench about 6 feet of a single width row or 3 square feet of a spinach bed.

Temporary shade and timed watering will be your best friends this month as you transplant the cole crops—broccolis first, then Napa and classic cabbages followed by kohlrabi, cauliflower, and Brussels sprouts.

Take a good look at citrus trees now to see signs of nutrient deficiency. If leaves are green but oddly

mottled, the tree either needs nitrogen or cannot access what is available. Overwatering and under-fertilizing can produce the unusual patterns simply because the container is too small for the growth rate of the tree. You water almost daily because the soil dries out, but that necessity leaches the nitrogen fertilizer out of the pot before the plant can access it. Repot to a larger container or root prune and repot the citrus tree if it is not in fruit now. Create a heartier potting mix by adding compost or another organic matter to a good quality product and add an inch of mulch to the top of the pot. Use a citrus fertilizer four times annually for container-grown plants.

ROSES
When you want thicker growth to create a low hedge of shrub roses or to fill the center spot in a rose garden, prune the roses harder now than if you only wanted more flowers. Fertilize at full strength now and again next month (except in Zone 7) and water well weekly.

PERENNIALS & ORNAMENTAL GRASSES
Two constant stars in our perennial plant constellation are essentially big hollow stems with spectacular flowers—angel trumpet (*Brugmansia*) and confederate rose, also called cotton rose (*Hibiscus mutabilis*). Both need plenty of hot sun and soil to grow well, so they are best left unmulched until June, and unlike other perennials, neither can be divided readily. By now their long trumpets and puffy powder puff flowers are in full bloom. After the flowers are finally done this year and the leaves drop, it'll be time to cut the canes to propagate them. Tell your friend who wants a start of these plants to wait for a while and get ready to:

- Cut down the canes (before they freeze).

- Put pieces of cane 2 feet long into an old vase with 6 inches of water in the bottom.

- Keep the water level constant, don't let the canes freeze, and be ready to pot or plant them early next year.

■ *Butterfly bush*

SHRUBS

Call it a shrub or a perennial, butterfly bush (*Buddleia davidii*) brings fountains of fragrant flower clusters to the summer garden and attracts butterflies like no other plant. Cuttings taken now will root in time to set out in late fall or early spring. Select tip cuttings from stems not now in bloom. Remove the leaves from the lower half of the stem; roll the cut end in rooting hormone powder, and stick into a small pot of clean rooting mix. Keep the pots damp and in the shade outdoors.

TREES

Water the ground well if it is dry and then lift seedlings around old-fashioned, single-flowered rose of Sharon trees (*Hibiscus syriacus*). Transplant directly to other garden sites if you can see to their water needs easily or pot them up if you cannot. Hybrid altheas (and most other hybrid plants) do not make seed with the same characteristics as the parent. Propagate them as you would the butterfly bush.

VINES & GROUNDCOVERS

Native passionflower vines prove that every rule has important exceptions. Deadheading is almost always a good idea, but not if you want maypops. The vines may be devoured by the larvae of gulf fritillary, but soon return. Leave the flowers on to set the soft, plum-sized fruits that may—or may not—pop when they fall to the ground to be devoured by backyard wildlife.

WATER GARDENS

Groom plants in and around both large and small water features to reduce leaf drop and prevent algae buildup. Propagate tropical plants to reduce overcrowding and begin preparing for the transition to fall.

When the ground is wet around a water feature when it shouldn't be, suspect a leaky liner. Find and fix holes and tears in pond liners right away or the situation may get worse.

HERE'S HOW

TO REPAIR A LINER

1. Remove plants and fish with enough water to sustain them in large plastic tubs.

2. Let the pond drain on its own until it levels off. In large water features, this can take days. Gauge its daily loss with a yardstick.

3. When draining stops, use a sponge to clean off the liner as you work your way around it to find little holes and slits. Don't stop until you have checked everywhere between the current level of the water and several inches above it. Mark the leaks with a wax pencil so you don't lose track of them.

4. Pump out 6 more inches of water so the patches you are about to make can stay dry.

5. Get a pond liner patch kit and use as directed to seal the leaks. Do not shortcut drying time!

6. Refill the pond and observe it for a few days. If leaking returns, repeat the process. If it does not, return the fish and plants to their home.

WATER

ALL

Our states are not among the most drought-prone and water restrictions are few. Still, an honest desire to conserve plus high water bills in dry summers can motivate you to garden with plants that thrive in drier sites. That sunny, hot bed might be better planted with xeriscape plants:

- Annuals—blanket flower, purslane, and Alabama sunset (*Coleus alabamensis*)

- Perennials—threadleaf coreopsis (*C. verticillata*), gaura (*G. lindheimeri*), candytuft

- Shrubs—dwarf yaupon (*Ilex vomitoria*), butcher's broom (*Ruscus aculeatus*), chokecherry (*Aronia arbutifolia*)

How much you will water this month depends on your plants and local weather conditions.

ANNUALS

Hot days and nights can stress annuals in pots. Small pots of any sort dry out quickly, black pots can heat up the soil and root zone, and clay pots dry out rapidly. Water small containers well each morning as needed and move pots out of direct sun if their plants wilt even with your good care. If you have removed saucers from under containers, replace them now to allow the plants to absorb water slowly from the bottom.

BULBS

Soak beds of spider lily, winter aconite (*Eranthis hyemalis*), and other fall-flowering bulbs, especially if this is their first year in your garden. If conditions have been very dry since June, water all bulb beds.

EDIBLES

For best flavor, harvest herbs in late morning when oils are most concentrated in the leaves. Water after harvesting. Step up irrigation of vegetables and fall-ripening fruits to compensate for water loss through leaves because of increased evaporation in hot weather.

LAWNS

If your lawn feels crunchy under your footstep or if you leave visible footprints behind as you walk across the lawn, it really needs a thorough soaking. If you are applying any products to the lawn this month, check the label for directions about timing of irrigation for best effect.

PERENNIALS & ORNAMENTAL GRASSES

Water plants in this category as needed to maintain good green color and flowering. Spray underneath lantana, verbena, and other large perennials that are persistently troubled by spider mites. The mites prefer the hot, dry conditions on the undersides of leaves and sometimes a weekly shower will deter them.

An oscillating sprinkler is a good choice for both small and large lawns because you can control the coverage efficiently by varying the water pressure.

Resist the temptation to soak established beds of native perennials such as purple coneflower (*Echinacea*) and gloriosa daisy (*Rudbeckia hirta*). Prolonged drought is not good, but no more than routine watering is ever necessary.

ROSES

Continue soaking weekly to promote fall flowering and water those that will not rebloom too. Set up the overhead sprinkler, if needed, to rinse leaves.

SHRUBS

You can slow down shrubs that grow faster than expected—cleyera (*C. japonica*) for example—by restricting the water they receive in summer to just under an inch a week. That is the average amount needed to grow most garden plants and we meet or exceed it in all but the hottest months. Yes, you are stunting their growth but only slightly to limit their ability to send out wild proliferations of new growth that must be pruned off later.

TREES

August can be the time when reservoir bags really help to sustain young trees that cannot be watered easily, or at all. It is also the time when adequate irrigation can determine whether crepe myrtles continue to bloom or slow down and develop seed pods for the year.

VINES & GROUNDCOVERS

Fall blooming clematis varieties and other flowering vines may not bloom without water this month. Likewise, berried plants like coral ardisia that grow in dry shade will benefit from irrigation this month if not at other times to ripen their berries.

WATER GARDENS

Consider draining and replacing some water in small water gardens if rainfall is below average. This will help replenish oxygen levels beyond what small volume pumps can do. Change the water in pond pots for the same reason.

FERTILIZE

ALL

Never fertilize a dry plant—water several hours before applying any fertilizer, conventional or organic. Even if the fertilizer does not burn the dry plant, it will not be absorbed.

ANNUALS

It is time again to use a three-month slow-release fertilizer as "insurance" in beds and pots. Whether you have done this before or not, it is a good idea to do it this month. The need for added fertilizer increases with heat and increased watering, and the slow-release product insures a baseline amount will be available even if you forget.

BULB

Use a granular garden flower fertilizer in beds of spider lilies (*Lycoris*). Go lightly on those with red flowers but provide yellow spider lilies with a full dose. Sprinkle a small amount around clumps of August lilies (*L. squamigera*), also known as surprise lilies or naked ladies.

The very tall white lilies that look like Easter lilies on stilts bloom this month. The 6 footers are Formosa lilies (*Lilium formosanum*), while those that only reach 3 feet tall are Philippine lilies (*L. philippinense*). They are elegant and prolific—each mother bulb produces two or more baby bulbs each year. Dig them up after blooming in the fall and fertilize when you replant.

EDIBLES

If it's an annual vegetable, fertilize it this month. Root feed young fruit trees and older trees that did not produce this season. Do not fertilize figs, pomegranates, and others with fruit on them now.

LAWNS

Fall feeding season begins this month and extends through next month. Little or no nitrogen will be in the formulas made for use at this time of year. Reasons to fertilize now with these specialty formulas include:

- To complete a fertilizer and weed control program that calls for fall application

- To promote healthy root growth in lawns more than 10 years old

- To ensure adequate nutrition is available to new sod installations

PERENNIALS & ORNAMENTAL GRASSES

Keep new roots coming without pushing top growth. Mix a root stimulator or compost tea and use it this month on newly planted—or transplanted—perennials and grasses.

ROSES

Fertilize roses this month to promote fall flowering. Use a formula made for roses or flowering shrubs. But do not fertilize roses that bloom only once in the spring such as 'Lady Banksia', 'Alchymist', and 'Fortuniana'.

SHRUBS AND TREES

Assess the shrubs and trees on your property to see if they are at their prime this month, as most should be. Good color and active growth without droop, sag, or wilt are hallmarks of good health in woody plants. If yours are lacking, root feed them this month with a formula containing no nitrogen such as 0-10-10.

Fertilize camellias—both the early-flowering sasanquas and japonicas with bigger leaves and flowers. Use a granular formula made for flowering trees or one made for azaleas and camellias to promote flowering during the fall and winter.

VINES & GROUNDCOVERS

Fertilize plants such as coral honeysuckle that grow on through the fall to bloom in winter. Use a complete granular formula like 10-10-10.

WATER GARDENS

Fertilize the "baby" plants you are growing outside the water feature in pond pots. Use the same fertilizer as you did for the plants inside the water garden.

PROBLEM-SOLVE

EDIBLES

Every season has predictable pests, and aphids will find fall squash unless you deter them. Plant squash around the garden so if one is attacked, others may escape detection by the fall aphid flight. If you use plastic mulch, spray it with silver spray paint to create a reflective surface that often dissuades insects.

LAWNS

Two lawn care tasks take precedence this month, in addition to the routines of mowing and watering. Use a selective product to spray for clumps of

■ *A walk-behind drop spreader is a good way to spread fertilizer on your lawn.*

perennial weeds in the lawn. Be sure the product is labeled for your type of turf; read and follow the label directions to learn about mixing and safely using any chemical spray. The second task is to follow up with your pre-emergent weed program to control those weeds that will sprout from seeds this fall.

PERENNIALS & ORNAMENTAL GRASSES

Those steppingstones are functional, but the lawn never did grow around them, and each time it rains, the situation gets worse. Spice up the texture in that area and add contrast with durable, low-growing perennials such as creeping speedwell (*Veronica repens*) or golden creeping speedwell (*V. repens* 'Sunshine').

Spider mites are nearly invisible, but the damage they do as they feed on your plants often shows up

HERE'S HOW

TO IDENTIFY SPIDER MITES

Before you spray anything, confirm that you have spider mites with this test:

1. Get a sheet of white paper and hold it under the branch that you suspect has spider mites.

2. Thump the branch and let the dust fall onto the paper.

3. Hold the paper still, and if the "dust" moves, you have located the spider mites.

■ *Spider mite*

in August. That's when lantana and other susceptible perennials slow down or stop blooming and develop a stippling or a burnished look to their leaves. Cut back and destroy affected plant parts now and spray the plants with a product containing Neem now and again when new leaves appear. These hardy perennials will rebound quickly and often bloom again before Thanksgiving.

ROSES

Watch for piercing and sucking insects (aphids, whiteflies, mealybugs) that will try to feast on new growth and rosebuds this month. In northern areas, keep an eye out for shiny metallic green Japanese beetles. Stomp and squish them or pluck off and drop them into a jar of bleach if you prefer.

As leaves emerge on susceptible varieties, spray with a fungicide spray to slow down the black spot fungus that may show up this fall if you do not deter it.

SHRUBS

When the center of juniper shrubs turn brown and die out in late summer, you may suspect mites are to blame. But the problem might also be twig blight, particularly if the branch tips stay green. Clean up the fallen needles and prune out serious damage. Use fungicide sprays in cool, wet springs to prevent this disease.

TREES

Veteran gardeners are familiar with the leaf spots that appear on woody shrubs and trees in the red top group (*Photinia* x *fraseri* and to a lesser extent *P. glabra*). The predictability of the disease has reduced red top's popularity because sprays are difficult to do and each time new growth emerges, more spots appear. If you can prune the spotted leaves off, the disease arrests for a time but returns when more of the prized bright red new growth emerges. It's a vicious circle; many other trees and shrubs can develop leaf spots but seldom with such dire results.

September

Few of us can imagine living in a landlocked state, especially in September, historically the month that brings us the most hurricanes. Our coasts have been ravaged too many times, and sometimes the damage reaches far inland, bringing unspeakable destruction. Yet we persevere, rebuild, and replant because that is our Tao, our way.

The water we live with may be salty, brackish, or fresh from rivers and rain clouds. It is our personal lifeline in many ways, as it is in the garden, and this month, there can be too much or too little rainfall—September is seldom moderate. Some years it seems you cannot water enough, but candelabra plants, perennial sunflowers, banana plants, and variegated shell ginger (*Alpinia zerumbet* 'Variegata') go right on and bloom anyway. We like hot, dry Septembers better than the stormy alternative and go fishing for bass in the shade of lily pads at Barnett Reservoir in Mississippi, seining for shrimp off the Louisiana coast, and take the charter to fish at night for swordfish out of Orange Beach, Alabama.

Wahoo is plentiful, but not just the tasty Gulf fish harvested now. The precious native shrub strawberry bush (*Euonymus americana*) is also called "hearts a' bustin" and "wahoo." Its bright red pods crack open this month, like bursting hearts, and wahoo—shiny red seeds—are revealed, and it looks like a strawberry. Red spider lilies (*Lycoris radiata*) are truly one of our states' best September features. Even if you never pick a flower, it's impossible to resist when stunning spiders pop up on leafless stems this month. The whirligigs look ethereal, like garden tiaras ready for a ball, and it is the most durable bulb. Many were planted decades ago and propagated themselves, blooming when available water allows them to do so.

The notion of fall color is usually more subtle in our states because there is still so much green in every view. However, every shade comes through—from the near-white of boneset (*Eupatorium perfoliatum*) to the russet of oakleaf hydrangea (*H. quercifolia*). In the Deep South, September also means sports and the green fields where we play. It's family and football for some, soccer and hunting camp for others. Turf gets almost as much discussion as wildlife plots, and we cultivate both.

PLAN

ANNUALS

Plan to plant overwintering annuals next month, beginning with the pansy family:

- Viola (*Viola cornuta*) compact mounds of 1-inch flowers, pastel and solid colors, and some with faces

- Pansy (*V.* x *wittrockiana*) larger plants and flowers to 3 inches, most with faces, bolder colors and mixes, and most show good thunderstorm resilience

- Panola (*V.* x *wittrockiana* et al.) bred for the best qualities of all the family members, panola has the colors, faces, neat clumps, plus improved hardiness and a longer bloom season

- Johnny jump-up (*V. tricolor*) loose mounds with dime-to-penny sized flowers in solid, faced, and mixed colors

Remember to plan for pansies under deciduous trees. As leaves drop, the winter sun bathes the pansies and offers shade as they leaf out in spring. This can help to prolong the blooms.

BULBS

It's fine to pick a bulb's color on a whim, but where and how many to plant takes planning. Think about these factors and make a planting plan.

- Groups of bulbs are more powerful than straight lines. Odd numbers are more pleasing than even numbers when planning a group.

- Tulips can pop up among pansies, but daffodils and snowdrops deserve a permanent place among perennial plants.

- Give each bulb the space it needs as measured from the center of one to the center of the nearest one:

» Giant allium, standard daffodils, snowdrops	12 inches
» Tulips	6 inches
» Hyacinths, Dutch iris	4 inches
» Anemone, ranunculus	2 inches

EDIBLES

Plants of both curly and flat leaf parsley (*Petroselinum*) grow best as overwintering annuals in our states, harvested in spring before they bolt. You may be devoted to one or the other, or grow both for their different qualities. Plan to get the right parsley for your taste:

- Curly or curled parsley has sharper taste when grown well, but it is more easily overwatered and can lose its flavor quickly in hot weather.

- Flat or plain leaf parsley tastes robust unless it is starved for fertilizer or water. In general, it is easier for most people to grow, and its leaves certainly are easier to clean.

LAWNS

When you will be planting a new lawn, consider the best turf grass for your conditions:

- Broiling, blazing sun and lots of children playing—bermudagrass takes the traffic but needs frequent mowing.

- Full sun and foot traffic—zoysia produces a lush, dark green lawn.

- Lots of sun, some shade in afternoon, average foot traffic—cheery, lighter green centipede grows more slowly, needs less mowing.

- Sun with high shade—St. Augustine grass in Zones 8b and 9; fescue in 8a and 7.

PERENNIALS & ORNAMENTAL GRASSES

Take notepad in hand (traditional or electronic) and list the perennials in each planting. Note what bloomed sooner or later than you expected this year, what colors boomed and which bombed— do this now, so you can wisely fill in any gaps with new plants this fall.

ROSES

Admire the fall flower show and plan for reblooming (remontant) roses such as these:

- Classic hybrid teas: 'Mrs. Pierre S. DuPont', 'Emily', 'Aloha', 'Chrysler Imperial'

- Antiques:
  » China: 'Louis Phillippe', 'Archduke Charles', 'Martha Gonzales'
  » Noisette: 'Lamarque', 'Fellenberg', 'Natchitoches Noisette'

- Climbers: 'Crepuscule', 'Cecile Brunner', 'Don Juan'

- 'Knockout' shrub roses in red, pink, and yellow

SHRUBS AND TREES

Few things in life are as inevitable as leaves falling in autumn. Plan now to put them to the best use for your garden. Nobody needs to bag leaves up for the landfill. Options to consider include:

- Make weekly raking part of your exercise routine. Pick a spot and create a leaf pile in the back of the garden or add them to the layers in a future no-till garden. Or:

- Let the leaves drop for a month. Use rakes, blowers, and children to get them all into the designated space.

- If you have a mulching mower, use it to chop up leaves that fall on the lawn so they can drop into the turf, decompose slowly, and give up their nutrients to the grass. This doesn't work well if they are very large like

sycamore or if the leaf cover is more than an inch deep.

- Run any mower over piles of large leaves to chop them into smaller pieces that compost faster.

TREES

Even veteran gardeners in our states can be fooled by the weather extremes. You can solve this problem by planting one of two trees, depending on where you live, because they do not leaf out until the last chance of frost has passed—black gum (*Nyssa sylvatica*) in the north and pecan (*Carya illinoensis*) in the south. Both have reputations for rugged beauty and because they have been prized for their "wisdom" for so long, they bring a strong sense of place wherever they are grown.

VINES & GROUNDCOVERS

Perhaps the best redo of a ranch-style house takes planning, but the result can be positively transformative. See this in your mind, dream a little, and plan to consult an architect: A long, wide pergola stretches from the driveway to the front door over the space that used to be the foundation planting. From each end grows a star jasmine, muscadine grape, or your favorite running rose and underneath are groundcovers and bulbs.

WATER GARDENS

Plan to expand your collection of hardy water lilies by adding colors:

- Red: 'Gloriosa', 'Aflame'
- Pink: 'Yuh Ling', 'Shady Lady'
- White: 'Perry's Double', 'Denver'
- Yellow: 'Texas Dawn', 'Yellow Queen'
- Color Changers: 'Pink Grapefruit', 'Georgia Peach'

PLANT

ANNUALS

Sow seed of cornflower, also called bachelor's button (*Centaurea cyanus*) and pot marigold (*Calendula officinalis*) directly in the garden or in pots outside.

Even the best seedbed can dry out this month, but mulch isn't the answer because its pieces present obstacles to emerging seedlings. Water gently to soak the seed bed and cover it with a board to hold moisture in. Check daily and remove the board when the seedlings sprout. Put floating row covers over the seedlings to protect the tender new growth if dry weather persists.

BULBS

Garlic is a true bulb that is edible and its close relatives in the *Allium* family are grown for exquisitely beautiful flowers too. Most often found in displays of Holland bulbs, flowering alliums like 'Globemaster' and 'Ambassador' can be planted as soon as they are available or until October.

HERE'S HOW

TO SOW SEEDS OUTSIDE

1. Use a trowel to dig a row in the garden soil outside. Dig the row about 1 to 2 inches deep.

2. Sprinkle the seeds in the row according to spacing instructions on the seed package. Some seed packets will advise you to sow the seeds "thickly." That means to sprinkle a lot of seeds in one area because the seeds don't sprout consistently. You can always snip off seedlings at the soil line to make room if more seeds than you need sprout and grow too close together.

3. Sprinkle seed starting mix over the seeds. While you can cover seeds outdoors with regular garden soil, seeds sprout more easily when they're covered with the lightweight seed starting mix. After covering the seeds, water them. Do not let the soil dry out until you see the seeds starting to sprout. If the seeds dry out while they're sprouting, they'll die.

4. Label the rows where you've planted seeds. Seed leaves can look similar to one another when they're sprouting, and you don't want to forget what you planted, where.

■ *Replant bearded irises with about 6 inches of leaf and 3 inches of rhizome sticking out of the ground.*

EDIBLES

Varieties listed here and elsewhere in this book are suggestions and should not limit you. Grow what you want!

Plant from seed this month:

- Carrots: 'Chantenay', 'Scarlet Nantes', 'Thumbelina'

- Radish: 'Scarlet Globe', 'White Icicle'

- Daikon radish: 'Summer Cross #3' (spicy), 'Alpine' (sweet)

- Swiss chard: 'Bright Lights', 'Rhubarb Giant', 'Fordhook Giant'

- Spinach: 'Bloomsdale Long Standing', 'Melody', 'Tyee'

- Leek: 'Titan', 'Dawn Giant', 'Blue Solaise'

Start planting this month:

- Parsley plants—both curled and flat leaf varieties

- Lettuce plants—including individual leaf lettuces and mesclun mixes

- Green onions from sets or dried bulbs of evergreen bunching onions

- Shallots from dried bulbs

Finish planting seeds by mid-month:

- Turnips: 'Purple Top', 'Shogoin', 'Red Round', 'Golden Globe'

- Mustard: 'Tendergreen', 'Florida Broadleaf'

- Collard: 'Georgia Southern', 'Champion'

- Kale: 'Dwarf Scotch', 'Vates', 'Toscano'

LAWNS

If you live where it is too cold for too long to successfully grow St. Augustine grass, explore tall fescue as a permanent lawn in sites with afternoon shade. Seed fescue and improved bermudagrass now and next month.

The reason most seeded lawns are topped with hay or wheat straw is right over your head. The hay helps to keep seed and soil from washing away in a thunderstorm and acts as camouflage for birds interested in eating your future lawn for lunch.

PERENNIALS & ORNAMENTAL GRASSES

Iris and daylilies are "bulbs" that also have clumps and so are considered equally as perennials. Plant separations you made earlier in the summer and potted up, as well as those you received from a friend's garden. Replant on a good day—one with cloudy skies, little wind, and rain in the forecast.

When you look at a new planting of iris or daylilies, the leaves of each clump are often cut into fan shapes. Each leaf is shortened to about 6 inches long, as you should do even if it means removing most of the height. The fans are easier to handle for transplant and do not dry out as quickly.

ROSES

Don't shy away from roses blooming this month in pots at garden centers—give them big containers to grow in for months or years ahead.

SHRUBS

When you're trying to sell a house before Christmas or have relatives coming to visit for the holidays, plant shrubs now. Choose shrubs for dramatic fall color or durable evergreen good looks, and add corresponding dwarf varieties to big pots by the door to unify the scene. Nobody needs to know you just planted them and nobody will, if you give the shrubs extra tender loving care to bolster them against heat stress. In this case, TLC means regular water twice weekly this month, 1 to 2 inches of mulch in beds and pots, and no fertilizer except starter solutions to promote rooting.

TREES

Grafting and budding are really propagation methods, but you can plant the rootstock now to get the process started. Dogwood may have pink-flowering wood grafted among branches that bloom white. Mulberry, Japanese maple, crabapple, and cherry are often grafted to achieve a weeping form atop a small tree. Citrus and some fruit trees are grafted onto hardy rootstocks so they can be grown outside their native ranges. When shopping for trees to plant for future grafting, use these tips:

- Choose a well-branched dogwood, even one with too many branches—for now. You'll select the strongest branches this winter with an eye toward grafting onto some of them. This project is limited only by familial plant relationships and your imagination. For example, you might want two colors of crepe myrtle or three different figs on one tree.

- Most weeping forms of a species are a selection discovered fortuitously and are not as root hardy as their standard counterparts. Choose a two- to four-year-old tree with a very straight, 4-foot to 6-foot trunk that has begun to thicken with few or no side branches. The canopy will eventually be replaced by the weeping form, and you want a straight base for the tree you will graft.

VINES & GROUNDCOVERS

Not every groundcover plant responds well to dividing and replanting now, but a bulletproof few can take it easily. Tall and thick in dry shade, cast iron plant thrives where others cannot survive. Use hedge shears to slice off the top half off of the leaves and then dig out groups of the plant with at least 3 inches of roots. Replant in shallow soil and cover the base of the plants with leaf mold and mulch. Keep watered for a month and then relax. Cast iron plant practically takes care of itself.

WATER GARDENS

It can be difficult to find pots made for growing plants in water gardens, but you can make alternatives from mesh bags, strawberry baskets, or plastic Easter baskets with handles and holes punched in their sides. Use the bag to pot up soil and new plants, and then settle it into one of the

TO MAKE YOUR OWN CONTAINER GROWING MIX

To make your own soil mix for containers that stay outdoors all year long, use this recipe and mix well:

- Start with a big bag of good quality potting mix without added fertilizer or water-holding gels.

- Dump the bag into a wheelbarrow and use it to measure:

  » ½ bag of your own compost or leaf mold

  » ¼ bag of your favorite composted manure

  » ½ bag of ground bark mulch–pine or hardwood

- To a pile of mix that would fit in a 30-gallon trash can, add:

  » 1 cup garden lime

  » 1 cup granular garden fertilizer (5-10-5)

■ *Select evergreen shrubs with their mature size in mind to reduce maintenance in the long haul.*

containers. Add a few pieces of gravel if needed to weigh it down. Plant the new container into a water feature or into a pond pot.

CARE

ANNUALS

There is nothing sadder than wilted flower beds or insect-ravaged plants. Summer annuals are capable of fast growth in stressful conditions if their care triangle has three strong sides. Tend to only water, fertilize, or pest control and the plants may survive, but with careful attention to all three, summer and fall annuals will grow and bloom to beat the heat.

BULBS

When Philippine lily blooms with its fragrant white trumpets in late summer, everybody wants some, but plants and bulbs can be hard to find. Fortunately, attractive seed pods soon follow and turn brown this month or next. Cut the stems of

■ *Red spider lily*

this rampant reseeder and put them in a brown bag, a bucket, or a box so the seed can fall out. Plant seeds in pots of good garden soil and transplant to the garden as small plants in early spring. For best blooms, grow Philippine lilies in full sun.

The best cut flower this month is, hands down, red spider lilies. Their stems will usually snap right off, but use clippers or scissors instead. Like other stems, it's better to cut these to avoid tearing on yanking them and possibly pulling the clump right out of the soil.

EDIBLES

Virtually every vegetable that you plant from seed must be thinned to proper spacing. If you seed in excess, as most of us do because we want to be sure some will come up, it's especially important. No matter how much it hurts your feelings, do it and eat the thinning as sprouts or compost them to complete the cycle of life. You'll find more information on seed packages and in catalogs, but unless you're growing mini varieties or outsized ones, here's how much space seedlings need between them:

- 1 inch between plants   Radish

- 2 inches   Swiss chard, mustard, and other greens

- 3 inches   Beets, carrots, green peas

- 4 inches   Onion, spinach, leaf lettuce

- 6 inches   Turnip

- 8 inches   Rutabaga

Companion planting is a strategy that uses one plant as defense against the pests of another. For example, marigold roots are known to attract nematodes and thus are planted with tomatoes that are susceptible to them. While there is a measurable effect, it stops when you pull up the marigolds. A better choice for companion planting is to grow garlic in the rose bed to repel insects. Like sprays of Epsom salts for bell peppers and

■ *Thin radishes to 1 inch between each plant.*

roses, some gardeners swear by garlic as a natural pest deterrent.

A windy thunderstorm can pound small vegetable plants right into the ground. Wait until the day after the storm and carefully reset any that do not return to the upright position. Use a chopstick or plant tag to wiggle stems loose so you can pick them up if they are stuck in the soil. If larger plants lean badly, press the soil on the opposite side and add soil if needed to reset them.

PERENNIALS & ORNAMENTAL GRASSES

The crown is what distinguishes a perennial plant, and its care is paramount to the plant's survival from year to year. Crowns can sink, get covered with mulch or plant debris, or be disturbed by voles and other digging critters. Work your way through the perennials this month, inspect them for sinking or stranding above the mulch, pull weeds, and groom each plant. Carry a bucket along so you don't have to make a second trip to collect the debris.

Daylilies bloom well in partly sunny sites, but reblooming varieties don't, even though they are not crowded and get plenty of water and fertilizer. Two issues may be involved: sunlight and seed pods. Move the rebloomers to a sunnier site. While deadheading is not required, do it to stop the plants from trying to form seeds.

ROSES

Deadhead and clean up around roses between flushes of fall blooms. Especially in Zones 8b and 9, climbing roses need pruning this month except those that only flower once in spring.

HERE'S HOW

TO PRUNE CLIMBING ROSES

1. Shorten any canes that are growing across or over the top of the trellis or arbor.

2. Cut the jute or remove whatever holds the rose to its supports. This step explains why it's so wise to attach climbing roses to the front of the support only, unless you are growing it into a 360-degree column.

3. Let the rose canes sprawl on the ground in front of the trellis.

4. Select the strongest, well-spaced canes and clip the rest out at ground level.

5. Reattach the remaining canes to the front of the support structure.

HERE'S HOW

TO PRUNE A LIMB

1. Sharpen your saw, put on long pants, a long-sleeved shirt, and closed-toe shoes. Wear safety glasses and have a partner nearby to hold the ladder if you use one.

2. Cut a slice into the underside of the branch about a foot out from the trunk to keep the bark intact.

3. Next, sever the branch off by cutting through it from the top an inch or so out from where you made the first slice.

4. Finally, cut the nub off behind the first slice. Do not work flush with the trunk—make this cut slope just a little to facilitate healing and so water runs away from the trunk.

5. Do not use pruning sealants, no matter what Daddy told you. You will seal in anaerobic bacteria and any other pests that are present, creating a laboratory for rot that you do not want.

TREES

After wind damage, you may see a broken branch, called a snag, hanging in a tree canopy. When you clean up after the storm, it is good to leave that snag for wildlife to enjoy unless it can create obvious havoc when it falls. If you are equipped to do some pruning, good—but this is not the time for on-the-job training and most people should consult a licensed professional.

Pruning a limb bigger around than your thigh requires a safe, efficient, specific method.

VINES & GROUNDCOVERS

Do not disturb cocoons you find in vines like Dutchman's pipe, hops, all wisterias (*W. floribunda, W. sinensis, W. frutescens*), and passionflower. Soon the butterflies and moths will be free and woody vines will leaf out again or go dormant.

If autumn clematis is sprawling over the hedge, leave it alone for now and plan to cut it back next spring. But if this vigorous vine is falling out of its appointed space, loop some jute around it and corral the vines for a better show.

WATER GARDENS

Algae patrol is always a must, but hot weather helps algae multiply. Their proliferation and subsequent loss of oxygen in the water is aggravated by excess nitrogen, usually from fish or fertilizer. Too many fish or too much fish food create nitrogen waste that feeds algae. When you use fertilizers made especially for aquatic plants and those growing in its margins, you can usually avoid the second issue.

1. Reduce the number of fish and/or the amount and frequency of feeding.

2. Increase the floating plants if less than half the water surface is covered.

3. Flush out small ponds and add fresh water.

4. Float barley straw bales to clear up existing algae and provide fish food.

HERE'S HOW

TO TROUBLESHOOT A WATER PUMP

1. Go through the system to be sure everything is connected and plugged in— check that your breaker is not tripped. Plug the pump in somewhere else to be sure both it and the electrical source are working independently of each other.

2. Look for dead leaves and other plant debris trapped at the intake or in the skimmer and remove it.

3. Be sure the water level in the feature has not dropped due to evaporation or a leak. In this case you can usually hear the pump running but nothing is happening because no water is reaching it. Add water to the pond or fix the leak and then add water.

4. Check for a vapor lock, which means an air bubble is trapped inside. You can usually dislodge it by gently rocking the pump back and forth a couple of times to burp it.

5. Look for other items that might be plugging up the works like gravel in a line or something in the pump that stops the impeller from spinning. Disconnect each element, inspect and clear it, then reconnect. You may need to spin the impeller once manually to get it to start up.

6. If none of these factors can explain it, call in a water garden professional and plan to replace the pump.

5. In severe situations, use an aquatic herbicide made to control algae and then take steps to prevent its regrowth.

Something is wrong and you think it's the pump. Before you go out and get a new one, try to solve the problem.

WATER

ALL

Summer container plant watering can be a constant chore or a fairly pleasant task that gives you time to really see the plants.

ANNUALS

It's tempting to believe that an afternoon shower will deliver enough water to annual flowers in beds and pots. But while light rain may wash the dust off leaves, it seldom comes in amounts adequate to grow these plants.

If crust forms on the surface of seedbeds or around new seedlings, the soil is staying too dry. Gently break it up with a hand cultivator, smooth the soil, and water it well.

BULBS

At this point in the season, daffodils and other perennial bulbs are storing energy for next year. You may not see them because their leaves are gone for the year, but you know where they are—remember to water bulb plantings if the weather is very dry this month.

EDIBLES

The symbiotic relationship between watering plants and mulching them shows clearly this month. Neither is as good alone as the two are

■ *Maintaining a rain gauge will help you determine how much more water your plants will need.*

together. Water hydrates the soil and thus the plants while mulch moderates its effects. In dry weather, mulch keeps water from evaporating from the soil surface and prevents crusting. When rainfall is great, mulch helps shed it so the soil doesn't get waterlogged. Keep new seedbeds watered and mulch around the new seedlings when they have two sets of true leaves.

LAWNS

If you decide to forego watering the lawn in dry weeks, several outcomes are likely: paler grass color, thinning growth, greater vulnerability to pests, and more weeds in the future.

PERENNIALS & ORNAMENTAL GRASSES

Water ornamental grasses to ensure their plumes will look as full and beautiful as they can. Water all perennial plants if the weather is dry with special attention to fall blooming perennials and those you planted this year.

ROSES

Water roses very regularly while they are in bloom. Whenever possible, water one afternoon or early evening and cut roses the following morning.

HERE'S HOW

TO WATER CONTAINERS

- Water all the soil in the pot, not just the base of the plant, to encourage root growth throughout the pot.

- Water slowly enough that mulch and soil do not wash out.

- After you see water running out the drain holes, move on to the next pot.

- When all pots are watered, go back to the first one and refill its head space, the inch between the top of the soil and the top of the pot.

SHRUBS, TREES, AND VINES & GROUNDCOVERS

Most plants in these categories may not readily show signs of drought or flood stress, but they suffer it nonetheless. Monitor woody plants, and if water stands in their beds, open a ditch to get rid of it. If drought causes wilt and premature leaf drop, berries will stop expanding and may not ripen. Remember the standard 1 inch of water per week and strive for it.

WATER GARDENS

Lots of the plants we grow around ponds need water in summer, but be careful not to wash soil and mulch into the water feature. Water slowly so it percolates deep into the soil.

FERTILIZE

ANNUALS

Just as you make sure that fall-blooming annuals are watered, be certain they have enough fertilizer, too, after they are well hydrated. If you use granular formulas, water lightly after sprinkling the fertilizer around to ensure none sits on the leaves and burns them. When heavy rain follows the use of a soluble fertilizer, most of it is washed away before it can do any good. Reapply or use a granular form.

BULBS

Fertilize red and yellow spider lilies after the flowers finish and leaves emerge from the clump. Use 4 tablespoons of bulb food or ¼ cup of granular flower garden fertilizer for a clump that is 6 inches across.

EDIBLES

Continue fertilizing actively growing vegetables on a regular schedule. If the soil is rich and fertile, that program might be a weekly watering with a soluble formula made for vegetables. If the soil is less than terrific, work in ½ inch of compost and then continue with the weekly soluble program.

Irish potatoes grow by sending up stalks from their eyes planted in a trench or ventilated container. As the potato stems grow, your task is to fill in around them with leaf mold, compost, and small amounts of granular vegetable garden food. Keep just the very top growth out of the mix to give the potatoes room to grow and make "digging" a lot easier.

LAWNS

September is the main month for fall lawn feeding in the Deep South. Its advocates swear by the practice to beef up the lawn's root system and provide a reservoir of nutrients.

- Lawn maintenance programs usually include a fall feeding component that may also include pre-emerge herbicide. If your lawn is doing well on such a program, do not skip this step.

- Those of us who grow organically do not generally fertilize in the fall. If the grass is thin or damaged, you can apply a ½-inch blanket of composted manure now. It will work its way into the soil and become activated by spring.

PERENNIALS & ORNAMENTAL GRASSES

Fertilize perennials that break dormancy now, such as Lenten rose and other hellebores in Zone 8a and iris in Zone 8b and 9. Use a flowering formula with a slow-release nitrogen component or a pellet slow release made for flower gardens.

ROSES

If roses are blooming, you can fertilize them if you live in Zone 8b or 9. Everywhere, mix a general purpose soluble fertilizer into water and use it on roses growing in pots such as floribundas that will bloom until frost and also on those cuttings you are rooting.

SHRUBS AND TREES

Use specialty formulas made to bolster root growth without stimulating new leaves such as 0-10-10 or 0-20-20. Young shrubs and trees, as well as mature ones, can benefit so long as there is little or no nitrogen in the fertilizer that you use now.

VINES & GROUNDCOVERS

Lightly fertilize young groundcovers and beds you pruned hard this year. Use half the recommended amount of a general purpose garden fertilizer in soluble or granular form now to sustain them until frost.

WATER GARDENS

Fertilize the hardy water lilies in your aquatic plant nursery. If you will be able to keep the nursery above 45 degrees Fahrenheit all winter, fertilize the tropical water garden plants too.

PROBLEM-SOLVE

ANNUALS

Pansy seedlings that grow faster than expected can dry out too quickly when their roots push out of peat cups or exceed the space in cell packs. Instead of fresh plants ready for beds and pots, yours look like they should be on deep discount at the end of the season. In north Mississippi and Alabama, September pansy planting is not unusual, but as you go farther south, October is the norm. Go ahead and plant, no matter where you live, and treat your pansies like other hot weather transplants. Water well, mulch, and put up temporary shade if needed—it's better to plant and coddle the pansies than to let them die in the flats.

BULBS

Different insects pester dahlias throughout their season, from slugs and snails that eat young sprouts to thrips that ruin the flowers. Many gardeners spray them preventatively once they know from experience what pests will come. Lacebugs, stinkbugs, and leafhoppers can be especially troublesome at this time of the year. Watch for them or the signs they have been feeding, such as tiny pricks all over the leaf surface called stippling. Control them with sprays containing permethrin or Neem oil.

LAWNS

Dog urine creates dead spots in your lawn. You can recognize them—deep green rings surround the browned places. The nitrogen-rich urine deposit acts like fertilizer and burns the center as surely as an overdose would. But around the edges, the urine becomes a nitrogen bath and greens up the area. Keep dogs off the lawn or rinse the spots routinely as you would their solid deposits.

Fleas and fire ants thrive in September. Keep a watchful eye out for them and repeat the treatments that were effective in spring. Like

To fix dog spots, first flush the soil by watering the area twice a day for three or four days. Then, dig out the top two inches of soil and replace it with new garden soil. Next, sprinkle grass seed on top and water the grass seed twice daily until it sprouts.

mosquitoes, these pests can present problems year-round. Just as you're getting out into the yard after a hot summer, fleas and fire ants can ruin the party, unless you control them.

Weed control in lawns this month can be as simple as digging out a few dandelions. Or it can be the sudden proliferation of some weed you never saw before the most recent tropical storm blew through. Herbicide programs can be effective, but many gardeners choose not to use them and battle weeds seasonally. Spot spraying with conventional or organic compounds labeled to control a particular weed are effective but may test your persistence. Common invaders likely to get your attention this month include:

- Chamberbitter (*Phyllanthus*) is a reseeding annual that looks like its other namesake, little mimosa, and grows low to the ground. If you do nothing else, scalp it before it blooms.

- Crabgrass (*Digitaria*) has longer, wider blades that are hairy and curled tightly, so it stands up higher than your lawn grass. Spot spray or dig annual crabgrass out when you see it.

- Dallisgrass (*Paspalum*), a clumping perennial, has thin blades and a reddish cast to its stems and somewhat resembles common bermudagrass. Dig out clumps when you first see them.

- Dollarweed (*Hydrocotyle*) is a perennial and spreads by underground rhizomes. Resist the urge to dig it up and clip this one to ground level several times. Spray successive rounds of new growth to achieve control and plant new plugs so the lawn can retake the area.

ROSES

Flooded rose beds don't happen after every storm, but even a few inches of water standing around the roots for prolonged periods can be deadly. Remove the water as soon as possible and watch for new growth in a few weeks to know if the roses are still viable. (We don't choose roses for their ability to grow in water, but one found rose surprised everyone. 'Peggy Martin' was collected by her namesake in New Orleans and prized for its thornless rambling canes covered with vivid pink flower clusters. Hurricane Katrina flooded 'Peggy Martin' with 20 feet of salt water for two weeks, yet the rose grew right on. Grow this rose, the living proof of our states' resilience in the face of adversity.)

SHRUBS

Deciduous shrubs fail to develop glorious fall color some years and instead, their leaves turn brown and drop off, or abscise. The natural phenomenon of changing leaf color happens as the daylight period shortens and the weather cools. We see fall color as deciduous plants respond to seasonal changes by moving nutrients from the leaves back into branches, trunks, and roots. When the weather is still hot as daylight ebbs, the process is disrupted and there is little you can do. Keep shrub beds watered and mulched now to reduce premature browning.

Late summer brings a surge in pest populations, sadly accompanied by more obvious signs of damage to plants. When you see azaleas with yellow specks dotting upper leaf surfaces and black dots on the undersides, you see the damage azalea lacebugs can do by September. Azalea lacebugs begin life as an egg laid now and left to overwinter unnoticed in bark crevices. Eggs that hatch in February soon grow through five stages (instars) and then adults mate and run rampant through your azaleas. They feed and breed in spring and summer, then lay eggs for the next year.

Effective control of azalea lacebug has three parts:

- Now: Good garden sanitation–keep damaged leaves raked out from under shrubs and discard, do not compost them.

- Sooner: Physical control–spray shrubs thoroughly with horticultural oil spray as soon as temperatures and label instructions allow. Repeat in January.

- Later: Spray program–in March, begin spraying at eight-day intervals with a control product such as insecticidal soap with pyrethrin, oil of Neem, or most synthetic insecticides.

Consider using systemic insecticides if serious infestations continue after the above program is completed.

TREES

Surprising fall rebloom of spring-flowering trees like deciduous magnolias and some fruit trees raises questions about its viability. You wonder if it will also put on new leaves that will be damaged by frost and if it will bloom on time the next year. This condition usually results from stress such as severe drought, overfertilization, or high winds that strip leaves off and lift the trees slightly. You cannot stop the wind, but you can keep trees on a routine schedule of water and refrain from fertilizing for a year, if that may have been an issue.

VINES & GROUNDCOVERS

The combination of wind and vigor can send vines to the ground and left to sprawl, soon creating a messy thicket. This can happen to all kinds of vines— whether they attach with tendrils, twine around their supports, or cling with adventitious roots. Before the star jasmine, passionflower, Carolina jessamine, or rambling roses can get away from you, trim or train them now while their wood is still fairly supple.

If groundcover clumps collapse now, drought may be to blame. However, if you have not pruned the liriope or monkey grass for several years, overcrowding is also probable. Take a couple of inches off now to reduce water loss through the leaves and mark your calendar to divide and replant them in late fall or winter.

October

October teaches lessons that run the garden gamut from personal to universal. You learn to prioritize and organize so the gardening gets done with time to decorate for the holidays. Pumpkins and decorative gourds like turk's cap (Cucurbita pepo), warty apple, and bule (C. siceraria) grace magazine covers, produce stands, school festivals, and front porches now. They mark the beginning of celebratory seasons that last until Lent in much of the Deep South.

According to the Victorian language of flowers, pansies are for thoughts, and now's the time to put those thoughts into action. It's wiser, perhaps, to go shopping for them with a plan in mind, but then you miss the eye-opening experience of gazing on racks and tables brimming with different varieties. That's why people stand and stare, to drink in the endless combinations of flower sizes, colors, and the silly faces we love in this fine plant family.

When you travel to our north now color flames in your face on every mile because cooler temperatures reveal striking red, purple, yellow, and orange leaves. Everywhere, the world glows orange with pumpkins, sumac (*Rhus*), and maples on parade. But not every tree with fall color is to be celebrated as we have learned from the beautiful exotic popcorn tree (*Sapium sebiferum*), also known as Chinese tallow tree. Perhaps no other tree consistently delivers red and purple color as far south as we live, and it grows absolutely anywhere. Its white seedpods resemble popcorn and have been used in decorating since America was a colony. The Chinese tallow tree was first imported to South Carolina in the 1700s. Sadly, it is grossly invasive through root sprouts and seeds distributed by birds, wind, and water. It is a rogue in the garden but a serious pest in the wild when it chokes wetlands and overruns native species that sustain our wildlife. Popcorn tree was adored at first sight and, like any relationship, built entirely on superficial features, time has proven it dangerous.

Maybe the biggest lesson October brings is how fast things can change. One day you're still irrigating like mad and the air conditioner is running. Overnight you have to haul in the last potted plants and get tender vegetables under cover, not to mention adding a coat to the Halloween costume.

PLAN

ALL

Not everyone who wants to compost has enough raw materials to satisfy the 1:3 green/brown ratio. With lawn clippings, spent annuals flowers, and vegetables—you've got plenty of green, but unless you have several trees, brown plant material may be in short supply. At this time of year, you can gather plenty of bags left at the curb by people who think it's trash. This time-honored form of early morning recycling is called "you rake, we take". You are advised to press on the bags to be sure only leaves are inside.

ANNUALS

Picture it: pansies planted on 6-inch centers in full bloom with tulips popping up between them to celebrate spring. Plan for a raucous or quiet mood as you combine these plants in your mind's eye.

- Solid colors make a bold statement even on a busy street. For example, consider yellow pansies and red tulips, or white pansies with purple faces combined with white and purple tulips.

- In a bed you'll see up close, pastel shades and color mixes work very well. Shades of pink, lavender, and blue pansies with a crown of pink tulips can make your heart sing.

- Because you'll be planting pansies first while tulip bulbs chill in the refrigerator, plan to slip a plant marker at the center of three pansies to mark its place. It's a fine way to repurpose some of the many plastic labels that you acquire with plants.

BULBS

To keep track of when you can begin planting Holland bulbs, grab your calendar.

- October:

  » Dutch iris (*I. x hollandica*)
  » Flowering allium (*Allium*)
  » Daffodils (*Narcissus*)
  » Grape hyacinth (*Muscari*)

■ *Compost piles can use plenty of your neighbor's leaves to get to the right ratio.*

  » Spanish bluebells (*Hyacinthoides hispanica*)
  » Snowflake (*Leucojum aestivum*)

Snowdrop is also the common name for *Galanthus*, a relative of *Leucojum* in the Narcissus family that does not grow nearly as well as our snowflake. You can tell the difference between the two when they are in bloom and snowflake's scalloped cup flowers are adorned with one green dot on a petal. It's a charming wink from this cottage garden favorite that blooms in winter.

- November:

  » *Crocus*
  » *Anemone*
  » *Ranunculus*
  » Squill (*Scilla siberica*) in Zones 7 and 8
  » *Fritillaria* in beds, north; in pots, south
  » Amaryllis in pots

- December after eight weeks in refrigerator

  » Hyacinth (*Hyacinthus orientalis*)
  » Tulip (*Tulipa*)

EDIBLES

To harvest lettuce (*Lactuca sativa*) all winter, learn what it takes to grow and protect the plants. Leaf and soft head lettuces like 'Buttercrunch', heading lettuces, and Romaines can all tolerate a few freezing hours if (and this is a big if) they have been in the bed long enough to harden off. Plan for steady growth with a moderate fertilizer program and keep an eye on the weather. When temperatures will be below freezing for more than a few hours, you'll need to cover the lettuce, so plan for that eventuality now—put raised bed covers close at hand or reserve space in your garage for pots.

If you have a greenhouse, plan to grow at least one tomato plant inside. Determinate and cherry varieties rate best with home gardeners for this environment for very different reasons. 'Celebrity' is a determinate tomato with good disease resistance. Its steady growth rate to 4 feet tall and abundant crop in a relatively small space recommends this and others with natural height limitations. Cherry tomatoes, except for basket types, will grow endlessly but respond very well to pruning that controls their girth. Because cherry tomatoes put on more stems in response to cutting back, there's still plenty of fruit. If you cannot grow your own, plan to befriend a local professional who grows greenhouse tomatoes—our states have the best.

LAWNS

Bermudagrass turns tan early and greens up later in spring than other lawns, making it the best candidate for overseeding. Although you can sow annual ryegrass seeds over the lawn until December and get some results, the best time is a month

■ *Greenhouses built from a kit can help you extend the growing season.*

before the average first frost date in your area. Plan to mow the bermudagrass low (1 to 1½ inches) and then sow 5 pounds of seed per 1,000 square feet of lawn. More seed can hamper the lawn's greenup in spring.

Overseeding ryegrass is no substitute for a healthy lawn and should not be done if the lawn is not in good condition. Figure out what's wrong and fix it, let the lawn recover, and plan for overseeding in the future.

PERENNIALS & ORNAMENTAL GRASSES

Plan for beautiful, long-lasting arrangements and accent pieces to paint for holiday decorating. Find a space to dry flowers and seedpods that is out of the sun and rain, well-ventilated, and less than 80 degrees Fahrenheit. A slowly oscillating table fan across the room is a good idea for this project, too. Survey the garden now with an eye toward healthy seed heads with strong stems— long and stiff for plants like black-eyed Susan and purple coneflower; erect and not drooping for short-stemmed hydrangeas.

ROSES

Plan now to plant roses in February: locate a sunny site, determine a water source, and gather the soil amendments you will need. Successful rose beds will be in place for years, so investments made in its good drainage and fertility on the front end are essential.

The edging you choose for a raised bed contributes to the mood of your garden and can reflect or complement its style. For example, the clean lines of flat lumber sides lend a no-nonsense, practical air to the rose bed. But a row of pointed bricks is more whimsical and can be a nod to retro or cottage garden styles.

SHRUBS

The worst thing about shrubs in a foundation planting is not always the overgrowth that reaches over the sill and across the windows. Their lushness might bring nice flowers or great berries that you enjoy. Sometimes it's a question of how often they must be pruned to avoid this overgrowth. Plan to keep pruning on the to-do list, or choose stalwart, evergreen shrubs that stay smaller than 4 feet without repetitive trimming.

- Dwarf wax myrtle (*Myrtus cerifera*)

- Crimson dwarf barberry (*Berberis thunbergii atropurpurea*)

- Drooping leucothoe (*L. fontanesiana*)

TREES

Lots of decisions go into tree planting. Site, water, soil conditions, flowers, and fall color, but also the reason for the tree should be in your plan.

- Legacy trees grow into stately forms and live for generations.

  » Ginkgo (*G. biloba*) turns brilliant golden yellow each fall and then drops its leaves neatly almost overnight. That makes duck foot tree a favorite for front yard planting. Plant only male trees to avoid smelly, messy flowers.

  » Oaks (*Quercus*) including swamp chestnut, post, white oaks, and more are the quintessential native Deep South tree. Every property needs at least one.

  » Bald cypress (*Taxodium distichum*) and its brother, pond cypress, do not need swamps to grow and deliver fine texture on a huge

■ *Ginkgo*

scale like no other tree. Bald cypress is also considered fast growing.

- Faster-growing native shade trees cool the garden and the house, lowering energy costs.

  » Sycamore (*Platanus occidentalis*) gets your attention with leaves bigger than your hand even on a young tree. As it grows, mottled bark makes for year-round interest.

  » Sweet gum (*Liquidambar styraciflua*) has star-shaped leaves with rich fall color and rugged bark. Gumballs are optional, as non-fruiting cultivars are widely available.

  » Tulip poplar (*Liriodendron tulipifera*) is a host plant for tiger and spicebush swallowtail butterflies. The tree has matte green, spatula-shaped leaves surrounding cupped, buttery yellow flowers that open to reveal orange petals and frilly yellow centers.

WATER GARDENS

Plan to bring the soothing sounds of water closer to you by exploring what it takes to install a fountain. Know what your wall, table, or patio floor can support in terms of weight, electricity, and plumbing. If the answer is not much, plan for a petite, sweet tabletop fountain. Sheetrock and drywall are not strong enough for a wall fountain and stucco can be difficult (read costly). Brick walls can work, as can modifying a retaining wall around the patio, but plan before you grab the sledgehammer.

PLANT

ALL

Weed barrier cloth can be quite useful, but this porous fabric mulch gets overlooked. Spread a blanket over the site of a new rose bed, perennial border, or annual planting and secure it all around with the handy pins sold with the cloth. Cut an "X" into the cloth, fold the "X" back, and plant. Cut in swaths and laid into a shrub bed that you've cleared of weeds, it shades the ground under organic mulch. Weed barrier cloth works because water still gets in, but weeds are suppressed along with sunlight. Several grades of the cloth are available; choose a tightly woven, quality product for long life in the bed.

■ *Planting into black fabric cloth can cut back on the weeds.*

ANNUALS

Living mulch is a classic concept employed to cover the ground beneath other plants and add color at the same time. Groundcovers are used this way and annuals can be, too, on a seasonal basis. Many low-growing annuals—sweet alyssum (*Lobularia maritima*) and diascia (*D. barberae*) for example—are quickly burned up by warm spring weather in more than half of our states' gardens. In an average winter, they grow as well as snapdragons in all but the coldest areas. Plant them now and plan to slip in some anemone and ranunculus bulbs for even more color.

Tall varieties of snapdragon are as hardy as the ground-hugging types, especially when you plant them now. Use single colors and mixes to fill the cut flower row where zinnias grew last summer. When you plant snapdragons, pansies, and other annuals *en masse*, take your time and be sure each one is at ground level. Sunken or elevated by as little as an inch, these small plants will be stressed and more mulch won't solve the problem.

Tempting benches, full of ornamental kale and cabbage, await—including the entire pansy family,

■ *Snapdragons*

snapdragons, stock, et al., and you buy many different overwintering annuals. When you get home without a plan, it's good to know a few guidelines for planting annuals.

- Because winter weather can be so unpredictable, choose garden sites with some protection on the north side and grow in a big pot—10-inch standards or larger.

- If the view will be from one side only, plant tall snapdragons, Canterbury bells, and foxgloves at the back of beds and pots. Otherwise, plant them in the middle and step down with smaller plants.

- Groups of different plants in the shades of the same color are calming but can look washed out if everything is pastel or too close in hue. Change to a mix of colors to let each plant pop—just avoid the chaos of planting the entire spectrum in one small space.

BULBS

Plant the bulbs of October: Dutch iris, allium, daffodils, narcissus, grape hyacinth, Spanish bluebell, and snowflake. Lay out large groups on a grid to insure proper spacing and a more formal-looking show but do not feel constrained by the geometry. You're in good company if you toss bulbs over your shoulder and plant where they fall. Bulbs planted too deep in heavy soils may never be seen again or will send up leaves and never bloom. Regardless of what you read, plant bulbs no deeper than twice their height. For example, a grape hyacinth or crocus 1 inch tall is planted 2 inches deep in the soil.

Save several dozen Dutch iris bulbs for forcing later and put them in the crisper drawer if you want to avoid the chilling treatment after planting in pots.

When you want Holland bulbs but haven't room for more perennial plants, skip the daffodils, Spanish bluebells, and grape hyacinths. Grow those we treat as annuals because their long-term survival rate is not good. Stock up on crocus, freesia, fritillaria, anemone, and ranunculus bulbs. Plant in pots outdoors to cool before blooming or tuck some into hedgerows and rose beds. Enjoy the show and if they do rebloom, consider it lagniappe.

EDIBLES

Make another sowing of thirty-day radish varieties. If you like 'Scarlet Globe', try 'Cherry Belle'. Spicy radishes like 'White Icicle' are the entrée to

For the best flavor, grow your own cauliflower in your vegetable garden.

the world of even hotter salad radishes like the pink 'Aka Karaine' hybrid and 'Shogoin Globe', a cooking radish that thrives in heavier soils than most. This one's an oddity because it grows most of its globe aboveground rather like kohlrabi. 'White Icicle' is a short crop, but other daikon and hot radishes take at least two months in the garden, so they are limited to Zone 9 without protection now.

In the warmest areas, plant kohlrabi and Brussels sprout plants and sow more greens of all kinds. If you find kale and collards bitter to taste, later planting can grow sweeter greens.

You can only cut one cabbage from a plant that takes weeks to grow, and it hardly seems worth the space it takes up. Grow multi-stemmed rapini or broccoli that you can cut and then let side stems come on for repeated harvest. Opt for premium-priced cauliflower that is, next to beets, the biggest revelation in the vegetable garden because its homegrown taste is so much better. Or dig another bed for the space takers: cabbage again in the spring followed by pumpkins or sweet potatoes next summer.

LAWNS

Begin overseeding with annual ryegrass (5 to 10 pounds/1,000 square foot of lawn) in the north

HERE'S HOW

TO PLANT LARGE GROUPS OF BULBS

1. First scrape the mulch away from the planting area. Then remove the soil from the planting area to make a trench or hole that is the depth of four to six times the height of the bulbs you're planting.

2. Then, set the bulbs in the planting area. For a natural look, mix several types of bulbs together in a bucket and then scatter them on the ground. Fix the bulbs so the pointy end is up.

3. Sprinkle ground cayenne pepper on the bulbs to keep the squirrels from eating the bulbs. (They don't like the taste of the pepper.) If you have serious problems with creatures digging up bulbs, consider making a makeshift cage out of chicken wire. Plant the bulbs in the cage and bury it.

4. Cover the bulbs with soil. You'll want to cover them with enough soil so that the bulbs are buried at least four to six times their height. If you don't feel like digging, you don't have to. Scatter the bulbs and cover them with soil at least four to six times as deep as the bulbs are tall. Your flower bed will be slightly taller in the spring, but you'll have saved yourself a lot of work!

5. Use a shrub rake or hard rake to spread mulch over the planting area for a finishing touch. You can use the same mulch that you use in the rest of the planting bed for this step. Remember to water the bulbs after you're done planting them.

Mississippi and Alabama regions, at mid-month in north Louisiana, central Mississippi and Alabama, and at the end of the month farther south. Use heavier rates on bare ground to prevent erosion and soil loss, lighter rates for a green carpet over bermudagrass and mow-what-grows lawns. Choose certified, weed-free seed for this project and use a proper seeder to distribute seeds evenly.

PERENNIALS & ORNAMENTAL GRASSES

You can plant all the perennials you want this month and sow seeds for native wildflowers. Work up the soil in beds and amend it as needed to increase organic content and drainage. Mix up equal parts of ground bark, compost or manure, and planting soil (not potting mix). Add a trowel full of mix to the planting hole for a 1-quart pot, more or less depending on the rootball. For a new wildflower patch, amend the entire area and cultivate it to a depth of 3 inches, then rake it very well before planting seeds.

When to divide perennials depends on the plant, and most grow nicely for three years before they grow crowded. That average is just that—if your plants grow faster or slower, dig and divide when their flowers get smaller or they become bullies in the bed. And know some of the big exceptions: Shasta daisies (*Leucanthemum superbum*) and perennial oxeye daisies (*L. vulgare*) may have fewer blooms unless you divide them annually. But wait longer than three years for those that are slow to spread such as plantain lily (*Hosta*), bleeding heart (*Dicentra*), and peony (*Paeonia*).

ROSES

The cuttings you raised outside and the rose that outgrew its pot can all be planted in the garden now. Treat roses like shrubs—do the soil work and plant them now.

String trimmers can slice small trunks, and weeds can grow tall quickly around small roses. If the ones you rooted are smaller in diameter than a pencil and shorter than 1 foot, they're vulnerable. Leave them where they are or move into larger pots to grow larger.

SHRUBS

The old adage is true: you don't want to plant a $20 plant in a 5-cent hole—soil preparation before planting often determines which shrubs thrive and

TO PLANT A SHRUB

1. Start with whatever you dig up—dirt, sand, clay, fill, or oyster shells; it's a source of minerals and microlife. Because the shrub will eventually grow out of the amended area and into it, you want some of it involved to ease that transition.

2. Add a quarter to one-third by volume of a mix of organic matters such as leaf mold, compost, ground bark. Mix them into the native dirt and refill the bottom 6 inches of the hole.

3. If you do not use starter solutions, look for big fertilizer tablets made for shrub planting and put one just under the soil at the bottom of the hole.

4. Loosen roots, place the shrub so it will be growing at the same level, and backfill the hole halfway. Tamp it down to get rid of air pockets and fill in the rest of the space.

5. Water well with a starter solution (compost tea, rooting hormone, or root stimulator fertilizer) and mulch the new planting.

which don't. If you have good garden soil and a bed ready to plant in, turn the soil in an area 6 inches deeper and 6 inches wider all the way around than the rootball. Slope the hole slightly so it is shaped more like a salad bowl than a soup can. Amend lesser soils, especially if you are planting into uncultivated native dirt. Your goal is friable soil: when you squeeze a handful, it does not turn to dust or globs, but crumbles through your fingers. Good soil is brown and smells nice, not moldy or wet.

TREES

More trees grow well from seeds than you think. Acorns and buckeyes go right into pots of leaf mold or garden soil now, but planting magnolia seeds takes more time and care. Right now the red cones are ripe and ready to start the process.

When planting more than a few small trees, such as for a windbreak or orchard, use a power-driven posthole digger to eliminate hours of work.

VINES & GROUNDCOVERS

Plant seeds from scarlet creeper, trumpet vine, and the layers you made from woody vines in spring and summer. Start the seeds in small pots of compost or planting mix and put flats of them outside in the shade. When a frost is predicted, move them to a sheltered place or cover them well until the weather warms again. When you separate layers from their mother plant, treat them like others you dig up—replant right away, heel them in, or pot them up, but do not let the roots dry out.

HERE'S HOW

TO START MAGNOLIAS FROM SEED

- Pick a healthy, ripe seed cone from the tree. Separate the red seedpods from the cone.

- Clean off the red covering around the seed and discard it.

- Put cleaned seed into a plastic bag of barely damp potting soil.

- Store in the crisper of your refrigerator until early spring.

WATER GARDENS

Water features surrounded by leafy green plants can be less interesting to look at in fall and winter. Plant a small weeping tree such as weeping dwarf yaupon (*Ilex vomitoria* 'Pendula') or dwarf Japanese maple (*Acer palmatum dissectum*, referring to its finely cut leaves). Consider two more maples: 'Brocade'—red spring leaves turn green-bronze in summer and red-orange in fall. Or 'Ellen', a beautiful spring green that deepens in summer and shows clear yellow in fall.

CARE

ALL

October finds you raking leaves, and you either pile them up behind the barn or start a more formal compost heap. While it is true that anything carbon-based will rot and so can be composted, few home heaps will achieve the high temperatures necessary for some. Pet droppings, proteins like meat and chicken, and oily substances like leftover fried foods should be left out. From a practical standpoint, pest-ravaged plant materials and seedpods may cause more issues than they are worth in the compost pile.

◼ *Use the fall leaves in your compost.*

HERE'S HOW

TO ROOT CUTTINGS

Set up a propagation box and put it in a brightly lit window. You'll need:

- Clear plastic box with a hinged or removable top that is 8 inches tall–for 3 inches of rooting mix, 6 inches of cutting (half above and half below the soil), and a 12-inch headspace above the cutting.

- Small clay pot that becomes a water reservoir

- Tube of waterproof bathtub caulk

- Soilless rooting mix–these are usually made of peat and perlite

Soak the clay pot if it is new and seal its drain hole. Use that dab of sealant to center the pot in the bottom of the plastic box. Surround the pot with damp rooting mix, stick the cuttings, put water in the reservoir, and close the top. The box increases needed humidity around the plants to facilitate rooting and your job is to prop the lid open for regular ventilation. Add liquid rooting hormone or soluble fertilizer to the water in the reservoir after a week. Or dip cut ends in rooting hormone powder.

When you pull out summer annuals, mix them into the leaves you just raked. Catch the last grass mowing and mix that in too. Sprinkle on a little fertilizer and turn weekly when it's not too cold to go outdoors. You'll have great leaf mold and some compost to use by May with this method.

ANNUALS

When you decide to dig up an annual to save it for the winter, take cuttings and root them for insurance. Some plants will die down and come back, but rooted cuttings will go on.

BULBS

Withhold water from caladiums in beds and pots to encourage their leaves to dry. You can dig and store them this month or early in November.

1. Dig the caladiums or unpot them and shake the soil off.

2. Find a place that is out of the sun and rain and lay them, leaves and all, to dry slightly before handling.

3. Wear a nubby glove to rub the soil off the caladium. Do not wash the bulbs.

4. Trim away any roots and leaves that have not dried up completely.

5. Use mesh bags (think onion bags) or shallow cardboard flats to store each caladium in a bed of sawdust or cedar shavings used for hamster bedding. Keep each from touching any others to prevent rot.

6. If it is very humid where you live, consider dusting the caladiums lightly with sulfur dust to prevent rot.

7. Check on them monthly and discard any that develop soft spots.

■ *Some bulbs, such as these peony tubers, need to be dried before storing.*

EDIBLES

The first cool nights don't bother tomato plants but do slow fruit ripening. Use this strategy when temperatures stay below 50 degrees Fahrenheit at night consistently:

- Ripen indoors in a bright room if the tomatoes have pink shoulders; that is, they have begun to ripen but very slowly. Rotate daily for even ripening.

- Ripen in a brown paper bag indoors the ones that have made the change from dark green to light green. This works better than you think!

- Enjoy green tomatoes that must be picked—fry or pickle them.

To keep its head white, cauliflower provides strappy leaves that make a great sun hat. Pull the leaves up over the head and tie it loosely like a Pebbles Flintstone top-knot. Use soft cotton that will not cut the leaves, such as a piece of old t-shirt.

LAWNS

Turf grass grows more slowly as the weather cools, and you will mow warm season grasses less often. But do not stop until the grass goes dormant, if it does. Keep it up even if it's no more than once a month in those areas—part of mowing now is weed suppression.

PERENNIALS & ORNAMENTAL GRASSES

Many who grow wildflowers (native perennials, mostly) from seed say the hardest part is weed control. Because you created a great seedbed when you sowed wildflowers, every weed in the area will try to take advantage of you. Learn to recognize your seedlings and keep everything else weeded out, both seedlings and new sprouts of perennials you missed. Keep this task on your weekly list—your seedlings cannot stand the competition at this point.

ROSES

When you let roses make their hips (seedpods), you sustain the fruit-loving birds that live in your garden and those that pass through in transit. Once the hips are gone, deadhead the roses as you would do after flowering. Keep leaves cleaned up from around roses as they fall.

SHRUBS

Go through shrub beds now and check how the natural process of decomposition is going. Use a hand cultivator or, if you don't like stooping, get a long-handled model with three tines or one claw. Scratch around, working rotted mulch into beds and around individual shrubs to incorporate this valuable source of organic matter.

Pine straw mulch is valued for its good looks and long life. Lift up the straw that has been there since spring or longer. If it is very dark in color or filled with white stringy mycelium, replace it with fresh straw. Chop and compost it or reuse it where its weight and water-holding capacity is handy, such as the utility area where you store trash cans.

HERE'S HOW

TO SPREAD PINE STRAW MULCH

1. Pine straw is sold in bales, just like hay. Bales can be prickly, and spiders and other insects like to hang out in pine straw, so use gloves when handling the bales. Look for bales that don't appear to have a lot of other material in them—cones, twigs, or pieces of ferns. Always buy clean, fresh pure straw.

2. To add the pine straw to the landscape, simply snip the twine holding a bale together, and the bale will break apart into clumps called "flakes." Sprinkle the flakes around the landscape bed or trees, being careful to keep the straw near the ground. If you fling pine straw around above your waist, you'll end up with needles hanging all over your shrubs, and that's annoying to clean up!

3. The newly spread straw will be fluffy, and it will most likely escape the landscape beds. To tidy up the beds, you'll want to rake and tuck the straw to keep it in place. Using a hard rake, pull the straw into the edge of the landscape bed. Step on the straw on top of the rake, and then, leaving your foot where it is, pull the rake out. This bunches up the straw at the edge of the bed.

4. To tuck the straw, after raking, plunge a sharpened spade or shovel into the ground about one inch inside the landscape bed. This will trap the edge of the straw in the soil, and will keep it from blowing out of the bed. You can use a chopping motion to do this.

Too many people shear eleagnus to within an inch of its life in a usually futile effort to control its growth. The problem is usually a case of wrong plant, wrong place. If an arching, multi-branched shrub like this one is overpruned, it never achieves its natural form. If you resisted the common practice and have eleagnus where it can really grow, you are rewarded with incredibly fragrant flowers this month.

TREES

Caring for trees this month is mostly a matter of observation and tidying up. Check leaves if they drop while still green and look for signs of insect feeding, cocoons or other nests, lichen, and swollen galls. Take pictures of those trees now to compare next year. Work rotted mulch into the area under trees and put on fresh mulch. Get ahead of the squirrels—get acorns out of flowerbeds now. They never eat all they pile up and too many sprout too soon in a carpet of woody weeds.

VINES & GROUNDCOVERS

Follow the steps to incorporate and replace mulch around these plants, including woody vines at the base of trees and mulched groundcover beds.

Propagate tropical vines now to have young plants indoors all winter that can return to the garden next spring. Look at stems of allamanda and similar vines to see that they are green at the tip and for some distance behind it. Plan to take cuttings 6 inches below the point where the green turns gray or brown, indicating a more mature stem that will root more easily.

WATER GARDENS

Cleaning concrete fountains is less of a chore if you do it annually and now is a good time to get it done.

When the water in your garden splashes too much, apply simple physics to solve the problem. The reservoir below the waterfall has to be big enough to accommodate the distance the water travels. If the lower level is 6 inches wide, splashing happens if the water falls more than 3 inches, or half its width. Increase the size of the lower level or reduce the distance the water falls to remedy the splash.

TO CLEAN A FOUNTAIN

1. Gather up plastic sheeting, a scrub brush with stiff nylon bristles, household bleach, your garden hose, a toothbrush you can sacrifice, and white vinegar.

2. Plastic wrap the plants below the fountain if it is situated in a garden bed. If yours sits at the center of a courtyard, shield any nearby plants.

3. Disconnect and take out the fountain's pump and rinse it with vinegar. Use the toothbrush to scrub it well and rinse it thoroughly.

4. Drain the fountain. Pour in a little bleach and use the scrub brush to clean every crevice.

5. Rinse completely with your hose. Trace amounts of bleach are decidedly not bird friendly.

WATER

ALL

It's hard to predict just how much you'll have to water this month. Less is sometimes more, since many plants are moving toward winter rest. But if the weather is windy with no rain, even those plants will stress without water, which could lead to damage later.

ANNUALS

Make another picking of summer annuals from the cut flower row, deadhead beds and pots, and water them well.

BULBS

Water Holland bulbs well when you plant, but unless the winter is uncharacteristically dry, don't worry anymore about them. To encourage spider lily clumps to bloom more and reproduce next year, water them well this month.

EDIBLES

You cannot control the weather, but you can be very regular about watering edibles that are growing actively—vegetables and fruits like pineapple guava and loquat (*Feijoa sellowiana, Eriobotrya japonica*) that ripen fruit in winter in Zone 9. While other kinds of plants do well with less water in fall, edibles do not.

LAWNS

Keep the areas you recently repaired and new sod well hydrated until night temperatures are 50 degrees Fahrenheit for a week. Even if you have an inground system, this task may be better done with an oscillating sprinkler. The classic back-and-forth motion of the sprinkler allows time for percolation without flooding these vulnerable lawns.

PERENNIALS & ORNAMENTAL GRASSES

If the weather is dry, water perennials in bloom, such as tall salvias (*S. guaranitica* 'Black and Blue', *S. leucantha* (Mexican bush sage). Their spectacular flower spikes provide essential nectar for bees now, and excessively dry conditions will spoil the nectar.

ROSES

Water the rose bushes this month, especially those in bloom. After flowering has finished, water deeply once more and not again for a month unless the weather remains dry and hot—above 75 degrees Fahrenheit in the daytime.

SHRUBS

Water established shrubs only if needed to prevent water stress. Refresh or replace the mulch in shrub beds and under hedges and then water the plants deeply to settle the mulch. Dry mulch absorbs much of the available water so it cannot reach the soil below.

TREES

Get water reservoirs ready for big tree planting projects. If you are reusing a bag system, clean it thoroughly when you take it out of storage or move it from one tree to another. We plant trees in fall and winter primarily because they need so much less water than in the spring or summer.

Still, newly planted trees that cannot be watered may be stressed, leading to bigger problems such as cankers on Leyland cypress.

VINES & GROUNDCOVERS

October brings fine conditions to dig and divide groundcovers. Some of the plants might be small and easily transplanted. Others can have thick crowns or long vines and must be coaxed and cut back to move them. Both kinds are subject to transplant shock if not watered well at planting and for several weeks afterward. Remember that these are young plants trying to put out new roots right after transplant. Water them slowly but do not overwater their beds or pots.

WATER GARDENS

Check water levels in water features and ponds as you take out pots of tender plants. Each one displaces a volume of water and can lower the level below the pump's intake. Change the water in pond pots you will be protecting this winter.

FERTILIZE

ALL

The indoor garden gets very busy now that you've moved the tender plants to windowsills and sunrooms, and arranged flowering plants under the warm glow of supplemental lights. Just as different plants need water more or less often, some of your houseplants—a loose term here that means anything growing indoors, not just tropical foliage plants—need fertilizer at different times.

- Add a slow-release complete formula fertilizer to every pot. That's enough for some, like snake plants, jade plants, and others that have grown as large as you want.

- Use a flowering formula mixed in water monthly on flowering plants like begonias, kalanchoes, and miniature gardenias.

- Water in a complete soluble formula monthly to tropical foliage plants you are growing.

- Do not fertilize pots you are holding in cold storage or those with bulbs that have gone dormant like caladiums.

ANNUALS

If you have actively growing annuals like pansies, ornamental kale and cabbage, foxglove, geranium, and dianthus, stick to a regular fertilizer program. You can use a slow-release, pellet formula and water with a soluble formula every two weeks too. Skip an application or two in really freezing weather, but otherwise keep fertilizing to keep annuals growing.

Clever, crafty ideas emerge from kitchens and gardens all the time, often melding two passions into one. Line up your favorite bud vases or antique bottles on the kitchen window, add water, and pop in bare stems of coleus and wax begonias (*Begonia sempervirens*). Instantly, you create a showcase to display collections and gain a place to root and grow.

Ornamental kale and cabbage plants too often end up looking like cartoon characters—fat faces over skinny legs, their leafless stems. You can usually solve this problem if you treat this pair like their vegetable relatives and fertilize them more than other annuals.

BULBS

The most effective fertilizer for bulbs at planting time is a formula made for them that you put directly into each hole as you go. You do not need to use bone meal, but if you do, be aware that it takes months to decompose and become available to plants of any kind. Bone meal applied now will be very helpful next year.

EDIBLES

Fertilize greens after each big picking to stimulate more new leaves. You'll keep the patch neater and more productive by grooming as you pick no matter whether you grow mustards, chard, or whatever. Take two bags or baskets with you to the garden, one for greens you'll take to the kitchen and the other for the compost.

Frequent picking of greens from mustards to leaf lettuces and mesclun mixes means clipping leaves beginning when they are 4 inches tall. Keep a small spray bottle handy to maintain the little crops' health. Use it to spray a soapy water mix if insects appear and to spray compost tea or soluble fertilizer on the leaves to avoid the issues wet soil can cause. Read product labels to be certain you are using a fertilizer designed to be applied to the foliage.

SHRUBS AND TREES

You can root feed the plants in this category with a formula that contains no nitrogen, such as 0-20-20. These formulas may be best applied to trees by the drill method that puts small amounts of fertilizer in holes around the base of the tree. How much to use depends on the diameter of the trunk. In general a 6-inch diameter tree will need about a pound per inch, but consult the product label for detailed instructions. Figure the amount to use and distribute it into 2-inch holes, 1 foot deep and 2 feet apart. Start the holes at the drip line and work in the direction of the trunk; you can crank a big hand-powered drill, but a power drill saves your arms and goes much faster.

Established plants in these categories should not be fertilized this month. Excess nitrogen fertilizer in the fall can promote leafy growth now that can be damaged by frosts before it has time to harden off. Read labels carefully to avoid using nitrogen now.

LAWNS

Three weeds with round leaves are especially troublesome in lawns across our states. Depending on where you live, one or more of these will find you: dichondra, ground ivy, and dollar weed. Each has their place, but it is not in the lawn.

- Dichondra (*D. carolinensis*) has cute little kidney-shaped leaves that thrive in sunny, cool conditions. It creeps into your lawn on stems that root each time they touch the ground. They compete successfully with the lawn where conditions are wet. Dichondra is the easiest of the three weeds to rogue out, or you can control it: pre-emerge in fall, spot spray in spring.

- Ground ivy (*Glechoma hederacea*) takes over shady lawn areas. Its scalloped round leaves rise on aboveground runners that spread quickly. Adjust sprinklers to water shady areas less and mow high so the grass blades can shade the weeds. Use sprays that are labeled to control ground ivy in spring and fall, or give over the area and enjoy their sweet spring flowers.

- Dollar weed (*Hydrocotyle* spp.) has the roundest leaves in the group, slick and shiny green lily pads just the right size for a fairy garden.

■ *Lettuce grows better in the cooler weather of autumn than in late spring or summer.*

■ *Dollar weed*

Dollar weed can float and grows where conditions are too wet for grass to grow. Its underground rhizomes sprout new leaves every time you pull them out. Get the excess water out of the lawn and follow label directions to spray dollar weed in fall and spring.

ROSES

Japanese beetles can skeletonize the leaves of roses and other plants in summer, but controlling them then solves only part of the problem. Take charge of the white grub population in your lawn now to get ahead of next year's beetles, their adult form. Both organic and conventional controls are effective, especially if you apply them in fall and spring consecutively. Milky spore fungus takes longer to become established in the lawn and works longer, while the conventional products are faster acting.

Beetles of all kinds are drowsy in the morning. Whenever and wherever you find them feeding, spread a cloth sheet on the ground under the plants—roses in summer, beans and cucumbers in spring and fall. Shake the plants to dump the beetles from their beds so you can dispose of them.

SHRUBS

The scruffy bunch of shrubs at the back end of a property may be serious pests within a native plant paradise, which you'll never see and enjoy, unless you control these invading plants. Some plants imported in the last century have turned out to be less than good guests; kudzu is the best example, but privet shrubs should be avoided in planting decisions and removed when possible. The Chinese privet, in particular, spreads rapidly by roots and seeds and shades huge areas previously populated with a variety of more desirable, native plants like wake robin (*Trillium*).

TREES

Hurricane-force winds knock down trees, but others turn brown within a year, especially pines. Those winds lift the trees up from their roots and then let them back down without knocking them over. The biochemistry involved with this process releases substances that cue southern pine beetles (*Dendroctonus*) and other insects that a tree is under stress. A female beetle locates the tree and calls in reinforcements to mate, bore into bark crevices, and set up snake-shaped galleries for the clan. Long after the storm, you see pine needles turn brown, but the beetles are probably long gone by then. Sadly, these insects devastate large areas of our forests and are a major pest with no good control. Have the trees removed, including their stumps.

Unlike lichens, mistletoe (*Phorodendron*) can be a problem when it takes over tree branches. This plant is alternately cursed and celebrated. Homeowners worry the mistletoe will kill the tree, but this seldom happens. Decorators prize it for holiday parties but often overlook the local sources. Its seeds are distributed by birds and sprouts root-like haustorias that penetrate the bark and rob the tree of water and nutrients. Chemical control is seldom very effective and regrowth happens, but pruning from now through the winter can be effective. Cut the mistletoe off by pruning the branch a foot behind it.

VINES & GROUNDCOVERS

Vines look lovely climbing high in a tree, but you worry if they are hurting the tree. As a general rule, a leafy vine can coexist with a tree so long as no more than one quarter of the tree's branches becomes obscured by it. Dense vines wrapped tightly can effectively girdle the branch, suppressing its ability to leaf out and conduct photosynthesis. Keep vines and trees in balance by limiting the number you allow to climb and choosing only big, healthy trees for this partnership. Cut excess vines now at ground level or wherever you can reach them and repeat the process in the spring.

November

November is a month of anticipation. You plant bulbs and trust they'll come up and bloom, bake zucchini from the fall garden into bread, and hope everyone likes it at the office party. The month builds to Thanksgiving, sometimes with tension about who cooks what or whether your aunt will be able to keep your uncle in check. When all is said and done, there is the garden. It's where we go to relax, to exercise, to escape, and to find the personal balance that keeps anticipation from turning to all-out worry.

Indoors, the saucers and watering cans work overtime as the houseplants readjust after their "vacation" on the porch. Outdoors, the green light is on to dig up woody plants and replant perennials, shop for new additions, and plant your propagations. Conversations run to the benefits of "planting high" for plants like dogwood (all *Cornus*) and azaleas (*Rhododendron*) that demand excellent drainage. The rootball is nestled about halfway into the planting hole with soil and mulch pulled up around it. The strategy, like so many of our inventions, seems counterintuitive, but it works here.

When experts tell us what to do, people in our states seldom follow suit. Sometimes, as with the trend to "eat local" and "nose to tail" cuisine, it's hard to suppress a laugh because that's how we live. The idea of eating what's in season and using all you've got comes natural to us, like sharing the flowers from our garden and saving their seeds. Most of us come from people who hunted, fished, and planted gardens simply to be able to eat. Today, need has mostly given way to the pure joy of the quest for game, the humble gambit of planting seeds. But our quirky souls make us ambivalent at times—we love Bambi until she eats the entire hosta bed for supper, and then venison sounds great.

Leaves drop in their own time for weeks and some, like red oak (*Quercus rubra*), don't shed one year's cloak until just shortly before the new one comes on. But one day in November, the wind picks up abruptly and showers of leaves fall in earnest. They swirl and lift, then float in waves to the ground, and the sight is oddly comforting, a sure sign that the season has finally changed and the holidays are here.

NOVEMBER

PLAN

ALL

Honeybees are in the news all around the planet since the first reports of commercial hive losses began shortly after the turn of this century. These large hives are trucked cross-country to pollinate such crops as almonds, which are almost completely dependent on them for successful crop production. Indeed, the problem has become so serious that almond breeders are working to develop self-pollinating varieties. More than 90 percent of everything in the average person's diet depends on insect pollination, either to produce the edible itself or the seed that grows the next generation. While beekeeping has never been without routine threats and serious challenges, this problem has puzzled the best.

The good news for honey lovers is that local honey production in our states continues strong as it does in most places. However, smart gardeners take steps to minimize threats to honeybees and other pollinators with these strategies:

- Reduce or eliminate the use of pesticides. Especially avoid pesticides with residual or long-term impact on the environment such as systemics.

- Allow some rogue weeds to bloom where they do not create a problem for cultivated beds.

- Grow blooming plants throughout the year at different heights from ground level to treetops.

- Install a water feature or mister or string a soaker hose on the lawn occasionally to create a water supply for pollinators.

ANNUALS

Plan color for a cause! Annuals in beds and containers can reflect your issues and passions, such as planting pink to support breast cancer research. There's time to get the whole block on board with plans for group purchases of seed and plants—and to get the best seeder (probably you) to teach everybody else. Consider pink possibilities: polka dot plants (*Hypoestes phyllostachya*) in front of double impatiens

■ *Flowers like this blue aster will help attract honeybees.*

(*I. walleriana*) or 'Fanny Munson' caladiums in shade, or classic pink zinnia shades in sun.

BULBS

Most tulips are grown as annuals in our states and are planted with them. But when you plan for perennial tulips in Zones 7 and 8 or for grape hyacinths anywhere, a different site will be needed. Because these bulbs are not tall and will be with you for years, identify a sunny site near the front of a bed with other perennials or shrubs.

Tulipa clusiana or 'Lady Jane' is a reliable perennial tulip in Zones 7 and 8 that was, for years, mostly a rumor. Increasing availability has made this diminutive pink and white tulip a reality, but you still may have to get on a waiting list to have it. Plan ahead.

EDIBLES

Even as fall settles in, smart gardeners start planning for fruit trees and a better vegetable garden next year. Select a sunny site with access to water, decide about space, sides, paths, and what you want to grow. With a road map to follow, and time to do it before spring, the soil and its amendments have time to blend together, or "mellow" in readiness for planting.

LAWNS

Start your holiday gift list early with a picture of the mower that will solve your lawn problems. Your mower may be too small for the job or it may create a cut that looks sloppy right after you finish. You may want more exercise or to save more time; research mowers to find the one that will meet your needs. Check out push mowers for very small lawns, top-quality rotary mowers for average lots, riding mowers for larger properties including zero-turn options. Learn the advantages of electric and battery power sources, consider mulching mowers, and take a look at reel mowers for a professional cut.

PERENNIALS & ORNAMENTAL GRASSES

Plan for borders that not only grow healthy plants but also work visually.

- Soil levels within beds can be adjusted slightly to make plants at the back look taller and to put their flowers over those in front. Raising the back area by 4 inches will not affect drainage but can transform the way the bed looks.

- A neat edge along and around borders and beds has an astonishing effect on how the planting looks. Like a pressed collar and combed hair, an edge kept clean and free of weeds makes everything else look better. Do it with plants or hardscape, but keep edging in your plan.

One lovely edging plant brings cottage garden charm and clove fragrance to the spring garden. Cottage pinks (*Dianthus plumarius*) and

■ *Cottage pinks* (Dianthus) *can be divided in fall.*

related hybrids are silver gray clumps of leaves that look like porcupine quills. The flowers are white or pink but also have zigzag edges that might have been cut by pinking shears. No more than a foot tall, cottage pinks can grow in a range of light conditions but will bloom best in full sun.

ROSES

Every garden needs more romance, and a rose in full bloom on a column or arbor is a great way to get it. If you don't have either sort of structure and want something unusual, plan a trip to an architectural salvage warehouse. To hold a big rose, supports may need to be set in concrete and allowed to cure before planting in February. Imagine what you'd like to see and plan for it now.

HERE'S HOW

TO EDGE LANDSCAPE BEDS

1. With your sharpened spade, stand on the outside of the bed and hold the spade at the edge of the bed at a 90-degree angle with the spade handle leaning back into the bed. Chop an angle with the spade along the entire bed. During this step, you'll remove soil or sod clumps from the edge of the bed.

2. Use a shop broom or pitchfork to clean up. Pick up grass clumps and compost them. If you're edging along a hard surface, use a shop broom to sweep the soil into a dust pan (put the soil in the compost pile), or to push back the soil into the bed, away from the newly cut edge.

■ *Many roses need to be supported by trellises or other structures.*

Rebar is the colloquial term for concrete reinforcing rods made of steel that have ridged lines in a whorl around them to provide more surface area that can strengthen concrete as it sets. Rebar is available at home-improvement stores in precut lengths from 18 inches to 3 feet or more, and it can be the best way to set up or reinforce small or medium-sized plant supports. Drive rebar into the ground like stakes where the "feet" on trellises extend at its base and wire the trellis on as you install it. If a support threatens to give way, use rebar to reinforce it.

SHRUBS

Propagating shrubs from semi-hardwood cuttings in summer does not always result in rooted cuttings. Don't fret—plan hardwood cuttings you can start this fall and winter. The time to take these cuttings is after the first freeze, or when the weather is as cold as you expect it to get, or sometime between November and February. Figure out where you will put bundles of cuttings in damp sand or vermiculite—plan to bury them in thin-walled plastic pots in a trench.

TREES

For the hard-to-please and environmentally conscious on your list, plan to plant a tree in someone's honor as a gift this year. Pick a spot at the family home or think bigger and organize the congregation to plant woods behind the church. Or contact local and state beautification programs for public projects such as Mississippi's Avenue of Magnolias. Each tree you personally plant or

sponsor helps to replace the millions lost to storms already this century.

VINES & GROUNDCOVERS

You do not have to know the name of the clematis vine to know when to prune it. Watch yours to learn its habits and plan to grow all three kinds.

- Summer- and fall-blooming clematis do not have to be pruned, and some will happily crawl over a pergola for years. The best known, autumn clematis, will soon eat up any available space. Prune both in early spring before new growth starts. Take the autumn clematis down to a foot, but prune the others only as needed to a healthy leaf bud, the swollen spot on the vine that will soon pop out leaves.

- Repeat blooming clematis usually put on a big show in spring or fall and flowers intermittently the rest of the time. If yours finished its prime time in fall, plan to prune it in late winter or early spring. Prune after abundant spring blooms, even though it may cost later flowers in the current year, to prepare for another great spring.

■ *You can prune autumn clematis back to a foot tall in early spring.*

- Spring blooming clematis flower on the wood they produced the preceding year. Plan to prune after flowering, as much or as little as needed to shape the vine. Keep these vines on your list of annual tasks so you don't have to cut into very old wood that is unlikely to rejuvenate.

WATER GARDENS

When you add fish to a water feature, you add an entirely different dimension to their appeal. Goldfish, mollies, and koi are obvious options, but plan to add mosquito fish (*Gambusia*) to make it a safer place. These attractive 3-inch-long silver fish will eat anything, but are particularly fond of insect larvae; they also eat algae.

PLANT

ANNUALS

Sowing sweet pea (*Lathyrus odorata*) and larkspur (*Consolida*) seeds can be like reading a map—those who are good at it cannot understand what's wrong with the rest of humanity. Some plant the seeds sooner or wait until spring, but seeding this month has advantages. Start early in the northern counties and by the end of the month or so in Zone 9. Many plant on Thanksgiving Day, saying it's a fine family activity, but also to avoid setting the table or clearing it.

- Sweet peas can be knee high or taller, to about 6 feet. Space smaller varieties closer together for mutual support and give the stately vines room to climb. To speed germination, nick the seeds and/or soak them in warm water before planting. Similar to their edible cousins, sweet peas grow faster in cool weather.

- Larkspur seeds sown now get the cold treatment they need to sprout and grow. Rake up and amend a seedbed that will be their home for years as they reseed as prolifically as candytuft (*Iberis sempervirens*) and Mexican hat (*Ratibida columnifera*). Work in organic matter now and fertilize the seedlings in spring.

BULBS

Like moss, woods sorrel bulbs are polarizing—you either love or hate them. Like many of the garden's ironic twists, it's usually those that see them as weeds that have the most. Your neighbor may have some to dig up or you can purchase plants or bulbs. All are low-growing with distinctive leaves and bell-shaped flowers.

- Purple shamrock (*Oxalis regnellii*), also known as love plant, has the deepest purple leaves in the garden and dainty pinkish white flowers. It is reliably perennial and not invasive.

- False shamrock (*O. triangularis*) has classic green leaves and white blooms, often in time for St. Patrick's Day.

- Yellow woods sorrel (*O. stricta*) has clover-shaped leaves and pink woods sorrel (*O. articulata*) are prolific and often considered weeds. Both make excellent groundcovers for difficult areas but do not belong in cultivated garden beds as the shamrock types do.

Where to find space for bulbs in the garden depends on what each one can take—how much sun they need, how much water they can stand. Plant anemone and ranunculus bulbs in raised rose beds and cut flower rows, crocus in pots by the front door, and Spanish hyacinths in the shade garden.

EDIBLES

It's time to plant sugar snap, snow, and English peas in Zones 8b and 9 in full sun spaces with a trellis for them to climb. Even short varieties will need support to keep leaves and peas clean; use short bamboo stakes or wattle fencing to gather them together for mutual support. Farther north, grow these and other spring garden vegetables in the greenhouse or other protected outdoor sites like high tunnels. Save space by growing container vegetable varieties with these space considerations:

- Three plants in a 1-gallon pot: radish, parsley, carrots, beets, green onion (up to 5 green onions per 1-gallon pot)

- Two plants in a 1-gallon pot: spinach, Swiss chard, lettuces, turnips, mustard greens

- One plant in a 2-gallon pot: broccoli, cabbage, cauliflower

LAWNS

Use a seeder to spread ryegrass on bare ground, browned bermuda lawns, and mow-what-grows areas this month. Seed at higher rates (8 to 10 pounds per 1,000 square feet) to protect bare ground from erosion and let the fibrous roots penetrate the soil to improve it. Use slightly less in mow-what-grows areas except in bare spots and still less (5 pounds per 1,000 square feet) to overseed bermudagrass. The lawn will be plenty green all winter and better able to rebound in the spring with a lighter seeding.

PERENNIALS & ORNAMENTAL GRASSES

Weather permitting, plant seeds for favorite perennials such as gayfeather or blazing star (*Liatris spicata*) and coral bean (*Erythrina herbacea*). Start them in pots in colder areas and direct seed them into the garden in Zones 8b and 9. In between, do both. If the seedlings don't make it, you have potted starts to transplant. Should you be successful with both methods, take the potted plants to a plant swap or donate them.

ROSES

Plant roses grown in containers—those roses you rooted or layered and any you find in shops. Prune one quarter of the top growth if it is lush or if the canes are damaged; otherwise, wait until February and prune with established roses. You can dig up and move roses when the weather pattern becomes consistently cool—days in the 60s, nights above freezing.

SHRUBS AND TREES

Ready, set, dig! From November through February conditions are close to ideal for moving woody plants from one place to another. Moderate temperatures, little wind, good soil moisture, and plants in a resting or dormant stage combine to reduce transplant shock. Some days are better than others, of course, but the longer a transplant has to adjust to a new site and recover its roots, the better. Then they are ready to leaf out as the seasons change without stress.

- When you dig up a tree from a group to transplant it to another site, take care not to damage nearby trees.

- Dig when the soil is moist, not wet enough to stick to your shovel or so dry it makes dust.

- Use a sharpshooter long-bladed shovel to create wedge-shaped, deep root balls for transplant.

VINES & GROUNDCOVERS

Find well-drained, shallow soils to grow these durable, but underused, groundcovers: creeping rosemary (*R. officinalis* 'Prostratus'), pennyroyal (*Mentha pulegium*), citronella (*Cymbopogon nardus*), and creeping sage (*Salvia sonomensis*). Do not be deterred by overcrowded pots and flats—use them to your advantage. Use a sharp knife to cut right through the soil and separate individuals or small clumps of plants. Plant as you go with this method so cut roots do not dry out. Water in with a starter solution and mulch around the groundcovers to suppress weeds.

WATER GARDENS

Dig up crowded clumps of perennial plants (except Louisiana iris) around the edges of water gardens. Divide and replant, then pot up the extras or transplant them to garden beds. Some, like flag iris, will have leaves—cut half their height to reduce stress in this process. Others such as canna lilies will be browned or nearly so and easier to handle.

CARE

ALL

When it comes to taking the best care of your garden, raised beds, or creating an elevated planting area, offer advantages to growing most plants in our soils. You are likely to improve them by increasing organic matter and moderate drainage. That results in a greater soil volume than you started with and a higher elevation that will settle. Raised beds require less stooping, especially if you add a seat to the sides. That makes them a boon to both plants and gardeners.

- You gain better growing conditions, neater looks, and perhaps lower maintenance. There are few garden tasks more time-consuming than mowing or trimming around individual

■ *Raised planting beds are easy to make from landscape lumber. In addition to elevating the plants so they're easier to reach, raised beds keep plants and leaves from spreading, limit diseases, and allow you to more easily customize your soil amendments. A colorful raised bed also provides yard decoration in nongrowing seasons.*

plants stuck out in the lawn. The results always look spotty even when there is no damage to plants from power equipment.

- Raised beds do not require sides but may have 2-inch landscape timbers, 4-inch bricks, or 6-inch boards, depending on location and plants. For example, a brick-edged kitchen garden with herbs and asparagus will be in place for years while a bed that will be replanted seasonally will need more access. Bolted wooden sides work here because they can be opened to work soil, mulch, and plant.

- The height of a raised bed without sides does matter. If it is more than 4 to 6 inches high, you will water much more often in dry weather. However, a lower elevation may sink to ground level in just a few seasons.

ANNUALS

Sunrooms and greenhouses are a delightful environment for garden annuals and tropical foliage plants, but you can create those conditions almost anywhere. You control water and fertilizer regimes; maintaining humidity levels can be as simple as grouping plants on trays of gravel kept damp and misting them regularly. Light intensity and duration can be the limiting factors until you

set up supplemental artificial light sources. Here's what popular groups need:

- Blooming plants need eight hours per day of sunlight or its equivalent, located 1 foot from them. These are windowsill plants well-suited for grouping under lights.

- Plants with variegated leaves may benefit from slightly higher light levels such as a table in a sunny room away from the window. You can put them to the side of a supplemental light, rather than directly under it.

- Tropical foliage plants do well in light that is bright enough to read a newspaper at midday, but has no direct sun.

Garden mums and annual asters dry up, flowers and some leaves turn brown. Whether or not this signals the end of them can be revealed by a closer look. Clip off the spent flowers plus the stems and leaves that are browned. If even a few inches remain, pull up the mulch and let the mums be—chances of rebloom next spring are good.

Snapdragons can take a hit from early frosts and you may be tempted to rip them out in frustration. Resist! Most varieties will recover on their own, but if the tips look burned or the flowers flop, cut

HERE'S HOW

TO PLANT NARCISSUS BULBS

1. Pick a flat-bottomed, preferably heavy container with no drain holes, 4 to 5 inches deep.

2. Lay 2 inches of pea gravel, 1-inch stones, or marbles into the container.

3. Cram the bulbs in, pointy end up, to fill the space.

4. Fill around the bulbs up to their shoulders with more of the same "rocks."

5. Water the pot once well.

6. To reduce stem stretching, put the pot into a dark, cool place like an unheated closet.

7. Check weekly, add water if the bulbs are very dry, and wait for white stems to be 4 inches tall.

8. Move the pot to a sunny windowsill and water as needed until flowers are done.

them back by a few inches. Fertilize the snaps as usual during a pleasant week along with other overwintering annual flowers.

BULBS

Start paperwhite (or gold) narcissus (*N. tazetta*) bulbs now for holiday gifts and decorating, a process that takes about six weeks to complete.

EDIBLES

Pick greens and lettuce often to keep new leaves coming and use cloches to trap the sun's warmth inside on cool days.

Finish the potato harvest if you have not and compost the stems and leaves—that green plant material is valuable this time of year. Work up the area, add organic matter, and mark it to grow something besides more potatoes or tomatoes next spring.

LAWNS

Mow and edge one more time before you clean up the equipment and store it out of the weather. Use up the last of any fuels or drain them, rinse the mower deck, and get needed repairs made now.

PERENNIALS & ORNAMENTAL GRASSES

Timely grooming now does more than enhance curb appeal. Remove stems and leaves as plants die back to benefit the perennial crown. It will not be pushed to releaf in warm spells, and stems will not conduct water into its center where rot can begin. Resist the urge to pull and instead, clip stems close to the crown without disturbing it, and remove all plant debris from the bed.

ROSES

Deadhead faded flowers and stems that have given up their rosehips to the birds. Clean up fallen leaves, pull weeds, and add flowering annuals and bulbs to rose beds for winter color and nectar.

Some roses growing in some places never lose their leaves, and a few flowers may try to bloom in warm weeks there. Evergreen rose care is not a common topic! This condition needs no encouragement with fertilizer but do not hesitate to water if needed. Take advantage of the situation and prune off the dead wood that stands out now as brown and thorny. But do not prune leafy canes except to deadhead flowers and hips.

SHRUBS AND TREES

Leave sprouts of shrubs and trees and to form thickets that contribute to wildlife habitat by creating protected spaces in the garden. Be selective about what you leave, harvest some, and rogue out those that are weak. Cut those stems slightly below ground to slow down regrowth. Begin taking hardwood cuttings.

You know how important trees are to the environment and the ecology of your garden. But some do need to be removed, and if they can be transplanted, complete that task now. Should they be unsuitable for replanting, plan to add a new tree elsewhere to keep the population in balance without hazards. Consider removing trees that are too close to your house or other structures, especially if they are thin for their height or already damaged by storms or pests.

Finish the task—if you must cut down trees, have the limbs, trunks, and stumps ground up. This material is precious, but not today. Let it rot for six to twelve months before using it as a soil amendment or mulch.

VINES & GROUNDCOVERS

Deep South gardeners face three native plants that are poisonous and should be removed or avoided for safe gardening. As in most situations, spray programs are most effective when accompanied by physical controls. But if you are allergic or have never dealt with them, consider hiring a person with more experience and less vulnerability. Do not burn these plants—their essential oils are toxic if inhaled. Poison sumac (*Toxicodendron vernix*) and poison oak (*T. pubescens*) are not as widespread as poison ivy (*T. radicans*).

Poison ivy patrol gets easier now as its fabulous fall color separates it from evergreen vines and groundcovers. Now, before the leaves are gone, cut the vines at ground level if they are climbing and flag the spot. You can use a landscape marker or spray paint the vine, just mark it so its first leaves

HERE'S HOW

TO ROOT HARDWOOD CUTTINGS

1. Select healthy stems as big around as a pencil and locate where this year's growth began. There will usually be a slight change in color or character at that point.

2. Take cuttings below the tip and above the old wood. You can often get several cuttings from one branch.

3. Make 6-inch cuttings, or whatever it takes to get three to five nodes on each. These growing points are often swollen or may be marked by a slight dot on thin stems.

4. Cut so the base end is slanted and the top cut is straight across to keep the wood right end up and sometimes create more area that can callus to promote rooting.

5. Bundle hardwood cuttings into groups of a dozen, label with plant and date, and plunge into containers of damp sand or vermiculite.

6. Store where it's cold but not freezing so a callus can form and rooting can begin by spring.

7. Check on hardwood cuttings monthly in storage to be sure they are not drying out.

■ *Poison ivy becomes easier to identify and target for control in the fall when it turns colors.*

will not escape your attention next spring. Mow ground level plantings of poison ivy to scalp them, exposing the vines to winter freezes.

WATER GARDENS

You don't have to drain your water feature for winter because the ground does not freeze, but you may want to anyway. Leaks and punctures, loose pieces of stone, too much soil in the bottom, and other issues are much easier to fix in a drained water feature.

Sometimes tasks get delayed, like putting the cover on the water feature to keep out the falling leaves. Clean them out before more than a few inches accumulate—if you leave them to rot all winter, they get slimy and very difficult to remove. Lift out hardy aquatic plants growing in pots in the pond and get in there, but take care not to damage the liner as you pull out the plant material. For this task, a spatula and rubber gloves can be handy.

WATER

ALL

With increased numbers of confirmed West Nile virus cases has come greater understanding of the important role water plays in the mosquito life cycle. There is not only the obvious need to remove sources of standing water but also to understand how little water can create habitat for them. A puddle in the compost pile or under the firewood rack, a pile of mulch that stays wet, a leaky hose bib, a plant saucer left full—these and more can become mosquito homes at any time of the year. November is no exception.

ANNUALS

Looks can be deceiving, but a fingertip tells you if soil needs watering in beds or pots. Even those still growing will use less water in cooler weather because less water is lost to transpiration through the leaves. Soil surfaces stay a darker color, but use your index finger to decide when to water them.

- Plants that need consistently damp soil such as ferns should feel moist up to the first knuckle all of the time.

■ *Use a hyacinth glass to add some color to your home this month.*

- Most plants thrive in a soil that dries out slightly between waterings. Your knuckle can feel damp, drying, and dry. This group should be watered when the soil is drying.

- Those that need to dry out completely between waterings to avoid rot, such as succulents, can feel dry for a month or more.

BULBS

Hyacinth glasses offer a way to grow bulbs with only their basal plate and roots in water. These shapely vases are transparent so you can see when to add water. Do not let the bulbs dry out!

Amaryllis kits make excellent gifts, especially if you start them growing. Pot the bulb as directed, water once, and put it in a bright window. Before you add a bow for delivery, water once again.

EDIBLES

Like annual flowers, vegetable plants may need less water this month but cannot be allowed to dry out without suffering stress. Greens and cole crops can become bitter without enough water and lettuce will be limp.

Water fruit trees monthly if the weather is very dry to prevent desiccation.

LAWNS

No water should be required for established lawns this month. Water new lawns and repaired areas in windy, dry weather.

PERENNIALS & ORNAMENTAL GRASSES

Water enough this month to keep salvias blooming but let truly drought-tolerant perennials such as the perennial sunflower (*Helianthus*) finish their season and begin to die down for the year. Few plants go completely dormant in our states, but many require a rest period during the winter if they are to perform well year after year. For example, feathery astilbes (*Astilbe chinensis*) are known to burn up in the hot summers of Zone 8b and 9. But, like preschoolers, they also suffer without a rest period. Like fruit trees that need more chilling hours than a mild, wet winter affords, their roots try to grow when temperatures are warm enough. That sets them back in the following season.

ROSES AND SHRUBS

Water mature plants sparingly if at all this month, but do not allow new plantings to dry out.

TREES

Indoor gardens often feature tropical trees like weeping fig and fiddleleaf fig (*Ficus benjamina, F. lyrata*) in large pots that can be difficult to water. Put their pots in saucers with 2-inch sides and put in 1 inch of water. If it is absorbed in less than 30 minutes, put in another inch.

VINES & GROUNDCOVERS

Water big pots of tropical vines very well once before you put them into storage. Check monthly and water pots in the garage, shed, or other unheated structure just enough to keep their soil from freezing.

WATER GARDENS

If you remove plants and fish from the water feature, check the water quality and temperature in storage frequently. Floating thermometers are handy for this purpose—think of them as inexpensive insurance and check them frequently.

FERTILIZE

ALL

No matter what kind of plants you grow indoors—coleus or clivia bulbs, woody gardenia or a pot of herbs, it matters how you fertilize them. There is a fine line between keeping plants alive and providing enough nutrients for them to actually grow indoors; one strategy or another will work for all.

- To keep mature plants nicely green and prevent leaf loss, use a slow-release, pellet fertilizer or a stake made for indoor plants. You will only have to remember to add more as the label directs, usually at three-month intervals.

- Use the slow-release pellet fertilizer in pots you want to grow actively and supplement them with those you mix in water. Apply solubles monthly or mix at half strength and use every other week. This method works well for recently rooted cuttings such as those you took from tropical plants at the end of summer.

- Keep flowering fertilizer in the reservoir of plants like African violet (*Saintpaulia*) and gloxinia (*Sinningia speciosa*) to bring on blooms in January.

Get a plastic caddy that fits under your sink and fill it with indoor fertilizing necessities:

- Two-quart or 1-gallon watering can with a narrow spout

■ *Plant African violets in special pots that allow you to keep them watered and fertilized in the reservoir.*

- Plastic funnel and measuring spoons

- Small containers of fertilizer – one general purpose and one for flowering plants if needed.

- Hand mist if you intend to apply fertilizer directly to leaves.

Add these to complete the kit:

- Soft cloth to dust leaves

- Scissors to groom plants

- Small paintbrush and bottle of alcohol for quick pest control

If you have lots of pots, consider a rolling water tank with a spray nozzle so that you can mix enough water and fertilizer to handle them all.

ANNUALS AND EDIBLES
Continue fertilizing actively growing plants in this category.

Organic fertilizers work more slowly than conventional products, and the numbers on their labels do not tell the same story. When you use organics before planting and at regular intervals, their synergism with soil elements produces similar results. In the long term, organics persist in the soil with long-lasting, positive effects. Look for organics that have higher first numbers, the nitrogen content, and some amount of phosphorus and potassium, such as 5-1-1. Organic fertilizers derive from many natural resources including fish, seaweed, poultry litter, and byproducts such as feather meal, manures, and processing byproducts such as bone meal.

EDIBLES
Brussels sprouts seem to sit there without making sprouts. Few vegetables test your patience more than this one. In the best of conditions, it takes up to a month longer to make sprouts than broccoli and even longer to reach edible size. Brussels sprouts cannot be hurried, but if you miss a fertilizer application, they will be further delayed. Feed them monthly.

■ *It takes patience to grow Brussels sprouts this time of year.*

LAWNS
If you planted ryegrass and forgot to fertilize it, use a fall feeding formula with a low nitrogen level now. On the other hand, if you forgot to sow ryegrass last month, do it now and fertilize with the same kind of fertilizer. Neither will affect the dormant bermudagrass but will benefit the ryegrass.

Plants in the following categories will not benefit from *nitrogen* fertilizer this month, and its use may stimulate new growth that can be damaged by freezing temperatures. Use fertilizers without nitrogen intended to feed the roots only on new transplants and those in stress.

Bulbs

Lawns

Perennials and Ornamental Grasses

Roses

Shrubs

Trees

PROBLEM-SOLVE

BULBS

You plant tulips and opportunistic squirrels dig them up. The rodents are as interested in the cultivated soil as the bulbs, and sometimes take the tulips and stash acorns in their place. Deter their efforts: lay something on top of the planting that will deter digging, such as chicken wire, window screen, or flexible fencing. Just remember to remove it when the tulips sprout unless the mesh is big enough for them to grow through.

PERENNIALS & ORNAMENTAL GRASSES

Some insect problems persist year after year, such as aphids on peonies or spider mites on lantana. Dealing with them only when you see the damage—summer's sooty mold or mottled leaves—is only part of the solution. The fall clean up plays an important part, but you should do more than cut off browned stems and pick up fallen leaves. Get rid of weeds nearby perennials that have been infested and use a two-stage spray program to remove other places they might spend the winter.

■ *To keep squirrels from eating your tulips, protect the tulip bulbs with a mesh screen.*

Once the perennial bed is cleaned up, spray crowns and mulch with a product containing Neem for its combined pesticide properties to control any lingering pests or eggs.

When temperatures range between 40 and 75 degrees Fahrenheit, spray perennial crowns with horticultural oil and if the weather is warm, repeat in February. Where infestations have been severe and there are trees nearby, spray their trunks with the same oil spray.

SHRUBS

Undesired seedling trees sprout in the middle of shrubs and stick out like sore thumbs in the garden. Left alone or overlooked, these woody weeds compete for available water, fertilizer, and sunlight. Herbicide choices are difficult to use here, and a combination approach can prove more effective in such situations. Crawl up under there this month and cut the little trees down below ground level. Take one of these with you—a can of spray paint, a box of salt, or a bag of cornmeal. As you reach into the soil to cut the little trunk, use your choice to suppress regrowth. If this strategy is successful, you won't need the brush killers or other herbicides, but they will be available for round two if you need them.

VINES & GROUNDCOVERS

Too often a few plants in a groundcover bed repeatedly succumb to unknown causes. To change to another plant in only those areas is not practical or attractive and an unconventional alternative seems in order. For example, the liriope bed, also called lily turf (*L. muscari*), is healthy except around the downspout where the plants rot. Creative solutions might include:

- Consider widening the area around the spout by removing the plants and replacing them with gravel or marble chips.

- Put a water collection barrel under that downspout, add drip lines, and use it to irrigate the bed. It's a win-win because you solve the rot issue and put rainwater to work on site.

December

*Holiday cards wish you well, beautiful prints of snow-covered spruce trees, snowmen (and women), and icicles hanging from eaves. December doesn't look like that here, but it can get cold and even snow for a minute, much to the delight of schoolchildren. The best depictions of our most festive days might be blue sky and brilliant sunlight illuminating possum haw (***Ilex decidua***), its scarlet berries glistening on leafless gray stems. Or the evergreens of our gardens, dawn redwood (***Metasequoia glyptostroboides***) and cedar (***Cedrus***), surrounded by early camellias, Lenten rose clumps at their feet. That's what our gardens look like now and why so many snowbirds flock here.*

We'll decorate anything, including our pets and vehicles, often in an eclectic mix of classic and down home traditions. Perfectly beautiful ornaments on carefully clipped Scotch and Virginia pine trees hang side by side with off kilter stars handcrafted by the family's children. One office lights the Norfolk Island pine in the atrium, and another hangs a Charlie Brown fir tree upside down in the break room. We embrace and transform natural beauty with both exuberance and humor. Magnolia leaves and dried hydrangeas plus gilt, wire, time, and a crafty attitude soon equals a magnificent topiary. But we're just as likely to slip golden bamboo into a green vase, slap clear nail polish on the fat red berries, and call it a centerpiece.

Should the merriment wear thin or your best slacks feel snug, the tulips call out from the crisper drawer and you're into the garden. Falling leaves don't take a holiday, pansies and Brussels sprouts are hungry. The calendar says winter begins when the night length hits its maximum this month. Daylight begins to increase, second by second, toward spring, and you can feel it even as you repurpose the Christmas tree into a bird feeder or a create a pond habitat. This is the season of lights, of prayerful hopes for a brighter future.

December comes in with bells on, lights bonfires to guide Papa Noel, and departs with fireworks ablaze to paint the night sky on December 31. The garden year ends now, too, often with a stocking full of seeds for the new one to come.

PLAN

ALL

When you give yourself a greenhouse, life changes for the better—if you get what you want. Seed starting, propagation, and growing plants can span the seasons with a sturdy house in full sun and outfitted with shade cloth to control summer temperatures. Choose your sunniest site; arrange water and electricity close at hand and put grow racks, soil bins, and a potting bench on your wish list. Glass paned houses are grand, but rigid plastic walls can be easier to afford, set up, and maintain. Plastic sheeting covers many greenhouses and can last several years before you have to replace it. Plastic sheet houses have another advantage—you can design them with sides that roll up for needed ventilation.

ANNUALS

Seed and plant catalogs fill mailboxes—both physical and virtual this month. If you're too busy, they pile up on your desk or desktop, ready for you to plan next year's acquisitions. There are obvious advantages of growing from seed: expanded availability, wider range of colors, sizes, and shapes to choose from, control over quality, timing, and cost issues.

HERE'S HOW

TO FORCE TULIPS

- Force tulips in clay pots (five bulbs/6-inch pot).

- Put 2 inches of potting mix plus ground bark (ratio of 1:1) in the bottom and arrange the tulips with flat sides out and pointy ends up.

- Cover with more mix, leave 1 inch of head-space, and water well.

- Let tulips root for two weeks in a cool area (50 to 60 degrees Fahrenheit) such as an enclosed porch.

- Move pots to cooler conditions (40 degrees Fahrenheit) such as a refrigerator, an unheated garage, or buried deep in a pile of leaves on the north side of your house. A Styrofoam cooler makes a good storage bin.

- Check pots monthly and water if dry. Sprouts should appear in twelve weeks.

- Bring tulips into bloom in a sunny window indoors.

Vague or no information about growing should be a red flag when planning to order seed. The best catalogs are detailed and specific and they:

- Offer a range of time frames. Look for short-season varieties that bloom sooner and have better chances in our unpredictable spring and fall growing seasons. When spring turns hot in May, ten days less from seed to flower can make a big difference.

- Provide specific temperature, light requirements, and time frames for seed starting and transplant. A heating mat made for starting seeds is usually a good idea, and most seeds must be covered to sprout, but particular seeds can differ and you'd never know.

- Tell you what kind of seed you are buying—heirloom, hybrid, or another class such as

A wood-frame greenhouse with sheet-plastic cover is an inexpensive, semipermanent gardening structure that can be used as a potting area as well as a protective greenhouse.

stable hybrid—so you know whether saving seed will be an option.

BULBS

Plan to force tulips in pots for spring—shop now and use winter temperatures to your advantage in the new year.

EDIBLES

When you want to give gifts that will encourage others to love gardening, look no further than the garden center. Put together your favorite seed starting needs or look for clever seed starting kits that may include:

- Peat cups, soil pellets that expand when wet, and seeds

- Peat pellets, trays, and seeds

- Cube pellets in ready to plant trays

- Kits for very young children may include books with seeds

Check the information about seed catalogs in the Annuals section. Plan spring vegetable gardens now and consider how much space it takes to feed the average family of four.

• Greens, turnips, carrots	10 feet of space based on a row 1-foot wide
• Kale, cauliflower, cabbage	5 plants each
• Broccoli	8 plants
• Radishes, onions, beets	5 feet of each

LAWNS

Plan for less headaches next year. Decide to replace areas too shady for the lawn to grow. Alternatives to consider include mulch beds, raked gravel, and groundcovers. Edgings to consider include a shallow trench to separate the area, rolls of plastic or steel that is driven into the ground at the margin, and a ring of mulch to define it.

■ *Seed starting equipment is a great idea to put on your Christmas wish list.*

Younger relatives often get drafted into a variety of tasks that help their elders stay in their homes. If you live nearby, you're it. When that list includes yard work and you have your own yard to mow, consider that relatives who live farther away could give the gift of a lawn maintenance service. Suggest it!

PERENNIALS & ORNAMENTAL GRASSES

Plan to cut down ornamental grasses of all types next month or as soon as the clumps turn completely tan. Grasses can be late to brown and early to green, so prioritize pruning them every January. Plan to find more hospitable sites for them—drier for maiden grass, wetter for Muhly grass. You'll be able to dig, divide, and replant the grasses after pruning.

ROSES

If you want rose varieties that are not locally available, plan to order bare root or potted plants for early season delivery from southern sources. With good timing, you'll be able to get bare root roses into containers so roots start growing before transplant to the garden.

SHRUBS

Using one plant in repetition can calm a chaotic scene by reinforcing that visual element. Plan for a low hedge around beds to gain their serenity and

■ American Holly 'Canary'

lend formal style to the scene. Boxwood (*Buxus sempervirens*) is the classic choice, but look at soft tip hollies (*Ilex crenata*) for equal good looks, faster growth, and fewer pests.

A shrub bed filled with spring flowers and fall color can look like sticks in December. Add evergreen shrubs for texture and color in winter such as sasanqua and camellia, Himalayan sweet box (*Sarcococca*), Oregon grape (*Mahonia aquifolium*), and leatherleaf mahonia (*M. bealei*).

TREES

Plan to grow your own fish bait with a catalpa tree (*Catalpa bignonioides*), a southern classic that grows 40 to 70 feet tall and almost as wide. Related to trumpet creeper, cross vine, and royal empress tree (*Paulownia tomentosa*), catalpa is also fast-growing and seeds as readily. Like them, it is not for front yards but creates shade in just a few years out back. Fabulous flowers and leaves made for munching make catalpa the only host for the catalpa sphinx moth. Eggs hatch and caterpillars defoliate the tree as they grow into fine fish bait, but don't worry—the trees soon releaf.

VINES & GROUNDCOVERS

Plan to clean up at the old home place or around the backyard shed to pull deciduous vines off before they eat into wood or mortar. The vine with five pointy fingers that make up each leaf might be Virginia creeper or five finger vine (*Parthenocissus quinquefolia*). While any vine is capable of causing a skin reaction in some people, this one is not the same as poison ivy, although they are sometimes confused.

WATER GARDENS

Plan for excellent last-minute gifts from your own aquatic plant nursery. Buy or recycle the biggest plastic drink glasses you can find, and decorate them with holiday ribbons and stickers. Add water and water lettuce or a bunch of anacharis for a lovely gift.

PLANT

ANNUALS

Most annual flowers we grow over the winter for spring bloom can also be started from seed now. Sometime between the end of January and the end of February, you'll be able to transplant them to the garden.

Gardeners in north Mississippi and Alabama swear by sowing seed of foxglove, Canterbury bells, stock, cineraria, and English daisy in late December. If you live elsewhere in our states, do it sooner.

Tiny seeds can be hard to sow without creating clumps that are hard to thin properly. You don't realize you've dropped twenty seeds where three would do nicely and the mass that sprouts put tiny stems very close together. Mix the seed with sand, sifted compost, or finely screened vermiculite to distribute it more easily. Choose whichever material is a different color than the seed. If the seed are very small, put the mixture in a salt shaker.

BULBS

Although daffodil bulbs appear quite natural in random plantings, tulips seldom do. Straight rows can be the answer, as when tulips grow in a narrow space with pansies underneath. But if two or more rows will fit, stagger the bulbs so they are not directly behind one another. It's a better view, as is grouping tulips. Put them front and center of any bed in groups of five or more, preferably in odd numbers, spaced evenly. For very large plantings, remove the top 2 inches of soil and lay out a grid first, then place bulbs and plant. Or dig holes first using a long-handled bulb planter for less stooping or a power drill for faster work.

EDIBLES

Horseradish and pineapple don't get enough attention, and both can be started this month.

To enjoy horseradish in a few months, plant some in pots this month.

They're available in markets (or you can order horseradish root), and you use the part you don't eat to grow the plant.

- Cut the top half of a 6-inch-long horseradish root for culinary use and bury the rest by slanting it into a pot of garden soil mixed with ground bark (ratio of 1:1) so the top edge of the root is 2 inches deep. Water, put in a protected place outdoors to root, look for sprouts in eight to twelve weeks, and transplant to the garden.

- The crown of a fresh pineapple doesn't make good compost anyway (too fibrous) so make a fresh cut just below the leaves and put it in a shallow saucer of water. It only takes enough water to touch the bottom of the crown; more will rot it. As soon as you see a few white roots in the water, pot up the pineapple and grow it like any other terrestrial bromeliad.

LAWNS

Bare ground at your new home construction site will one day be your lawn, and erosion is not your friend. Sow a combination of fine-rooted ryegrass and alfalfa seed to push in now and hold it in place. As a bonus, the roots break up compacted soils so you don't have to work as hard to put in the lawn next year. Do a soil test to determine whether to lime or add nutrients before installing the lawn.

PERENNIALS & ORNAMENTAL GRASSES

By now the perennial wildflower seeds you planted should be recognizable enough to weed between them and scatter a little mulch around them. Use scissors if necessary to cut weeds out at ground level if pulling them might disturb the roots of your seedlings. Sow more seed now if there are gaps where the first sowing did not come up after six weeks.

ROSES

In Zone 9, you can separate, dig up, and plant roses you layered last summer. Mix potting soil and ground bark in equal amounts and move rooted cuttings up to small containers to grow on.

SHRUBS

Plant shrubs at will! Whether you dig one up or plant one grown in a container, woodies can be transplanted with little stress this month. In small gardens, spread shrub features across the year by planting quartets like this one:

- Spring: Mock orange (*Philadelphus coronarius*) brings white flowers that resemble dogwood on a plant that can grow in a wider range of sites.

- Summer: Indian hawthorn (*Raphiolepis indica*) has thick, stubby leaves and pink flowers in very well-drained soil.

- Fall: Virginia sweetspire (*Itea virginica*) is known for chains of white flowers in spring but overlooked for brilliant red and purple fall color.

- Winter: Winter jasmine (*Jasminum nudiflorum*) makes mounds of neat green leaves dotted with yellow flowers in late winter.

TREES

Plant all the trees you want this month and consider these that are underappreciated:

- Fruiting mulberry (*Morus alba*) is prized by birders for long chains of berries in summer that would be more popular with humans if they had fewer seeds.

Fruiting mulberry tree (Morus) *is a favorite for gardeners with wildlife in mind. Its berries bring in the birds!*

- 'Nellie Stevens' holly (*Ilex* x 'Nellie R. Stevens') tolerates almost any soil and grows several inches a year to become a medium-size tree, 30 feet by 10 feet. Berries are most plentiful when pollinated by one of its parents, cornuta holly (*I. cornuta*).

Palms and cycads bring tropical flair to your garden if you grow the right ones for your zone:

- Zone 7   needle palm (*Rhapidophyllum hystrix*)

- Zone 8   needle palm, windmill palm (*Trachycarpus fortunei*), pindo palm (*Butia capitata*), and palmettos (*Sabal minor, S. louisiana, S. texana*)

- Zone 9   all above and cabbage palm (*Sabal palmetto*) and Washington palm (*Washingtonia filifera*)

VINES & GROUNDCOVERS

Two vines with great potential for our gardens are overlooked often enough that they become conversation pieces when you grow them:

- Armand's clematis (*C. armandii*) has leathery evergreen leaves that separate it from the more familiar hybrid clematis. Fragrant white flowers with yellow centers appear in late winter and look different, too, with narrower petals and bloom clusters at the end of each stem. Armand climbs by wrapping its leaf stems like tendrils around anything nearby.

- Persian ivy (*Hedera colchica*) grows at a moderate rate with thick stems, coarse texture, and heart-shaped leaves that are dark green, variegated, or splashed with light green. Better behaved than its relative, English ivy, and hardier than Algerian ivy, this vine grows best in part shade.

WATER GARDENS

Separate plants that have grown crowded in pond pots and aquatic planters even if it means composting some material. Overcrowding, especially at cool temperatures, works to insulate water plants to some extent but can exacerbate rot in the pots.

CARE

ANNUALS

Be careful of stretching! When green stems do not get enough light, they respond by elongating their cells to compensate. They are not able to thicken up and soon flop over in the indoor garden or the seedling tray. Increase the light duration and/or intensity (how close the light is to the plants) to encourage thrifty growth.

BULBS

Check the mulch around established bulb plantings to keep weeds under control. Limit mulch to 1 inch over new tulips and other bulbs after planting. Lay on the mulch blanket and put squirrel barriers on top of it.

You take all the right steps to force paperwhite narcissus, but the weather is so warm in December that they stretch anyway. Keep the pots from falling over on the buffet table—grab a tall gift bag and slip the pot of bulbs into it with a few inches of stem and flowers showing at the top. The bag supports the stems and adds to the holiday theme.

When someone gives you a stocking full of unchilled tulips, don't despair that their season has passed. Force them in pots so the bulbs get cold treatment outdoors or in your refrigerator. Or put them in the crisper now and plant them in eight weeks—it's a gardening gamble that often pays off.

EDIBLES

The slightly warmer microclimate inside cloches and other covers means you are able to pick greens weekly as new ones keep coming.

LAWNS

No matter how your lawn became uneven, due to construction, erosion, moles, or another cause, it will not fix itself. Use sand to fill holes and dips in the lawn while it is dormant and the low spots are easy to see. Be aware that moles do not just go away, but by

HERE'S HOW

TO TELL WHAT KIND OF SOIL YOU HAVE

1. Take a handful of soil and dampen it with water until it is moldable, almost like moist putty.

2. Roll the soil into a ball, as if working with cookie dough.

3. Using your thumb and forefinger, gently press the soil until the ball begins to roll out of your closed hand. The ribbon will begin to form, and will eventually break under its own weight. If the soil crumbles and doesn't form a ribbon at all, you have sandy soil.

4. If a ribbon more than 1 inch long forms before it breaks, you have silty soil.

5. If a ribbon 1–2 inches long forms before it breaks, you have clay soil.

6. If a ribbon greater than 2 inches forms before it breaks, you have very heavy and poorly drained soil. It will not be suitable for a garden without some major amendments.

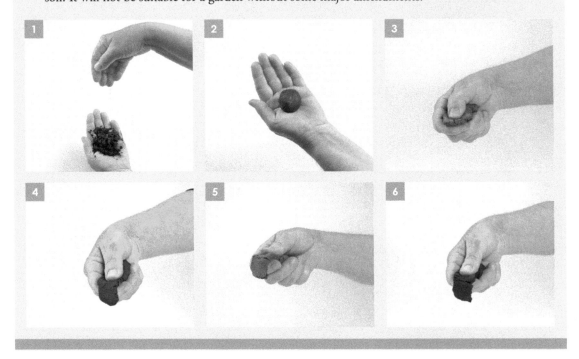

crushing the runs and filling in holes you may deter them. Rarely, a French drain collapses, causing a dip in the lawn. Check yours to be sure it stays open and keep cars off of it to prevent compaction.

PERENNIALS & ORNAMENTAL GRASSES

Sometimes big ornamental grasses like those known as pampas grass (*Cortaderia selloana* and *Erianthus ravennae*) put on very heavy plumes. The stalks may not hold them, especially if you have not pruned the grasses for several years. Instead of tall, upright, and feathery, the plumes spill out of the clump every which way. If the stalks break, the plumes hit the ground, and make a dirty mess. Cover up—these leaves are edged in little knives—and get around those plumes with jute string like a loose belt and pull them up.

When a plant that is supposed to be perennial does not make it through the first winter, you should review conditions in the bed or container. If they do not match the particular plant's needs, it may not survive. When you remove a dead perennial, use your senses to know if drought, rot, or something else is the culprit:

- Feel the soil to know if it is staying too wet or too dry. With a few exceptions, perennials grow best in well-drained soil that has the opportunity to dry out at least slightly and never puddles. Otherwise they rot starting at the roots.

- Smell the soil where the plant was—it should have a pleasant odor, not a foul one that would indicate water has been standing in the hole with the plant. Drowned roots stop functioning.

- Look where the crown meets leaves to see if the stem is dark and soft there or if it is crispy brown. See if the plant has any roots left or if they have shrunk up and turned brown. Depending on the symptom, you may have a fungal or bacterial infection that has spread into the stems.

- Touch the soil. If it feels slick, it has more clay than some can tolerate. Gritty, sandy soil may be draining water too fast and losing nutrients in the process. Solve this problem before you replant.

ROSES

If you have been collecting fresh rose petals from the fall bloom and letting them dry, they should be ready for potpourri. There is no nicer gift than one made by hand with care.

TREES

Gifts of wind chimes and tire swings beg the question: how can you attach them without hurting the tree? In every case, nails and hooks

HERE'S HOW

TO MAKE POTPOURRI

1. Use a quart pitcher to measure your stash of rose petals. Pour 1 quart of petals into a large bowl.

2. Add 1 tablespoon of chopped, dried lavender as a natural preservative. Use more lavender if you want more of its fragrance in the finished product.

3. Add 1 teaspoon of cinnamon and three crushed cloves.

4. Add 6 drops each of two essential oils, rose and another such as orange or vanilla.

5. Put the mix into an airtight container and close it tight. Shake the jar daily.

6. In ten days, the potpourri is ready to enjoy or wrap for gifting.

are not the answer! Use string or rope instead—a simple loop around a branch with an S hook attached works for light weight ornaments; use heavier materials for bigger items as long as nothing digs into the bark. To hang from a higher branch, tie a weight to a piece of sturdy rope, fling it over the branch, and pull it to the right level for that tire swing.

WATER GARDENS

Recycling is a great practice but take care when reusing water garden materials. First, use soapy water to scrub clean all plastic surfaces and parts, then rinse well. Mix household bleach and water (ratio 1:5) and wash everything again, then rinse very well and allow to dry before reassembling.

WATER

ALL

Drought stress causes plants to withdraw the water inside them into their roots in an effort to stay alive. Roots need water to survive; they take and shed it in the normal cycle. When root zones are flooded, however, root hairs become saturated and can no longer function to move water and nutrients in and out of the plant system. Ironically, that means the roots stop working, dehydrated in a saturated environment. Like dominoes falling, this situation makes the roots vulnerable to infestation by rot fungi that are present in soil. As the struggle to survive continues, the pathogen may get into the plant's vascular system and symptoms show in stems and leaves, such as dark patches or spots.

Every plant has a vascular system. The tissues of this system, xylem and phloem, form structures that transport water and nutrients from the roots to the shoots. Xylem moves water and dissolved minerals to the leaves, and phloem takes it from there to the rest of the plant. Without the vascular system, not much happens in plant growth. Its collapse explains what happens in blossom end rot of tomatoes, a graphic example of what wilting due to improper watering practices can do.

ANNUALS

Cooler temperatures reduce the need to water pots outdoors, but some soils and potting mixes need

more water than others because of their ingredients. Container size and the depth of garden beds play a role too, along with wind exposure and microclimate in the growing location. For example, small pots of herbs on a windy porch will need water almost daily. Larger containers with soil mix that contains moisture-holding polymers in the same place can be watered weekly or less. Adjust your watering practices to fit your growing conditions and the season.

BULBS

The soil mix in amaryllis gift boxes is very light and is intended to be watered regularly. If you pot up your own this month, use a soilless mix with a similar profile so you can water often to accommodate the bulbs' fast growth. Dry conditions indoors can shorten the life of paperwhites. Water their pots regularly to extend bloom and keep the fragrance wafting through the house.

Soilless mixes can be finicky to water from the top. If they are dry, components can float, and if they are wet, percolation can be poor. Water soilless mixes from the bottom most of the time and water from the top to leach the soil at least monthly.

EDIBLES

Puddling is not acceptable in vegetable gardens or around fruit trees. Take steps right away to get excess water out of these plantings. You can dig a ditch but keep the dirt in a pile nearby to make it easier to refill.

LAWNS

Unless you are growing ryegrass and the weather is very dry, no supplemental water should be needed on lawns this month.

PERENNIALS & ORNAMENTAL GRASSES

No water beyond rainfall is usually needed for established plants now. Monitor newly divided clumps and water if needed to prevent wilting.

ROSES

For the most control over watering in rose beds, install a drip system. Each plant gets its own skinny tube that runs to a larger pipe connected to your hose bib or water collection system. Do this task now while the roses are leafless to make the piping easier.

SHRUBS

Shrubs that are in bloom or will be soon need water to open their buds. Check on these to be sure they are hydrated: camellia, pussywillow, forsythia, flowering quince, and almond.

TREES

Water young trees and those recently transplanted this month or be sure their reservoir bags stay filled. If the weather is very wet, knock down any low dams around young trees intended to hold water around them. Puddling at the base of trees is unacceptable to most—dig a swale or shallow ditch to get the water out.

VINES & GROUNDCOVERS

If there is no rain this month, water berried plants and those that are setting buds now for late winter bloom, such as hardy periwinkle and coral honeysuckle.

WATER GARDENS

Change the water in pond pots you are growing in protected environs with care to maintain the same temperature.

FERTILIZE

ALL

Few plants benefit from fertilizer this month unless they are growing in greenhouses, indoors, or propagation chambers. To make this task neater and more efficient, consider a siphon mixer. This device accurately mixes your favorite soluble fertilizer into water as it goes through your hose. It consists of a brass fixture (the siphon) and a rubber tube with an uptake fitting. The siphon dilutes concentrated fertilizer solution at a rate of 16:1 into your water. It has a backflow preventer and, at average water flow rates, dispenses a gallon of concentrate in five minutes. Soluble fertilizers have mixing instructions on the label or website for use with a siphon mixer.

ANNUALS

Winter hardy annual flowers grow best in cool weather and need fertilizer to do it. Don't skip this

month or any other unless temperatures are below freezing for weeks at a time. Give them a soluble formula as usual this month.

BULBS

Broadcast a granular garden fertilizer such as 10-10-10 over beds of established daffodils as they come up. If you used bulb food when planting new bulbs, no additional fertilizer is necessary and may promote excess leafy growth.

EDIBLES

Fertilize vegetables that are growing now in beds, pots, and under covers. Use a soluble fertilizer mixed at half strength for all but heavy feeders, such as Brussels sprouts. When temperatures are above 45 degrees Fahrenheit at night, fertilize lettuce weekly.

Plants in these categories that do not require fertilizer this month:

Lawns

Perennials and Ornamental Grasses

Roses

Shrubs

Trees

Vines and Groundcovers

Water Gardens

PROBLEM-SOLVE

ANNUALS

Last summer slugs and snails tried to consume every annual you planted. Take action now to roll up their welcome mat by disrupting their habitat. Rake back the mulch in annual beds and spread on a layer of diatomaceous earth (the kind made for gardening, not swimming pools). You can do this between existing plants with no ill effects. Repeat when you replant the bed. If you have areas that stay warm, damp, and dark such as underneath a brick pile, spread diatomaceous earth around them.

EDIBLES

If you are growing greens under cloches, larvae and even eggs may be inside, too, and they're hungry. Holes that appear in leaves of cabbage, turnip greens, and related vegetables are usually caused by cabbage loopers. Control them with *B.t.*, the specific bacillus that preys on these and related caterpillars, sold as Dipel dust or Thuricide liquid.

ROSES

When the first roses of spring fail to open properly, your heart aches to know you have thrips. Tiny and tough, these insects demand a preventative defense best done now. Clean up around roses, lay new mulch if you haven't done so this fall, and spray bushes with horticultural oil now and in February.

SHRUBS AND VINES & GROUNDCOVERS

Horticultural oil sprays are an efficient way to smother some fungi, insects, and their eggs. Be sure you get the highly refined oil made for this purpose and sold at garden centers. Dormant oil is a different product, heavier and more viscous. It is used to spray dormant fruit trees but not other trees or plants in these categories.

TREES

Squirrel nests might be considered aeries because they are located high in trees, but their occupants are much less welcome in the garden than birds. You may think squirrels are cute, but when their population builds, you're likely to find it

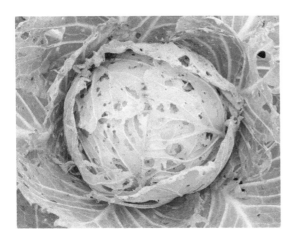

■ *Holes in cabbages are usually caused by cabbage loopers.*

impossible to control the fleas they carry. You'll hear tales of fireworks and shotguns used to vacate them, but those methods are not recommended. Better to hire a pro to remove this problem.

When you notice sap running out of a tree trunk, it is cause for concern and possibly action. Should you notice small holes in the trunk are seeping, check for boring insects. Some can be treated successfully, but most cannot. When the tree is more damaged and bark is missing (usually due to mechanical injury) recovery is also unlikely. If the tree can fall and create havoc, consult a tree pro and possibly have it removed. If not, try these strategies:

- Physically clean the wound with soapy water and/or alcohol

- Start a weekly spray program that combines insecticide and fungicide or

- Spray once and enclose the area with tree wrap, a porous fabric protector that looks like an ace bandage.

- Monitor the situation and take more action if needed to control secondary insects, the opportunistic invaders that slip in and do more damage.

VINES & GROUNDCOVERS

Bramble vines in the flowerbed may be nothing but pesky weeds unless you can identify and move them. For example, dewberries (*Rhus trivialis*) grow thorny vines in shady flowerbeds but make fine berries with more sun and a little encouragement. Known as early blackberries, these native vines form thickets that bloom in early spring and fruit weeks sooner. Find a spot and cultivate this problem into delicious desserts and jellies.

WATER GARDENS

Troubleshoot problems you experienced earlier in the year and solve them now. You may need a new or larger filter system, want to add a skimmer, or have concluded that another pond is necessary because fish and plants are multiplying. But if any problems were caused by algae, consider the benefits of anacharis on the bottom of your pond and mosquito fish for their silver beauty and algae appetite.

Great Eights: Plants You Can Count On

There are many, many plants imbued with a Deep South sense of place. Here are eight great plants in each category that are not included elsewhere in the book.

ANNUALS FOR SHADY SITES

Bamboo palm (*Chamaedorea seifrizii*)

Blue bells (*Browallia speciosa*)

Nerve plant (*Fittonia verschaffeltii*)

Nun's orchid (*Phaius tankervilleae*)

Persian shield (*Strobilanthes dyeranus*)

Wax begonia (*Begonia* x *semperflorens-cultorum*)

Wild basil (*Perilla frutescens*)

Wishbone plant (*Torenia fournieri*)

BULBS FOR NATURALIZING

Paperwhite narcissus

> *Narcissus tazetta* x 'Geranium'. Fragrant bunch flower, white with orange cup

Large cup daffodils

> *N.* 'Ice Follies'. Yellow cups age to white in long-lasting flowers.

> *N.* 'Carlton'. Bold yellow flowers, an early heirloom with vanilla

■ *Blue bells* Browallia speciosa

■ *Daffodil* 'Ice Follies'

> *N.* 'Fortune'. Bright yellow perianth (petals) and striking orange cup.

Trumpet daffodils

> *N.* 'Mt. Hood'. Solid white flowers, excellent for cutting.

> *N.* 'Unsurpassable'. Best yellow trumpet for perennializing.

Southern heirloom daffodils

> *N. poeticus* var. *recurvus* Pheasant's Eye. Late bloomer in Zones 7 and 8.

> *N.* 'Butter and Eggs'. Favored for its double cups and mixed coloration.

EDIBLES FOR ALL SEASONS

Annuals
> Edamame (*Glycine max*) for warm soils and summer steaming.

Overwintering Herbs. Plant alongside parsley and chives.

> Cilantro (*Coriandrum sativum*)

Dill (*Antheum graveolens*)

Florence fennel (*Foeniculum vulgare*)

Spring Herbs. These thrive in warm soils.

Borage (*Borago officinalis*)

Lemongrass (*Cymbopogon citrates*)

Pineapple sage (*Savia elegans*)

Salad burnet (*Poterium sanguisorba*)

PERENNIALS & ORNAMENTAL GRASSES

For Spring

Clasping coneflower (*Dracopis amplexicaulis*)

Moss phlox (*Phlox subulata*)

Red columbine (*Aquilegia canadensis*)

Wild blue phlox (*Phlox divaricata*)

For Summer and Fall

Autumn sedum (*Sedum* 'Autumn Joy')

Butterflyweed (*Asclepias tuberosa*)

■ *Cilantro* Coriandrum sativum

Cardinal flower (*Lobelia cardinalis*)

Muhly grass (*Muhlenbergia capillaris*)

SHRUBS FOR NATIVE BEAUTY

Buttonbush (*Cephalanthus occidentalis*)

Lyonia (*Lyonia lucida*)

Mountain laurel (*Kalmia latifolia*)

Native azaleas

Yellow flame (*Rhododendron austrinum*)

Honeysuckle azalea (*R. canescens*)

■ *Sedum* 'Autumn Joy'

■ *Mountain laurel* Kalmia latifolia

Summer azalea (*R. serrulatum*)

Sevenbark (*Hydrangea arborescens*)

Snowbell (*Styrax americana*)

TREES FOR GARDEN DIVERSITY

Black cherry (*Prunus serotina*)

Honey locust (*Robinia pseudoacacia*)

Ironwood (*Ostrya virginiana*)

Longleaf pine (*Pinus palustris*)

Sassafras or Gumbo (*Sassafras albidum*)

Sourwood (*Oxydendron arboreum*)

Sweet olive (*Osmanthus americanus*)

Walkingstick (*Aralia spinosa*)

VINES & GROUNDCOVERS OFTEN OVERLOOKED

Blue star (*Amsonia tabernaemontana*)

Dwarf huckleberry (*Gaylussacia dumosa*)

Evening primrose (*Oenothera speciosa*)

Poppy-mallow (*Callirhoe papaver*)

Rose vervain (*Glandularia canadensis*)

Soapwort (*Gentiana saponaria*)

Widow's tears (*Commelina erecta*)

Wild strawberry (*Fragaria virginiana*)

LAGNIAPPE—A LITTLE SOMETHING EXTRA

Spirea shrubs with great fall color

'Goldflame' (*Spiraea* x *bumalda*)

'Anthony Waterer' (*S.* x *bumalda*)

'Nana' (*S. japonica*)

'Neon Flash' (*S. japonica*)

Trees that grow faster than average

Green ash (*Fraxinus pennsylvanica*)

Bald cypress (*Taxodium distichum*)

Shumard oak (*Quercus shumardii*)

'October Glory' maple (*Acer rubrum*).

■ *Honeylocust* Robinia pseudoacacia

■ *Widow's tears* Commelina erecta

HERE'S HOW

TO PLANT IN CONTAINERS

1. Choose a container with at least one drainage hole in the bottom so excess water can escape. Cover the drainage holes with a few layers of newspaper to prevent the soil from washing out. If your container is large, you may want to consider a layer of pot shards or some other loose material to reduce the amount of potting mix you need to use.

2. Fill the container about half full with planting mix. Add a slow-release fertilizer according to package directions, and then add enough additional mix to come within about an inch of the rim.

3. Experiment with the design while plants are still in their containers. Place the tallest plant in the center and fill around it with lower-growing plants. Plant trailing plants near the perimeter.

4. Starting with the middle plants and working outward, remove the plants from their pots and plant them, keeping the soil level about an inch below the container rim to allow for watering. Water well once all of the plants are set.

HERE'S HOW

TO BUILD A SIMPLE RAISED BED

1. Cut the wood and assemble the frame upside down on a flat surface. Drive deck screws through pilot holes at the corners.

2. Reinforce the corners by nailing metal corner brace hardware. Use galvanized joist hanger nails to fasten the braces.

3. Position the bed frame in your garden location. Bury the bottom at least 2 inches below grade.

4. Fill the bed with a suitable planting soil and rake smooth. The surface of the soil should be at least an inch or two below the top edges of the frame.

HERE'S HOW

TO CUT BACK ORNAMENTAL GRASSES

1. The main maintenance task with ornamental grasses is cutting back the browned foliage each spring.

2. You can use an electric hedge trimmer, hand pruners, or even a mower, depending on how big your plants are and how many.
Cut back to about 2 inches from the ground.

3. Be sure to cut the clumps back early enough so that you don't cut off any new green growth. Avoid cutting back grasses in the fall as winter injury may result and the winter beauty of the plants and their value to wildlife is lost.

HERE'S HOW

TO PLANT A BALLED-AND-BURLAPPED TREE

1. Dig a hole no deeper than the depth of the rootball but at least twice as wide, preferably three or four times wider.

2. Amend the soil, if needed, to create a well-drained soil in the correct pH range. To do this, mix the planting soil with organic matter such as well-rotted compost or manure.

3. If the wrapping is real burlap, you simply have to cut and remove the fabric on top of the ball and peel the burlap down the sides so it stays below the soil line. It will eventually decompose. Synthetic burlap must be removed completely. Remove the wire basket that surrounds the root ball and burlap, if present.

4. Place the plant in the hole and adjust the hole depth so that the plant is about 1 inch higher than it was planted in the nursery to allow for settling of soil. Use a shovel handle laid across the hole to help determine the proper depth.

5. Shovel in the amended soil around the rootball, stopping to tamp down the soil when the hole is half full.

6. Fill the rest of the hole with loose soil and tamp down again to ensure good contact between the soil and the roots.

7. Soak the planting area with water. Once the soil has settled, build up a 2- to 3-inch basin around the plant to catch rainfall and irrigation water. However, do not build a basin if your soil is very heavy and doesn't drain well.

8. Apply 2 to 3 inches of organic mulch such as shredded bark or wood chips, keeping the mulch a few inches away from the trunk.

HERE'S HOW

TO MAKE COMPOST

1. You will need some way to contain your compost. You can simply pile up the debris, but it is more effective to build or purchase some type of bin.

2. Build your compost pile as materials become available, layering carbon materials alternatively with nitrogen materials. If you have an abundance of carbon (brown) materials, put some of them on the side until more nitrogen (green) materials become available. Too many green grass clippings can mat down and prohibit the composting process. Mix them with looser materials such as straw or dried leaves or allow them to dry in the sun before adding them to the pile.

3. It's a good idea to add thin layers of topsoil or finished compost to a new pile to introduce the decay organisms that create compost. Add water as needed to keep the pile moist but not soggy.

4. Turn your compost regularly—once a week if possible—to get air into the pile. If you don't turn your pile, you'll still get compost, but it will take a lot longer. If you want to speed up the composting process, turn the pile more often, add more nitrogen-rich materials, and shred or chop the carbon materials before adding them to the pile so they break down more quickly. Ideally, you will have several piles going at the same time so you will always have some finished compost available. You'll know your compost is ready for the garden when it is dark, crumbly, and most of the plant parts are decomposed.

HERE'S HOW

TO CLEAR BRUSH

1. Begin by using a tree pruner to cut woody brush that has a diameter of less than 1½ inches. Cut the brush and/or small trees as close to the ground as possible, dragging brush out of the way and into a pile as you clear.

2. Next, clear out larger plants—brush and trees with a diameter of about 1½ inches to 3½ inches. Use a bow saw or chain saw to cut through the growth, and place the debris in a pile. Trees larger than 4 inches diameter should be left to grow, or removed under the supervision of a professional.

3. Use a heavy-duty string trimmer or a swing-blade style weed cutter to cut tangled shoots, weeds, and remaining underbrush from the area.

4. Clear the cut debris and dispose of it immediately. Curbside pickup of yardwaste usually requires that sticks or branches be tied up into bundles no more than 3 feet long. If you plan to install a hardscape surface, make sure the brush does not grow back by using a nonselective herbicide to kill off remaining shoots or laying landscape fabric.

HERE'S HOW

TO REPAIR LAWN DAMAGE

1. Moisten the damaged area, and use a garden fork to break up the soil. Rake out dead grass or other debris.

2. Spread grass seed over the repair area. Select seed that matches the grass type in your lawn—this often is a blend of several different types. Broadcast the seed at the coverage rate recommended on the package.

3. Fertilize the new grass plants with a grass seed starter formulation. Again, use the coverage rate specified on the package.

4. Water the repair area thoroughly, but not so much that you cause fertilizer granules or seeds to wash away. Install stakes and strings around the repair area to discourage foot traffic. Water the area daily until the new grass has established.

Bibliography

Armitage, Allan M. *Armitage's Garden Annuals: A Color Encyclopedia*, Timber Press, Portland, OR, 2004.

Bender, Steve, editor. *The Southern Living Garden Book*, Oxmoor House, Birmingham, AL, 2004.

Brown, Clair Alan. *Wildflowers of Louisiana and Adjoining States*, LSU Press, 1980.

Chaplin, Lois Trigg. *The Southern Gardener's Book of Lists*, Taylor Publishing Co., Dallas, TX, 1994.

Coombes, Allen, editor. *The Timber Press Dictionary of Plant Names*, Timber Press, Inc., Portland, OR, 2009.

Dirr, Michael A. *Dirr's Trees and Shrubs for Warm Climates: An Illustrated Encyclopedia*, Timber Press, Portland, OR, 2002.

Hill, Madalene, and Barclay, Gwen. *Southern Herb Growing*, 2nd ed., Shearer Publishing, Fredericksburg, TX, 1997.

Lowenfels, Jeff, and Lewis, Wayne. *Teaming with Microbes: A Gardener's Guide To The Soil Food Web*, Timber Press, Portland, OR, 2006.

Midgley, Jan W. *All About Alabama Wildflowers*, Sweetwater Press, Raleigh, NC, 2003.

Odenwald, Neil, and Turner, James R., *Identification, Selection, and Use of Southern Plants (4th rev. ed.)*, Claitor's Law Books and Publishing, Baton Rouge, LA, 2010.

O'Rourke, Edmund N., and Standifer, Leon C. *Gardening in the Humid South*, LSU Press, Baton Rouge, LA, 2002.

Pleasant, Barbara. *Warm-Climate Gardening: Tips, Techniques, Plans, Projects for Humid or Dry Conditions*, Storey Books, North Adams, MA, 1993.

Reich, Lee. *The Pruning Book*, Taunton Press, Newtown, CT, 1999.

Sullivan, Barbara J. *Garden Perennials for the Coastal South*, UNC Press, Chapel Hill, NC, 2002.

Thomas, Charles, and Heriteau, Jacqueline. *Water Gardens*, Houghton Mifflin Harcourt, Boston, MA, 1996.

Thompson, Peter. *Creative Propagation*, Timber Press, Portland, OR, 2005.

Timme, Stephen L. *Wildflowers of Mississippi*, University Press of MS, Jackson, MS, 2007.

Welch, William C., and Odenwald, Neil. *The Bountiful Flower Garden: Growing and Sharing Cut Flowers in the South*, Taylor Trade Publishing, Dallas, TX, 2000.

Glossary

Alkaline soil: soil with a pH greater than 7.0. It lacks acidity, often because it has limestone in it.

Annual: from a botanist's perspective, an annual lasts no longer than one year. To the gardener, an annual is a seasonal plant, growing until winter's cold or summer's heat causes it to decline or die.

Balled-and-burlapped: tree or shrub grown in the field whose rootball was wrapped with protective burlap and twine when the plant was dug up to be sold or transplanted.

Bare root: plants that have been packaged without any soil around their roots. (Often young shrubs and trees purchased through the mail arrive with their exposed roots covered with moist peat or sphagnum moss, sawdust, or similar material, and wrapped in plastic.)

Barrier plant: a plant that has intimidating thorns or spines and is sited purposely to block foot traffic or other access to the home or yard.

Beneficial insects: insects or their larvae that prey on pest organisms and their eggs. They may be flying insects, such as ladybugs, parasitic wasps, praying mantises, and soldier bugs, or soil dwellers, such as predatory nematodes, spiders, ants, and beetles.

Berm: a temporary narrow raised ring of soil around a newly planted tree, used to hold water so it will be directed to the root zone.

Bract: a modified leaf structure on a plant stem near its flower that resembles a petal. Often it is more colorful and visible than the actual flower, as in dogwood or poinsettia.

Bud union: the place where the top of a plant was grafted to the rootstock; usually refers to roses or fruit trees.

Canopy: the overhead branching area of a tree, usually referring to its extent including foliage. Also called the crown.

Cold hardiness: the ability of a perennial plant to survive the winter cold in a particular area.

Complete fertilizer: powdered, liquid, or granular fertilizer that contains the three key nutrients—nitrogen (N), phosphorus (P), and potassium (K).

Compost: organic matter that has undergone progressive decomposition by microbial and microbial activity until it is reduced to a spongy, fluffy texture.

Corm: the swollen energy-storing structure, analogous to a bulb, under the soil at the base of the stem of plants, such as crocus and gladiolus.

Crown: the base of a plant at, or just beneath, the surface of the soil where the roots meet the stems.

Cultivar: a CULTIvated VARiety. It is a naturally occurring form of a plant that has been identified as special or superior and is purposely selected for propagation and production.

Deadhead: a pruning technique that removes faded flower heads from plants to improve their appearance, abort seed production, and stimulate further flowering.

Deciduous plants: unlike evergreens, these trees and shrubs lose their leaves in the fall.

Desiccation: drying out of foliage tissues, usually due to drought or wind.

Division: the practice of splitting apart perennial plants to create several smaller-rooted segments. The practice is useful for controlling the plant's size and for acquiring more plants; it is also essential to the health and continued flowering of certain ones.

Dormancy: the period, usually the winter, when perennial plants temporarily cease active growth and rest. Dormant is the verb form, as used in this sentence: Some plants, like spring-blooming bulbs, go dormant in the summer.

Established: the point at which a newly planted tree or shrub has generated enough roots in its new location to keep it alive without supplemental watering.

Evergreen: perennial plants that do not lose their foliage annually with the onset of winter. Needle or broadleaf foliage persists and continues to function on a plant through one or more winters, aging and dropping in cycles of three or four years or more.

Foliar: of or about foliage—usually refers to the practice of spraying foliage, as in fertilizing or treating with insecticide; leaf tissues absorb the liquid directly.

Floret: a tiny flower, usually one of many forming a cluster that comprises a single blossom.

Germinate: to sprout. Germination is a fertile seed's first stage of development.

Girdling root: root that encircles all or part of a trunk/woody stem or other roots and interrupts the movement of water, minerals, and sugars.

Graft (union): the point on the stem of a woody plant with sturdier roots where a stem from a highly ornamental plant is inserted so that it will join with it. Roses are commonly grafted.

Hardscape: the permanent, structural, nonplant part of a landscape, such as walls, sheds, pools, patios, arbors, and walkways.

Herbaceous: plants having fleshy or soft stems that die back with frost; the opposite of woody.

Hybrid: a plant that is the result of intentional or natural cross-pollination between two or more plants of the same species or genus.

Included bark (bark inclusion): bark embedded between two adjacent stems or between a branch and a trunk, which indicates a weak union or attachment.

Mulch: a layer of material over bare soil to protect it from erosion and compaction by rain, and to discourage weeds. It may be organic (compost, wood chips, bark, pine needles, shredded leaves, compost) or inorganic (gravel).

Naturalize: (a) to plant seeds, bulbs, or plants in a random, informal pattern as they would appear in their natural habitat; (b) to adapt to and spread throughout adopted habitats (a tendency of some nonnative plants).

Nectar: the sweet fluid produced by glands on flowers that attract pollinators such as hummingbirds and honeybees for whom it is a source of energy.

Organic material, organic matter: any material or debris that is derived from plants. It is carbon-based material capable of undergoing decomposition and decay.

Peat moss: organic matter from sphagnum mosses, often used to improve soil texture, especially sandy soils. It is also used in seed-starting mixes and in container plantings.

Perennial: a flowering plant that lives over two or more seasons. Many die-back with frost, but their roots survive the winter and generate new shoots in the spring.

pH: a measurement of the relative acidity (low pH) or alkalinity (high pH) of soil or water based on a scale of 1 to 14, 7 being neutral. Individual plants require soil to be within a certain range so that nutrients can be available to them.

Pinch: to remove tender stems and/or leaves by pressing them between thumb and forefinger. This pruning technique encourages branching, compactness, and flowering in plants, or it removes aphids clustered at growing tips.

Pollen: the yellow, powdery grains in the center of a flower. A plant's male sex cells, they are transferred to the female plant parts by means of wind or animal pollinators to fertilize them and create seeds.

Raceme: an arrangement of single stalked flowers along an elongated, unbranched axis.

Rhizome: a swollen energy-storing stem structure, similar to a bulb, that lies horizontally in the soil, with roots emerging from its lower surface and growth shoots from a growing point at or near its tip, as in bearded iris.

Root-bound (or potbound): condition of a plant that has been confined in a container too long, its roots having been forced to wrap around themselves and even swell out of the container. Successful transplanting or repotting requires untangling and trimming away of some of the matted roots.

Root collar: region between the base of the trunk and the roots which swells as trees grow. Also called root crown, root flare, and trunk flare.

Self-seeding: the tendency of some plants to sow their seeds freely around the yard. It creates many seedlings the following season that may or may not be welcome.

Semievergreen: tends to be evergreen in a mild climate but deciduous in a colder one.

Shearing: the pruning technique whereby plant stems and branches are cut uniformly with long-bladed pruning shears (hedge shears) or powered hedge trimmers. It is used when creating and maintaining hedges and topiary.

Slow-acting/slow-release fertilizer: fertilizer that is water insoluble (contains more than 50 percent water insoluble nitrogen) and therefore releases its nutrients gradually as a function of soil temperature, moisture coating, and related microbial activity. Typically granular, it may be organic or synthetic.

Sucker: a new growing shoot. Underground plant roots produce suckers to form new stems and spread by means of these suckering roots to form large plantings, or colonies. Some plants produce root suckers or branch suckers as a result of pruning or wounding.

Tuber: a type of underground storage structure in a plant stem, analogous to a bulb. It generates roots below and stems above ground. A dahlia is a tuberous root. A potato is a tuber.

Variegated: having various colors or color patterns. The term usually refers to plant foliage that is streaked, edged, blotched, or mottled with a contrasting color, often green with yellow, cream, or white.

White grubs: the larvae of scarab beetles, including Japanese beetles, masked chafers, and May and June beetles. They have plump, cream-colored, C-shaped bodies and distinctive yellow to brown heads. Most have life cycles lasting from several months to three years.

Wings: (a) the corky tissue that forms edges along the twigs of some woody plants such as sweetgum; (b) the flat, dried extension of tissue on some seeds, such as maple, that catch the wind and help them disseminate.

Index

Photo Credits

Contech Enterprises: pp. 73

Dreamstime: pp. 184

Tom Eltzroth: pp. 27, 28, 58 (left), 60, 111, 159 (right), 187 (left), 188 (right)

Katie Elzer-Peters: pp. 12 (all), 29 (all), 38, 62, 68, 81, 85, 88, 97 (all), 106, 117, 154 (all), 157, 164, 168, 173 (all), 178 (all), 187 (right), 195

Pam Harper: pp. 66 (lower)

iStock: pp. 9, 10, 39, 64, 91 (left), 120 (top), 199

Jerry Pavia: pp. 49, 58 (right), 128, 140 (lower), 145, 202

Shutterstock: pp. 6, 14, 15, 16, 30, 34, 46, 47, 48, 50, 56, 59 (top), 65 (top), 66 (right), 75, 76, 78, 79, 80, 82, 84, 91 (right), 93, 94, 95 (both), 98, 100, 103, 105, 108, 110, 114, 116, 119, 120 (lower), 123, 124 (right), 131, 132 (both), 134, 136, 138, 140 (top), 141, 143, 144, 151, 158, 159 (left), 162, 166, 170, 171 (both), 172, 175, 181, 183, 186, 192, 193, 194, 196, 197, 203, 204, 206, 209, 210 (both), 211 (all), 212 (both)

Neil Soderstrom: pp. 31, 35, 53, 63, 73 (top), 121, 155, 176, 177

Lynn Steiner: pp. 215 (all)

Meet Nellie Neal

Nellie Neal is a garden writer and radio host who sojourned outside the Deep South just long enough to find the road home. She learned to garden in her native north Louisiana and spent her childhood visiting relatives all over Mississippi, Alabama, and Tennessee. She went on to earn a B.S. degree from LSU where she studied her mutual passions, English and Horticulture. Nellie has grown, bought, and sold plants, tested new varieties of plants, and helped sustain old plants. She has planted and maintained landscapes and movie sets, mowed lawns, watered greenhouses, waited on customers in garden retail, and taught gardening to students of every age. An avid grower since age eight, Nellie never met a plant she didn't want to propagate!

After years in California and south Louisiana, Nellie found a home in central Mississippi and began her radio programs and website, www.gardenmama. com. Today, gardeners ask "GardenMama" and she answers on radio, online, and in print. She is a serious advocate and practitioner of lifelong, year-round gardening who says the kindest compliment is to hear that her advice worked.

Nellie Neal is the author of *Gardener's Guide to Tropical Plants* (Cool Springs Press), *Questions and Answers for Deep South Gardeners, 1st and 2nd Editions, Organic Gardening Down South, How to Get Started in Southern Gardening, GardenMama, Tell Me Why,* and *The Loose Dirt Garden Primer*.

She served as contributing editor for *Ortho's All About Houseplants* and *Ortho's All About Greenhouses*, and a contributing writer for *Annuals for Dummies* and *Rodale's Low Maintenance Gardening*.

Nellie is a member of the Garden Writers Association, the Mississippi Nursery and Landscape Association, the Mississippi Sustainable Agriculture Network. She shares a home with her husband Dave, their dearest friend, Pam, 5 cats, and an odd assortment of potted plants.

CPSIA information can be obtained
at www.ICGtesting.com
Printed in the USA
LVHW050527090120
642815LV00003B/3